Ireland's District Court

MANCHESTER 1824

Manchester University Press

Ireland's District Court

Language, immigration and consequences for justice

KATE WATERHOUSE

Manchester University Press

Published by Manchester University Press
Altrincham Street, Manchester M1 7JA, UK
and Room 400, 175 Fifth Avenue, New York, NY 10010, USA
www.manchesteruniversitypress.co.uk

Distributed in the United States exclusively by
Palgrave Macmillan, 175 Fifth Avenue, New York,
NY 10010, USA

Distributed in Canada exclusively by
UBC Press, University of British Columbia, 2029 West Mall,
Vancouver, BC, Canada V6T 1Z2

British Library Cataloguing-in-Publication Data
A catalogue record for this book is available from the British Library

Library of Congress Cataloging-in-Publication Data applied for

ISBN 978 0 7190 9527 6 hardback

First published 2014

Typeset in Sabon and Gill by
Servis Filmsetting Ltd, Stockport, Cheshire
Printed in Great Britain
by CPI Group (UK) Ltd, Croydon, CR0 4YY

For the mothership, for everything

Contents

List of tables and figures

Tables

Figures

Preface

This book originated in a PhD research thesis carried out in the School of Social Work and Social Policy in Trinity College Dublin under the supervision of Dr. Eoin O'Sullivan, and within the context of the then Trinity Immigration Initiative (TII); it was financed in part by a Trinity College studentship and in part by the TII. The field research period spanned 2009 and 2010 and involved eighteen semi-structured interviews with solicitors, barristers and interpreters, as well as seven months (or a total of forty-five days, or 183.5 hours) sitting as a fascinated observer in a number of District Courts: one, a busy city centre court in Dublin; the second, a custody court outside Dublin city centre; and the third, which appears in the text collectively as a 'rural court', a set of three courts in medium to large towns outside of Dublin, between which the same judge moved on different days. A total of twelve judges and a vast number of defendants and cases, probably in excess of a thousand, were observed.

The research, which began as part of a wider immigration project, initially aimed to observe how the cases of immigrants with few or no English-language skills (Limited English-proficient, or LEP) were dealt with by the Irish District Court on the basis that rising numbers of LEP defendants were being processed by the justice system; that the District Court was inevitably dealing with the vast majority of them; and that while language and interpreting issues were being identified as a major issue in Irish courts (and have proven historically and theoretically to be of great import), nothing was known about the new reality of enforced contact between court and LEP immigrant or the implications for justice and the justice system of how both sides reacted and interacted. As observations began, however, and the structure of District Court proceedings meant also being present for hundreds of non-LEP cases, it quickly became apparent that not only were such cases extremely interesting *per se* in terms of understanding the structure and nature of proceedings in the District Court, but that the question of how LEP defendants were processed, and any analysis of how interpreting facilitated that process, was intrinsically linked to the basic structure and discourse of the generic District Court case and to the characteristics and dynamics of the District Court itself.

The result is an original decriptive analysis of the language, discourse and procedure of the District Court as well as an analysis of the significant changes made to the caseload and processing of the District Court by the advent of the LEP defendant, and the implications of those changes for justice.

Acknowledgements

It is difficult to express and impossible to quantify the degree of support I have been given in completing this book. The funding and support of Trinity College and the Trinity Immigration Initiative, and the additional support and opportunities afforded by the School of Social Work and Social Policy and its heads – first Prof. Robbie Gilligan and then Dr. Eoin O'Sullivan – have been far-reaching and are much appreciated. For the other hats of supervisor, mentor and supporter that he has worn in this process, I owe Eoin further debts of sincere gratitude. For their enthusiasm, support and invaluable feedback as my PhD examiners, I sincerely thank Prof. Ivana Bacik and Prof. Donncha O'Connell. Thanks for further financial support go to Westmeath County Council and to the Polish Embassy for providing a wonderful scholarship to study in Warsaw. Many, many people facilitated and took part (often unknowingly) in the research process that has led to this book, and I would like to express my appreciation of the help and support provided by the Irish Courts Service, the President of the District Court and the President's Office, the registrars who took time out of their busy day to help me, and the judges, court staff, court participants and all of the research participants who gave so generously of their time, expertise and experience. For the support, belief and unfailing encouragement of my friends and family, I cannot thank them enough; I will not forget the calls, the coffees, the lunches and the Lemsips that somehow materialised when needed. Particular appreciation and recognition is due for the support and contributions of Niall MacGiollabhuí, Natalie Woodward and Alana Smith, and, as ever, deepest thanks to Tom Waterhouse for being both a rock and a brick. Finally, I would like to thank Manchester University Press most sincerely for their support.

Abbreviations

CJA	Criminal Justice Act
CitC	City Centre Court
CusC	Custody Court
Directive (the)	EU Directive on the Right to Interpretation and Translation in Criminal Proceedings
DPP	Director of Public Prosecutions
ECHR	European Convention on Human Rights
ECtHR	European Court of Human Rights
ICCPR	International Covenant on Civil and Political Rights
IPRT	Irish Penal Reform Trust
ITIA	Irish Translators' and Interpreters' Association
LEP	Limited English-Proficient
MJELR	Minister for Justice, Equality and Law Reform
NCCRI	National Consultative Committee on Racism and Interculturalism
ORAC	Office of the Refugee Applications Commissioner
RAT	Refugee Appeals Tribunal
RC	Rural Court

Guide to extracts from District Court field notes and interviews

Chapters 2, 4 and 5 are based directly on interviews and ethnographic research carried out in a number of Irish District Courts in 2009 and 2010 (Appendix A (Methodology); Appendix B (Participants)). All citations are from interviews or court observations.

Interviews

The eighteen interviewees are anonymised as follows:

Interpreters: Svetlana, Anna, Marta, Mihai, Belén, Molly, Stella, Jevgenius and Ewa
Barristers: Aoife, Eleanor and James
Solicitors: Matthew, Gerard, Thomas, Gwen, Stephen and Mark

District Court field notes

The courts and judges are referred to as follows.

The first, a Dublin city centre criminal court, is called *City Centre Court* and is abbreviated as 'CitC'. The relevant judges from this court are anonymised as N, R, T, U, V, W and X.

The second, a custody court outside Dublin city centre, is called *Custody Court* and is abbreviated as 'CusC'. The relevant judges from this court are anonymised as O, P, Q and S.

The third, a set of three courts in medium to large towns outside of Dublin between which the same judge moves on different days, is collectively called *Rural Court* and is abbreviated as 'RC'. The relevant judges from this court are anonymised as Y and Z.

Where standard or common phrases and terms are quoted, the court/judge is not distinguished. Notes, quotations and dialogue from court were recorded by hand during proceedings and are not taken from transcripts. Text which represents the *essence* of what was said, rather than being a *verbatim* (or as close to that as possible) transcription, is denoted by square brackets.

In the course of observations for this study, oaths rather than affirmations were observed, such that the term 'oath' is used here throughout. However, there are undoubtedly circumstances in court where an affirmation rather than an oath is administered.

Introduction

> Years ago, we had trouble here in the city from other sailors who came from his part of the world. They did a great deal of damage, stayed for a considerable time and caused a lot of upset to the people of Dublin. I want him to understand that this kind of behaviour cannot be allowed to happen again. (Kotsonouris 2011:132)

Such was the message that a District Court judge urged the consular official from the Norwegian Embassy to explain – presumably in the Norwegian tongue – to a crew member from a Norwegian ship recently docked in Dublin, who was up before that judge on charges of being drunk and disorderly. Kotsonouris (2011:132) goes on to reveal: 'The startled official was obliged to enlighten his compatriot on the Viking invasion of a thousand years before, still a sensitive issue in Court No. 6 of the Bridewell!'

Those unfamiliar with the Irish District Court might be tempted to shrug this off as folktale, fable or fantasy, having in their minds an image of the grandeur and solemnity of the formidable arm of justice that is the courts system. Yet, while there is something of pageantry and formality in the archaic forms of address, the occasional barrister in robes and the incidental interpreter addressing the judge as 'Your Majesty', the District Court is fundamentally a world of incomprehensible, organised chaos where those accused of stealing rabbits and misplacing chinchillas rub shoulders with murder suspects and TV licence renegades, and where judges mysteriously ask for directions, solicitors request dates and defendants are promised books.

This book aims to unravel the mystery and the chaos. It examines the institution of the District Court, dissecting its procedure and the language that both forms the basis of and facilitates the court's heavy workload. It sets out in particular to capture an important change in the District Court over the last twenty years: the advent of the immigrant or the Limited English-Proficient (LEP) defendant. These defendants can bring an element of humour, like the Polish defendant on drunk driving charges who suggested he had 'eaten too many apples'; they sometimes create confusion, like the French defendant who insisted that his occupation was 'pestry chefffff' or the 'Polish' defendant that did not speak any Polish; and they may just as easily *become* confused, like the silent defendant sent off by the judge to 'write to "Santy"' or the fluent English speaker from Pakistan whose case was inexplicably remanded for an Urdu interpreter. The interpreter that appears might remain bafflingly silent, they may unobtrusively interpret proceedings, or they might get deeply involved, like the Romanian interpreter that challenged the Garda expert witness or the interpreter – a former priest – who tried to convince a client to confess to murder.

Issues of language and language barriers in the Irish courtroom have a lengthy history. Following and almost identical to the 1731 Courts of Justice Act in England, the Administration of Justice (Language) Act (Ireland) 1737 made English the language of law and the administration of justice, replacing French and Latin on the basis that 'many and great mischiefs do frequently happen to the subjects of this kingdom from the proceedings in courts of justice being in an unknown language; those who are summoned and impleaded having no knowledge or understanding of what is alleged for or against them'. The Acts aimed '[t]o remedy those great mischiefs, and to protect the lives and fortunes of the subjects of this kingdom more effectually than heretofore from the peril of being ensnared, and brought into danger' by ensuring that henceforth 'all proceedings ... which concern the law and administration of justice, shall be in the English tongue and language, and not in Latin or French, or any other tongue or language whatsoever'.

While great mischiefs may well have been avoided where English was also the tongue of those appearing in courts, the Irish Act was not necessarily designed or destined to avoid the same in the Irish courtroom. On the contrary, some accounts from the nineteenth century suggest that the 'foreign' English tongue was a source of very great mischief indeed.

> 'Come, come – English. Swear him to know whether he does not understand English. Can you speak English, fellow?'
> 'Not a word, plase your honour'

The scene is a fictional nineteenth-century court in which an Irish speaker, Phil Naughten, feigns ignorance of English and frustrates the court with his halting words and simple demeanour (Griffin, 1979:379–80), but non-fiction accounts present the same theme. Waldron (1993), for example, in documenting an infamous murder trial that took place in Maamtrasna on the Galway/Mayo border, describes a key witness who 'would not answer when asked did he speak English – a well-known ploy in courtrooms. Many non-English speakers could understand it adequately, but to think out their replies while the interpreter was translating, they feigned total ignorance.'

Hickey (1999), who analysed these and other examples, found two opposing stereotypes of those using Irish language interpreters in courts under British rule, the first being fearless, manipulative peasants with a passion for the court and an innate understanding of how to exploit the system: 'extrovert' witnesses who avoided direct answers in a 'whelter of rhetoric and skilful wordplay', and 'introvert' witnesses – as above – who said nothing or very little as '[i]gnorance of law and language was easily feigned and could form a most effective, if less entertaining, barrier between the court and the truth' (Hickey, 1999:94). The second stereotype was that of the downtrodden peasant, oppressed by laws of which he or she was ignorant and suffering the 'crippling handicap' of lacking fluency in the English language.

Indeed, there is evidence of judicial attitudes that correspond to both stereotypes. A study of Mayo petty sessions from the nineteenth century showed that magistrates, tiring of ploys that involved feigning ignorance of English, used interpreters grudgingly, if at all, to hear prosecutions in Irish after the early 1830s (MacCabe, 1985). Ní Dhonnachadha (2000) found that interpreters were present at a great number of important trials throughout Irish history, and that judges traditionally viewed them as rogues who would not obey their oath, though they did not consider them to have any outright effect on proceedings. In the Irish case of *R. v Burke*, on the other hand, where the necessity of an interpreter for a key defence witness was challenged on the basis of their having spoken to two other witnesses and sung a song in English, the leading judgment showed sensitivity to the difficulties of communicating through a language that is not one's own, and acknowledged that a few words in a language does not a fluent speaker make:

> I apprehend it is perfectly possible that the witness was actuated by an honest motive in wishing to be examined in Irish. He may have wished to express himself in the language which he knew best, in which he could most clearly express his thoughts, ... and certainly if every lady who sings an Italian song is to be taken on that account to have a perfect knowledge of the Italian language, I can only say that a great number of ladies may very easily find themselves placed in a very unpleasant position indeed. (*R. v Burke*, 1858)

More than 150 years later, the situation of the LEP defendant in the Irish court presents issues not dissimilar to some of those discussed. This book traces the rise of such defendants through a number of years of sustained immigration and looks at the development of services designed to respond to that rise. Set in the District Court, which deals with the vast majority of LEP (and Irish) defendants, it provides an account and an analysis of how the District Court processes those defendants, and how this new defendant profile has impacted on the court. It is hoped in so doing to fill an existing void in what we know about how the District Court functions in practice, and specifically about its procedure in dealing with non-Irish defendants.

The book is organised into three parts. The first comprises Chapters 1 and 2 and is concerned with the role, function and day-to-day operation of the District Court. Chapter 1 introduces the Irish District Court as the lowest yet busiest court in the ordinary courts system, examining the type of crime it deals with and the extent of its criminal jurisdiction in terms of offences and sanctions. It then moves on to look at the nature of proceedings, how offences are processed and at the characteristics of some of the main participants (notably the prosecution, judges and defendants). Finally, it explores the legal process in terms of legal language and courtroom discourse on the basis that the District Court is a predominantly verbal arena. Chapter 2 then goes on to provide an original description of discourse and procedure in the Irish District Court based on a research study involving seven months of ethnographic observation of a vast number of cases in several different courts, and on a series of interviews with solicitors, barristers and interpreters – though the interpreter accounts mainly apply to the third part of the book. Further in this chapter, an account is provided of the type of language used in court and how language use differs among participants, and the typical or generic District Court case is broken down into its constituent parts in a detailed examination of how the characteristics of District Court language can impact on and be observed in different aspects of procedure.

The second part, which consists solely of Chapter 3, sets the scene for the changing context resulting from the impact of immigration on the Irish District Court. Here, a discussion of how the need for language services in the Irish courts system grew, and was responded to, moves into a more theoretical dialogue on the role of interpreters in the criminal process and the basis on which LEP defendants have recourse to interpreters in that process. Consideration is given to how the need for interpreters is balanced against other demands of justice and procedure; and consideration is also given to how the developing interpreting system in Ireland has been evaluated in terms of quality and satisfaction.

In the third and final part of the book, which is made up of Chapters 4 and 5, an account is provided of the practical impact of immigration on the District Court. This section is also based on the research study and involved observation of over 370 LEP cases and detailed interviews with interpreters and legal professionals. Chapter 4 looks at the operation of the District Court in cases involving LEP defendants. It considers how and when interpreters are provided, evaluates the interpreter's role in court and creates an original typology of District Court interpreters, which classifies how and the extent to which interpreters variously interact in and with the interpreted case. Chapter 5 describes in detail how interpreting has been incorporated into, become a feature of and impacted on District Court proceedings, and how the characteristics and dynamics of District Court proceedings impact on the interpreted criminal case in unprecedented ways. It also provides a modified description of the generic District Court case described in Chapter 2, detailing how the interpreted case can differ both linguistically and substantively.

The book concludes with a discussion of where theory, practice and reality meet, ultimately considering how the District Court has altered as an institution and how this is affected by and responds to the need and ability of LEP defendants to access justice in Ireland's District Court.

PART I

The Irish District Court: its role, function and day-to-day operation

1

Introducing the District Court

> Within the court itself, no room. Three hard benches, and the unlucky ones line the walls. It gets too hot, too cold, too stuffy, too noisy, too quiet. Even the gardai[1] don't know how to use the microphones. The Justice is irritated. Justice is flawed. The solicitor arrives late. Justice is delayed. The lists are long and the bailsmen have to come back the next day. People don't know what to do and other people are too busy to help them. Tempers flare, spirits flag, and the long hopeless grind grinds on.

McCafferty (1981:3–4), above, describes her experience of the Irish District Court where she sat as a journalist for ten years. Her often critical accounts portray the 'astonishing parade' of characters she witnessed; the diverse nature of the court's proceedings, from the trite and trivial and occasionally uproarious, to the frustratingly imperfect and sometimes heart-breaking; and the busy and informal nature of a forum where personal lives are laid bare to the sometimes sympathetic, occasionally curious and often cynical ear of the District Court judge. As a retired District Court judge, Kotsonouris' (2011) account from the other side of the bench also emphasises the variety of characters that play a role in the District courtroom, the often informal nature of proceedings, and the court's mixed jurisdiction of humorous incidents that catch the eye and those that involve 'drama, fury and despair' (2011:64). Though few descriptive accounts of proceedings in the District Court exist, in those mentioned above judge and journalist identify common features that characterise the court: its busy and somewhat informal nature, the wide variety of people and cases processed by it and its capacity to invoke a wide range of reactions, from amusement, humour, surprise and curiosity to frustration, anger, distress and hopelessness.

The District Court, in exercising its criminal jurisdiction, is the setting for this book and for the study on which it is based. This opening chapter therefore seeks to provide a foundation for those that follow in providing some detail about the District Court as an institution.

The first two sections look at the place of the District Court in the hierarchy of the courts system, considering its workload, the type of crime it deals with and its jurisdiction.[2] The remaining three sections detail the nature of District Court proceedings and how offences are processed, examine the characteristics of some of the main participants (notably the prosecution, judges and defendants[3]), and introduce the District Court as a verbal institution by exploring the language of the law and the courtroom.

The lowest and busiest of courts

The District Court is a busy place. Sometimes called the 'workhorse' of the criminal justice system (Rottman 1984:68), the District Court has a caseload far greater in size than other courts in the courts system, processing, as Bartholomew (1971:6) puts it, 'a fantastic number of cases'. In fact, it processes the vast majority of criminal cases that come into the system, possibly making it, as Byrne and McCutcheon (2009) suggest, the most significant criminal court, even if it is also the lowest in the hierarchy of the Irish courts system.[4] Aside from criminal matters, the District Court has substantial jurisdiction in other areas, including family law (e.g. maintenance, barring, custody, access, domestic violence) and licensing (e.g. granting certificates for intoxicating liquor licences, auctioneer licences and lottery licences), and in dealing with miscellaneous actions such as applications related to citizenship, birth and marriage certificates and the Environmental Protection Act, 1992 with regard to noise reduction, as well as actions under the Control of Dogs Acts. The small claims procedure operates within the District Court and it also has a limited appellate jurisdiction in respect of decisions made by statutory bodies.

It has been a busy place for quite some time. The system in its current form dates from the 1922 Constitution; the Courts of Justice Act, 1924 defined its structure and jurisdiction; the 1937 Constitution has been its constitutional basis; and the Courts (Establishment and Constitution) Act, 1961 is the official legal basis for the current court structure. The District Court, confusingly, is a single court but it is regionally organised into twenty-four districts, with each district further divided into District Court areas, meaning that multiple courts make up the single court. The court consists of a President and ordinary judges, the number of which is fixed by statute and is currently sixty-three;[5] at least one is assigned permanently to each district. The Dublin Metropolitan District Court is differentiated somewhat from the other twenty-three districts in that the President of the District Court is permanently assigned to it and, while courts in other districts deal with the full spectrum of District Court work, jurisdiction is separated here so that certain courts, for example, will deal exclusively with criminal matters.

All of this means that for almost a hundred years District Court judges the length and breadth of the country have been busily dealing with a vast number of diverse legal issues. In criminal matters, District Court judges have been hearing, trying and sentencing a huge number of defendants across a wide range of criminal offences.

Kotsonouris (2011) recorded the description of a Co. Clare solicitor, John Casey, as to what District Court practice was like when he qualified in 1941. He spoke of charges for being drunk and 'begging', and of summonses for cycling without lights, having a dog or wireless without a licence, for driving with one light or no rear lights or sometimes for speeding, careless or dangerous driving. He noted that common assaults were more often verbal than physical and that robberies were mostly confined to rare cases involving orchards; he recalled cases of unlicensed bulls and animals wandering on the public road as well as applications for dancehall licences, though he also recalled sad and shocking cases involving violence in the home and family law cases. In the foreword to Kotsonouris' book Ó Tuathaigh observes that:

> The courts and the issues with which they deal must inevitably reflect the changing circumstances and values of the society that they serve .... The Courts are a vital site of discourse on our values and standards as a society. What is done and said, what is determined and declared, what is 'conducted' in the courts, resonates within the wider society, affirming or calling into question its notion of what, in colloquial terms, it considers 'right' and 'wrong.' (Kotsonouris 2011:xiv–xv)

Casey's almost idyllic recollections of the nature of District Court offences in the 1940s reflect the low level of crime at that time as well as the types of crimes that were recorded and prosecuted: for example, in 1950 six murders, fourteen larcenies of motor vehicles and accessories, sixty-five burglary offences and some specific offences such as those under the Agriculture Produce (Eggs) Act, 1939 and the Noxious Weeds Act, 1936, reflecting the agricultural nature of Irish society at the time (Young, O'Donnell & Clare, 2001). By comparison in 1998 there were thirty-eight murders, over 700 burglaries and 1615 larcenies of motor vehicles and accessories; in that year 80 per cent of all non-indictable crime involved traffic, reflecting the extreme influence on crime that the rise of the motor vehicle has had in Ireland (Young, O'Donnell & Clare, 2001; Kotsonouris, 2011). In fact, as can be seen in Table 1, road traffic offences continue to make up the largest proportion of the

Table 1 Types of offences dealt with by the District Court

All cases disposed of	2012	2010	2008
Road traffic	233,234	313,565	358,371
Public order/assault	48,284	63,550	69,248
Theft	32,568	32,275	30,821
Drugs	15,838	16,939	15,658
Sexual	2,199	1,815	2,017
Other*	68,768	70,528	74,579
Total	400,911	498,672	550,694

*Other includes breach of bail, litter offences, street trading and offences prosecuted by Government Departments and State agencies.
Sources: Courts Service, annual reports, 2008, 2010, 2012

Table 2 Sentences of imprisonment by court

Prison sentences	2012	2010	2008
District Court (imprisonment/detention)	18,522	20,435	18,440
Circuit Criminal Court	2,498	1,906	2,326
High Court: Central Criminal Court (murder/rape and sexual assault)	76	72	70
Special Criminal Court	18	**	**

Sources: Courts Service, annual reports, 2008, 2010, 2012
** No statistics given

offences processed by the District Court. The other categories of greatest significance are public order/assault, theft, and drug and sexual offences. While drugs constitute a major category of offence *per se*, the rise in drug use in Ireland has also contributed indirectly to the commission of other offences to an unknown degree, and the impact of drugs on District Court proceedings and its defendants is touched on later in the chapter.

Despite crime levels having risen since the District Court was set up, Ireland is still considered a relatively low crime country (Adler, 1983; O'Mahony, 2002). At the same time, the Irish prison population is at an all-time high and continuing to rise, prisons are operating at or above full capacity and there has been a continued commitment to expanding the prison system (O'Donnell, 2005; Irish Penal Reform Trust (IPRT), 2013b). As the District Court deals with in excess of 90 per cent of all criminal matters that come before Irish courts, it is of little surprise that it also hands down vastly more prison sentences than any other court (see Table 2).

Recent prison data also suggest that the numbers of those actually committed to prison have also risen significantly in recent years (see Table 3). Imprisonment rates still seem low when compared with the US or even the UK (760 and 153 prisoners per 100,000 of population, respectively) but they have been growing substantially: between 2007 and 2012 alone, rates increased from 76 to 96 per 100,000 of population; they increased by 100 per cent between 1997 and 2011; and they have increased by 400 per cent since 1970 (Hamilton, 2013; IPRT, 2013a). After the 1997 Bail Act widening the circumstances under which bail could be denied, the numbers of those committed on remand or without having being convicted of a criminal offence rose significantly and, although decreasing, remains high (O'Donnell, 2008; Prison Service, annual reports). This is particularly relevant to District Court proceedings as bail is dealt with for most cases, at least initially, at this level. In addition, while those serving long sentences make up most of the prison population at any given time (O'Malley, 2010), most of those committed to Irish prisons are committed for short sentences. The numbers of those committed for periods of less than three months have increased substantially in recent years, more than trebling between 2007 and 2012 (2,293 to 8,837; Prison Service, annual reports). It will be seen in the section on jurisdiction below that the District Court deals with 'minor offences' that carry penalties of less than twelve months' imprisonment. From Table 3 it is also clear that many of these committals result from the failure to pay a court-ordered fine. Fines are and have been the most common form of punishment in the District Court, yet increasing numbers of people are being imprisoned for non-payment thereof and while legislation has been introduced to tackle this issue, it continues to be a substantial one (Campbell, 2008; Prison Service, annual report, 2012).[6] Thus, even where non-custodial penalties are

Table 3 Committals to Irish prisons

Committals	2012	2010	2008
Under sentence	12,991	11,861	7,461
Sentences < 3 months	8,837	7,356	3,526
Non-payment of court-ordered fine	8,304	6,688	2,520
On remand	3,632	4,836	5,052
Committals under immigration law[1]	400	479	1,034
Contempt of court	3	3	10
Total committals	17,026	17,179	13,557

Sources: Courts Service, annual reports, 2008, 2010, 2012
Note: [1] Immigration detentions will be touched on in Chapter 3.

imposed by the District Court, committal to prison may result where financial difficulties are involved. This also applies to homeless people who, when fined by the court, are often effectively given custodial sentences, as those unable to pay a fine immediately or provide an address are sent to jail (Hamilton, 2005).

A court of local and limited jurisdiction

The Irish Constitution (Art. 34) provides for the setting up of courts of 'local and limited jurisdiction'. The District Court is such a court. As a court of local jurisdiction, it can only hear cases commenced in the correct District Court area; for criminal cases this is generally where the offence was committed or where the defendant was arrested, resides or carries on business (District Court Rules). As a court of limited jurisdiction, the types of cases it can decide are restricted, and in criminal matters it is a court of summary jurisdiction,[7] meaning that it can try cases summarily or by a judge sitting alone and without a jury. The essence of a summary trial is described by Gannon J. in *Clune v D.P.P. & Clifford* (1981:19) as:

> a trial which could be undertaken with some degree of expedition and informality without departing from the principles of justice. The purpose of summary procedures for minor offences is to ensure that such offences are charged and tried as soon as reasonably possible after their alleged commission so that the recollection of witnesses may still be reasonably clear, that the attendance of witnesses and presentation of evidence may be procured and presented without great difficulty or complexity and that there should be minimal delay in the disposal of the work load of minor offences.

As a court of summary jurisdiction, the District Court is permitted by the Constitution (Art. 38(2)) to hear minor offences. The phrase 'minor offence' has no constitutional or statutory definition but is a matter of legal interpretation that has been ruled on in a number of cases over time.[8] It has come to be understood that the most important factor in determining whether a particular offence is minor is the severity of the punishment involved, while the 'moral quality' of an act may also be relevant (O'Malley, 2009; Campbell, Kilcommins & O'Sullivan, 2010). Byrne and McCutcheon (2009) provide a general 'rule of thumb' that minor offences are those that carry a maximum prison sentence of twelve months and fines of up to €5000, though the maximum fines that the District Court can impose vary over time.[9] While the District Court can ordinarily impose prison sentences of up to twelve months, it can

Table 4 Cases processed by the District Court: summary, indictable, sent forward

Cases processed	2012	2010	2008
Summary offences disposed of	332,085	428,472	482,203
Indictable offences dealt with summarily	68,826	70,200	68,491
Sent forward for trial	14,317	12,475	12,965

Sources: Courts Service, annual reports, 2008, 2010, 2012

impose aggregate sentences of up to two years for two or more offences (Criminal Justice Act, 1951 (as amended) (CJA, 1951)).

Offences, however, are created by statute and the basic statutory distinction is between summary and indictable offences.[10] The former lead to a summary trial while the latter, usually involving more serious offences, traditionally lead to a trial on indictment or a trial by jury. Various statutes over time have created a collection of summary offences, and because they are 'minor' offences, the Constitution permits that they be heard in the District Court. They generally involve penalties of a fine or imprisonment of not more than twelve months. Summary offences include public order offences such as intoxication in a public place, disorderly conduct in a public place and failing to comply with a direction of a member of the Gardaí;[11] road traffic offences such as speeding, careless driving, dangerous driving and driving without insurance;[12] as well as less serious violent and drug crimes. The vast majority of offences that come before the District Court are summary offences (see Table 4).

Indictable offences are those that can be tried by judge and jury in the Circuit or the Central Criminal Court. Some indictable offences must always be tried before a judge and jury, including treason, murder, attempted murder, conspiracy to murder, piracy, rape and aggravated sexual assault (Campbell, Kilcommins & O'Sullivan, 2010). However, not all indictable offences have to be so tried and some may be tried summarily in the District Court. These fall into two categories: indictable offences triable summarily (also called either-way offences) and hybrid offences.

For either-way offences (which include perjury, obstructing the administration of justice and attempting to engage in a sexual act with a child under the age of fifteen or seventeen) to be tried summarily, three conditions must be met (CJA, 1951). First, the Director of Public Prosecutions (DPP) must consent to summary trial; secondly, the judge must be satisfied on hearing the relevant facts that the case is minor in nature and fit to be tried summarily; and thirdly, the accused person, having been informed of the right to trial by jury, must elect to be tried summarily. Although persons charged with these offences have the right to a trial by jury, the potential penalties on conviction on indictment are considerably more severe than if the offence were to be tried summarily, such that when given the choice most will opt for a summary trial. In a study of the Galway District Court in 1984, for example, Boyle (1984:208) found that jury trial 'is remarkably underutilised', with 90 per cent of those charged with indictable offences electing trial in the District Court. As to the judicial discretion in classifying an offence as minor, O'Nolan (2011a:212) highlights the fact that this can lead to extremely different results, as judges' attitudes to the gravity of particular offences can vary greatly. Judicial discretion will be considered in more detail below.

The second type of indictable offence that may be tried summarily – hybrid offences – are similar to indictable offences triable summarily but with one crucial difference: the accused person has no right to elect a trial by jury.[13] As such, hybrid offences are those which may be tried summarily or on indictment as decided by the DPP subject to the District Court judge's agreement. Some examples of hybrid offences are possession of a controlled substance for the purposes of unlawful sale or supply, threats to kill, or soliciting for the purposes of the commission of a sexual offence. It has been noted that most new statutory offences are hybrid offences, such that the District Court's jurisdiction is continually increasing while the constitutionally held right to trial by jury is being curtailed (Conway, Daly and Schweppe, 2010; Coonan & O'Toole, 2011). It has also been asserted that there is a fundamental lack of logic in denying the right to a trial by jury to those accused of some indictable offences (e.g. threatening another with a syringe), but not others (e.g. robbery) (Working Group on the Jurisdiction of the Courts, 2003).

With regard to both either-way and hybrid offences, as the District Court is in all cases permitted by the Constitution to try only minor offences, the judge may send a case forward for trial at any time if not satisfied that the facts of the case render it a minor offence fit to be tried summarily (CJA, 1951). The District Court judge may also impose sentence for many indictable offences not otherwise triable summarily where the accused pleads guilty and the court is satisfied that the person understands the facts alleged and the nature of the offence, and where the DPP consents. However, if the court considers that a more severe sentence is warranted than that available to it, the accused can be sent forward for sentencing. The District Court can never sentence for such offences as treason, piracy, terrorist offences, murder and attempted murder (CJA, 1951).

Finally, where indictable offences are not triable summarily and where the prosecutor consents, the District Court acts as a 'clearing house', dealing with bail issues for most offences and serving the book of evidence[14] (Byrne & McCutcheon, 2009). The result is that, although permitted to try 'minor' cases, the District Court's jurisdiction to try cases summarily is actually very wide-ranging and it can try a considerable and increasing number of offences that could potentially be considered serious enough to warrant trial on indictment, including offences where the accused is not given the right to choose trial by jury. Some of these offences might be considered in layman's terms not to be minor at all. Even where an offence is not considered minor in the legal sense and cannot be tried summarily, the District Court may impose sentence under particular circumstances, and in most cases that are sent forward for trial on indictment the District Court will deal with matters including legal aid, bail and the book of evidence. As such, almost every person that is charged with a criminal offence will begin their journey through the criminal process in the District Court and the vast majority of those will have contact *only* with the Gardaí and the District Court.

The nature of proceedings

The District Court deals with a huge number of criminal offences. The definition of its summary proceedings was given earlier in the chapter, where it was described as involving a degree of expeditiousness and informality to enable the court to dispose of that workload with as little delay as possible as well as to ensure that offences are dealt with as soon as possible after their alleged commission. An important element in ensuring expeditiousness is the guilty plea, and as the majority of cases in the District Court proceed on a plea of guilty (Bacik *et al.*, 1998; Jackson & Doran, 2003; O'Malley, 2009) only a relatively small number of the cases tried here are contested. From the review of jurisdiction it is also clear that most of those cases do not involve particularly grievous matters and O'Nolan (2011a:142), in her ethnographic observations of the court, found that many of the matters processed were 'unexciting and commonplace in character'.

Related to the minor and trivial nature of offences is the perception highlighted by O'Donnell (2007:137) that in day-to-day dealings in the District Court it is better 'simply to proceed on the evidence and facts alone, and leave any questions of law for higher courts to resolve'. The idea that the law or legal argument is not an integral part of District Court proceedings is underscored by the fact that although the DPP has ultimate control of prosecutions in Ireland, an important and defining characteristic of the District Court is that the great majority of prosecutions are both initiated and conducted by the Gardaí rather than a legal professional. Indeed, this is usually done without any help or guidance from legal practitioners (Coonan & O'Toole, 2011), and it means that in practice most criminal cases are not only investigated but also prosecuted by the Garda Síochána. The investigating Garda or the local Garda Superintendent (who sits as the 'court presenter'[15]) will usually act as the prosecutor in court (Dwyer, 1991; Byrne & McCutcheon, 2009).

Aside from the implications for legal argument – or lack thereof – in court, there is another consequence of the policeman-as-prosecutor in terms of the nature of District Court proceedings: the idea that the word of the Garda will invariably be taken over that of the accused in court. Carey (1999:138) quotes Michael McDowell talking from the perspective of a parliamentarian and Senior Counsel in this regard:

> there is a natural tendency ... not to disbelieve a policeman in his account of an altercation with a civilian. After many years on the bench dealing with local Gardaí on a day-to-day basis, the [district] judges are not sufficiently objective to conduct a trial where people they know, with whom they have regular dealings, are swearing the details of an incident with an ordinary member of the public.

A tendency to prioritise the accounts given by the Gardaí is strongly reflected in many of McCafferty's (1981) descriptions. Moreover, in O'Nolan's observations of the District Court (2011a:151) she found that prosecution evidence was most often in the form of witness testimony – often that of the arresting Garda – and that where a conflict arose between this and a defendant's version of events, 'it is likely to be difficult to persuade the judge that the defendant's version of events is closest to the truth', with some judges especially unlikely to question a Garda's account.

Interestingly, some of the literature also reflects instances where the prosecuting Garda mitigates on behalf of the defendant. In discussing cultural values in the criminal justice system, Hamilton (2013:161–2) refers to a 'tradition of Gardaí speaking up for criminal defendants at the sentencing stage' and notes that where the prosecuting Garda tacitly acknowledges the hardships a defendant has faced in their life, this can affect the judge's decision. In one account relayed by McCafferty (1981:172), the prosecuting Garda suggests to the judge that a twenty-one-year-old defendant up on a charge of breaking into a clothing firm was probably 'a victim of circumstance', and when the judge expresses doubts about the defendant's excuse that he had sold the goods in question – on the basis of it being an old story that he was 'sick and tired' of hearing – the Garda again supports the defendant, telling the judge that 'strangely enough' he believes him, an averment that the judge clearly takes into account in suspending the sentence he imposes and providing him with a probation officer: 'the guard has not said anything against you. If anything, he has spoken in your favour ... What more can we do for you?'

Whether the Garda speaks for or against the defendant, these sources suggest that the Garda's word holds much sway with the District Court judge. Like much of what does and does not happen in the processing of crime in the District Court, however, the degree to which this holds true is at the judge's sole discretion and thus depends on the individual judge, who administers justice alone and has absolute authority over the proceedings in their courtroom. Indeed, broad judicial discretion is one of the most defining characteristics of Irish judges generally, and the District Court judge perhaps in particular (Bacik *et al.*, 1998). District Court judges, unlike lay magistrates, are fully qualified and experienced lawyers,[16] which means not only that they have a constitutional duty 'to defend and vindicate the personal rights of citizens' and to guarantee that the principles of natural justice and fair procedure are complied with (O'Malley, 2009:257; Campbell, Kilcommins & O'Sullivan, 2010), but that superior courts 'adopt a sparing approach towards the exercise of a supervisory jurisdiction over the District Court' (O'Malley, 2009:564) and are 'very slow to interfere with a decision made at summary level' (Conway, Daly & Schweppe, 2010:127).

The exercise of judicial discretion is perhaps most apparent at the sentencing stage. Although limited in the sentences they can impose, concerns have been widely expressed about the appropriateness and consistency of sentencing in the District Court (see e.g. O'Malley, 1991; Bacik *et al.*, 1998; O'Mahony, 2002). Hamilton (2005) has described District Court sentencing as a 'geographical lottery' and this description is borne out by McCafferty's (1981:2) account of the District Court where the law often depends on the personality of the judge: 'One likes to jail drug addicts, another likes to put them under probation.' Similarly, O'Nolan (2011a) notes the lack of a coherent sentencing policy in the courtroom and her observations suggest an acute awareness on the part of practitioners that sentencing can depend on a judge's particular inclinations as well as on their humour or attitude on a particular day. Canny (2003:xxxiv–v), having provided a comprehensive list of what a judge might take into consideration when sentencing an offender, concludes that 'each judge will view each case differently and the only indication a practitioner will have as to how a court will react to a number of convictions is the past sentencing policy of the judge in question'.

In terms of jurisdiction, as we saw, the District Court judge has discretion in the classification of certain offences as minor or otherwise based on the facts of the case, and, as most bail applications are heard in the District Court (Conway, Daly & Schweppe, 2010), the issue of bail is also, at least initially, largely at the discretion of the District Court judge. The District Court judge also possesses considerable discretion when it comes to granting free legal aid, which is determined at the District Court level (Law Society of Ireland, 2012). The entitlement to free legal aid applies to those charged with an offence whose means appear to the District Court to be insufficient to pay for legal representation and where, because of the gravity of the charge or offence or because of exceptional circumstances, it is considered in the interests of justice that they have legal aid for their defence (Criminal Justice (Legal Aid) Act, 1962). Byrne and McCutcheon (2009) make the point that defendants in criminal cases are usually represented and that this is probably due to the availability of legal aid, but it will be seen in the next chapter that judges vary considerably in how they decide to award or deny it.

It will also be seen in the next chapter that an important feature of day-to-day proceedings in the courtroom itself is the granting of adjournments and remands. This, too, is at the discretion of the District Court judge, who may adjourn proceedings at any time and on any terms he or she thinks fit (District Court Rules). One example of where a judge might decide to grant an adjournment is if either the accused or the prosecutor fails to show up. Where the accused is absent, proceedings may go ahead if the judge is satisfied that the summons was properly served, or the case may be adjourned and a bench warrant issued for his or her arrest.[17] Where the prosecutor does not show up, the court may adjourn or strike proceedings out (District Court Rules). Proceedings may be adjourned or remanded for many other reasons and, in fact, issues of continuity are identified as a problematic feature of the District Court, where successive and sometimes lengthy adjournments can create problems for parties and for the judge in remembering what evidence has been given and in what manner; this can be particularly troublesome due to the huge number of cases processed by the court (O'Malley, 2009; Conway, Daly & Schweppe, 2010). Resulting delays may impact on the defendant's right to an expeditious trial (O'Malley, 2009) and they add to and are part of wider issues of organisation and efficiency in a system criticised for its 'infrastructural, practical problems that severely inhibit the system' (O'Mahony, 2002:331).

In a nutshell, the District Court might be characterised as a place where minor criminal offences proceed mostly uncontested on a plea of guilty and are dealt with quickly and with little or no legal argument. They are usually prosecuted by a member of the Garda Síochána, whose account of events is likely to hold considerable sway; however, the outcome will depend on the individual judge, whose discretion in the processing, adjudication and sentencing of an offence is considerable and rarely interfered with by superior courts but is nonetheless tempered by the duty to uphold the principles of natural justice and fair procedure.

The judge and the judged

One characteristic by no means unique to the Irish District Court but nonetheless worthy of consideration, particularly considering the degree of judicial discretion involved in the District Court, is the differing backgrounds of the judges and those they are judging. At the outset of the chapter, there was a reflection upon the broad spectrum of society to be found passing through the Irish District Court. Despite this diversity, the majority of defendants that come before the courts, in particular persistent or repeat offenders, are young men from a low socio-economic background. Boyle's study of the Galway District Court in 1983 found the bulk of those appearing in court were male and unemployed and Rottman's (1984) study confirmed this, further highlighting that those entering the criminal justice system were characterised by early school-leaving. McCafferty's impressions lend support to this finding; she notes that the 'real crime' she observed was 'all too often committed by men who began their careers in children's reformatories and were processed through St. Patrick's, Mountjoy, Dundrum Mental Hospital, and back to Mountjoy again, with occasional breaks in the fresh air and no hope of a life outside institutional walls' (1981:1–2).

The increased role played by drugs in relation to criminal offences was also mentioned earlier. Kotsonouris (2011) refers to the 1980s as 'bleak times' in this regard, suggesting that many offenders coming before her were of questionable functionality as a result of drugs; she remembers in particular the overworked mothers of such offenders who would come to court for their children with their 'legs … swollen from cleaning hospital floors' and clutching their post office savings books. In their observations of District Court procedure, McCafferty (1981) and O'Nolan (2011a) also note patterns involving those with substance abuse or addiction problems – and often other problems – being 'sent back to the jail again and again and again' (McCafferty, 1981:2), which O'Nolan identifies as particularly problematic as high numbers of temporally proximate convictions tend to evidence substance abuse problems rather than serious or organised criminal activity, yet persistent offenders are typically sentenced more harshly than those with no or fewer convictions. McCafferty (1981) recounts a number of drug-related proceedings, including one in which a youth, recently sentenced for possession, appeared in court on charges of assault and attempting to break and enter. She describes his demeanour during proceedings (1981:45–7):

> He lolled on the bench, his head thrown back on the partition behind him. At times he drifted into sleep, to come awake with a jerk. He had trouble focussing his red-rimmed eyes. ... [H]e was seldom capable of paying attention to the proceedings.

O'Nolan (2011a:176), in her ethnographic study of the District Court, found that substance abusers in court were often identifiable by their physical appearance: '[a] sickly pallor, an unsteady gait, slurred speech and uninhibited behaviour' and that such characteristics were frequently apparent in District Court defendants, some of whom had difficulties staying awake for their appearance and some of whom were all but catatonic; while some were there on drug-related charges, she found that most were on charges not directly related to drugs. A related feature of these accounts of the District Court is the idea of judges having 'heard it all before', effectively listening to the same stories over and over again (also Kotsonouris, 2011:129) and having ever diminishing sympathy for the individuals behind the generic stories.

Bacik *et al.*'s (1998) study provides further support for the notion that those who come into contact with the District Court are not typical of the population at large, though they found the degree of difference to be considerably starker than expected, with District Court appearance so heavily biased towards males, young people and people living in economically deprived areas that, they submitted, 'one might be forgiven for suggesting ... that the Dublin District Court system appears to be there *for* people from deprived areas' (1998:25). The study found that more males and people from deprived areas were given custodial sentences, suggesting that the backgrounds of those appearing and of those adjudicating may have an impact on sentencing. Irish judges and lawyers, like those elsewhere, tend to come from middle class backgrounds; as Bartholomew (1971:41) found in his study of Irish judges: 'None ... had been of humble family origin. On the contrary, almost two-thirds came from admittedly upper middle class social and economic backgrounds and almost all of the remainder from the middle class.' This, Bacik *et al.* (1998) posit, is suggestive of a *de facto* bias against the poor.

The Irish prison population appears to affirm the tendency to punish this section of society. In O'Mahony's (1997b) study of Mountjoy prisoners, he found that prisoners were overwhelmingly 'young, urban, undereducated males from the lower socio-economic classes'; many were also alcohol or drug dependent and had unstable family backgrounds and mental health issues. In a study on recidivism, O'Donnell, Baumer & Hughes (2008) found that those being released from prison were overwhelmingly male, unmarried and young, many with low levels of formal education and just over half unemployed before imprisonment. Nearly half of those released were reimprisoned within four years and rates of recidivism were significantly higher for males, younger people, those with less formal education, and unemployed and illiterate persons. Rates were also found to be significantly higher among those who were held on remand as part of their confinement, and for those having a recent prior prison committal.

The Law Society of Ireland (2012:248–9) recognises the potential gap between advocate and client in its advice on court advocacy skills:

> sometimes one's client in a criminal practice may emanate from a less privileged background than that of the practitioner. By analogy, the dearth of literacy skills may prejudice the client's ability to comprehend the content of the charge sheet, witness statements, reports from expert witnesses retained, and the contents of the book of evidence, where applicable. It is important to be mindful of such impediments.

An overwhelmingly linguistic institution

It seems somehow fitting that the above passage, reminding criminal practitioners that their language and literacy skills may be more advanced than the related skills of some of their clients, is written in a style and using such vocabulary so as to be almost certainly prejudicial to the ability of clients emanating from a particular background with a dearth of literacy skills to comprehend. In being so written, it illustrates both the law's position as a 'profession of words' (O'Barr, 1982:15) and the distinction of legal language from that of common usage in its incomprehensibility and its elitist and exclusionary function.

The law has been described as 'an overwhelmingly linguistic institution' (Gibbons, 2003:1) and the criminal process as being made up of language events from beginning to end, from the charge made against the defendant, through police questioning and consultations with lawyers, to the trial (Solan & Tiersma, 2005). This book is concerned with a very particular part of that process – what happens in the Irish District Court, which has been recognised as a predominantly verbal arena (Carey, 1999; Hamilton, 2005; O'Brien, 2006). In fact Kotsonouris (2011:64) suggests that the comparable informality of District Court proceedings has much to do with how account is made; '[T]here is quite a lot of verbal evidence which makes participants, not least the lawyers, spark off each other.'

The exclusionary nature of legal language has also been acknowledged in the Irish context more broadly, where the 'often arcane legal terminology' of the system is considered to be challenging even for competent speakers of English (O'Brien, 2006). In fact, legal language has existed as long as the law itself and it has always been distinct from the language of common usage. Before English became the language of the law and of the courts in England by virtue of the 1731 Courts of Justice Act, for example, Latin and French had variously been used, despite not being understood by most people (Maley, 1994), and the linguistic influences of Old and Middle English, Latin and Norman French are retained in today's 'legal jargon' – usually the lexical aspect of language. Consider, for example, a feature of legal language where synonyms of different origins are coupled to create commonly used terms (O'Barr, 1982):

acknowledge and confess	(Old English/French)
act and deed	(French–Latin/Old English)
breaking and entering	(Old English/French)

Of course, the introduction of English as the language of the courts in the Irish context by means of the Administration of Justice (Language) Act (Ireland), 1737, served, as we saw in the Introduction, more to perpetuate the distinction between the language of the law and that of ordinary people than to eliminate it. In any case, even where the same language is spoken by ordinary people as is used in the legal system, legal language can differ from the language of common usage in fundamental ways. In fact, while lawyers have argued that comprehension difficulties stem from the complexity of legal concepts, linguists have demonstrated that the ability to understand legal discourse is determined by its 'grammatical, semantic, and contextual complexity' – or the features of legal language (Sales, Elwork & Alfini, 1977:165; Charrow & Charrow, 1979).

Legal language is not a single generic entity but differs across legal systems and parts thereof, among different legal professionals and between legal writing and speech. Nonetheless, some of the technical features of legal jargon from across a wide descriptive literature on legal language (written and spoken) in the English-speaking common-law world can be identified and distilled in contrasting the nature of legal language with that of common usage.[18] Features include the use of common words with specialised meanings ('action' for lawsuit); technical terms; formal words and expressions; words and expressions with flexible meanings (adequate; promptly); and professional argot or words used for in-group communication (damages, due care). In spoken language, using abbreviations such as acronyms or referring to statutes by number is common, and grammatically, written legal language (sometimes called 'legalese') can feature long, complex sentences; an impersonal or abstract tone using the passive voice or the conditional tense; negatives and multiple negatives; and repetition, nominalisations (nouns made from verbs) and unique determiners ('such', 'said' + nouns, e.g. in any such event). Legalese can be vague or wordy; it can lack cohesion or be extremely precise; and it can appear pompous and dull, sophisticated and elegant, solemn and ceremonial, or even ritualistic.

Little wonder, then, that there is an equally lengthy tradition of criticising the language of the law as 'a paradigm of linguistic inaccessibility' (Morawetz, 2000:xi), 'often incomprehensible' (Schane, 2006:2) and 'a completely foreign language to the layperson-juror' (Elwork, Sales & Alfini, 1977:165). In fact, it has been suggested that the inaccessibility of law is an impediment to the basic principle of justice that 'ignorance of the law excuseth not' – the law's presumption that the person who committed the unlawful act knew that it was a crime (Morawetz, 2000; Gibbons, 2003). Goodrich (1987:7) goes so far as to call it a 'major paradox of contemporary legal culture' that although it is incumbent on us all to know the law, the structure of legal language and practice prevent any other than a 'highly trained elite of specialists' from acquiring this knowledge.

Danet (1980) says that even well-educated speakers often have difficulty understanding the language of court and O'Barr (1982) agrees that almost everyone has some degree of trouble with it. Serious concerns have thus been raised at the idea that criminal defendants are often unable to understand their own trial. Hood, Shute & Seemungal's (2003) study on perceptions of fairness, for example, found that 'posh' language and legal jargon created difficulties for defendants, many of whom did not fully understand the sentencing comments of judges and magistrates, and 60 per cent of respondents said the language used in court had put them at a disadvantage. Similar issues have been identified in the Irish context where the Courts Service (2005:53) has acknowledged that for ordinary members of the public the language of the legal system is an impediment to understanding the 'rules that dictate the practice and procedure of all courts'; the 'exclusionary operation' of legal language has been recognised as a particular hurdle for the unrepresented defendant (Carey, 1999); and Hamilton (2005) observes that anyone unfamiliar with the unspoken language of the District Court will find it very difficult to understand judges' sentencing comments.

Elitism and exclusion have long been associated with legal language. Mellinkoff (1963) suggested that the reason for the historical divergence of legal language from that of common usage was the urge of those in the legal profession for their own, secret language. Maley (1994:12) points to a strong historical and cultural pattern of powerful and elite groups having their own, special language to identify them socially and perpetuate their power 'by depriving the less powerful classes of access to its mysteries'. Naturally, the complexity of legal language poses little difficulty for legal professionals, initiated into the language of the law in university or law school and having spent entire working lives immersed in it (Conley & O'Barr, 2005). In fact, it is a widely recognised feature of legal discourse that most lawyers and judges not only master the specificities of legal language but tend to be excellent and exceptional language users (Tiersma, 1993; Maley, 1994).

In fact, the few accounts we have of the Irish District Court draw attention to the way language is used by lawyers; even where the case is minor and uncontested, the lawyer chooses words carefully to achieve the desired purpose of reducing the client's sentence. In this context O'Nolan (2011a:155) observes that '[a] good defence advocate is a wordsmith who can craft his client's life history into something heroic at best, or at worst present the court with the possibility, however slim, that the defendant is still redeemable and capable of reformation'. She also gives the example of a case where, in an effort to lessen the judge's negative reaction to his client's delayed guilty plea, a solicitor employed an unforgettable choice of words in putting it to the court that accepting one's guilt is a 'process of osmosis' (2011a:146). Kotsonouris also refers to this 'endless ingenuity of lawyers' (2011:29) and gives the example of a case in which she was asked to hold that 'a man could not form an intention to drive if he were engaged in sexual intercourse at the time'.

Legal language is thus frequently viewed as a membership marker of the prestigious elite group to which lawyers and judges belong. It is also frequently depicted as an instrument of authority, power and control. According to Saville-Troike (2003), social control is greater in situations where speech events are formalised, and the courtroom is a highly ritualised setting where strict rules govern what can be said, when and by whom; power belongs to those most entitled to speak and to choose and control topics, with lawyers and judges at the top of the hierarchy (Berk-Seligson, 1990, 2002). On the one hand, lawyers use language to support their own version of events and try to make their own witnesses 'look credible, sincere, and competent' (Berk-Seligson, 2002:20); lexical and grammatical choices can play an important role in mitigating or obfuscating guilt (Danet, 1980). On the other hand, language can be used by lawyers as a powerful tool to manipulate, mislead, confuse, annoy, trap, intimidate or obtain an advantage over less sophisticated users of language and vulnerable witnesses (Ellison, 2001; Eades, 2002; Mattila, 2006). The adversarial trial has thus been likened to a verbal duel (Conley & O'Barr, 1977), 'a war of words' (Danet & Bogoch, 1980:37) and a 'joust or a battle' fought with words in 'an arena of opposition and drama' (Maley, 1994:35–6).

Based on the review of the District Court, this type of adversarial interaction is limited and while accounts suggest the presence of some degree of drama, much of what happens involves minor and commonplace offences that proceed uncontested on a plea of guilty. Even where a case is contested, it is not a battle between two legal professionals but between the defence – an unrepresented defendant or more usually a lawyer – and the prosecution – almost always a member of the Garda Síochána. Legal argument is rare and it has been suggested that the Garda-as-prosecutor brings its own particular dynamic, with some judges possibly more inclined to favour the Gardaí's version of events and with Gardaí sometimes even speaking up for the person they are prosecuting – both scenarios tend to render the interaction less adversarial.

Nonetheless, a basic principle derives from and transcends the use of language in an adversarial battle to inculpate or mitigate: that how things are said in court may be more important than what is said (O'Barr & Conley, 1976). Possibly the most cited experiment to illustrate this principle is that of Loftus and Palmer (1974), where a film depicting a car-crash was shown to two subject groups. One set was asked to estimate how fast the cars were going when they 'smashed' into each other, while the others were asked about the cars' speed when they 'collided', 'bumped', 'hit' and 'contacted'. Subjects in the first group estimated the speed as having been significantly higher than those in the second. Moreover, when re-called a week later, one third of the first group claimed that there had been broken glass at the scene while a smaller number of the second group believed this to have been the case. There was no broken glass.

How a person speaks in court has been shown to affect how they are perceived and even how they are sentenced. Conley, O'Barr & Lind (1978) found that speech styles affect juries' perceptions of witnesses; those who used more 'powerless' speech (speech that conveys a lack of forcefulness through frequent use of particular words and expressions) were evaluated more negatively in terms of credibility, veracity of testimony, competence, intelligence and trustworthiness than those using a more 'powerful' style of speech, which they associated with witnesses with higher social status (e.g. well-educated, white collar men; male and female expert witnesses). Wodak-Engel's 1984 study found that defendants' linguistic behaviour, along with the propensity to plead guilty, influenced how a judge sentenced them. Although using a small sample (fifteen people), she found that defendants who pleaded guilty *and* were able to construct a valid and consistent story using technical vocabulary were given less severe punishments than those who did not enter a guilty plea and/or were unable to present a coherent story and exhibited stereotyped behaviour. Dividing defendants by class, those most successful in achieving the image most palatable to the judge were middle class, while defendants from the working and lower middle class were less successful. Conley & O'Barr (1990) similarly found that where people were able to present their accounts to the court in a framework that approximated the official discourse of the court – often people with experience in business or law – the account was better received.

These studies highlight the idea that how a person speaks can affect how they are perceived and judged in the courtroom, that a person's speech style is usually reflective of their social status, and that speech styles associated with a lower social status may be more negatively perceived and judged. This fits within the wider paradigm of the court as an arena of linguistic inaccessibility, where judges and lawyers belong to an elite group marked by their language use, both in terms of legal jargon/legalese and their general exceptional mastery of the English tongue, and as a linguistic arena in which language is a central tenet of control.

While in much of the literature the features of legal and courtroom language are studied to understand power and control in the adversarial setting, the next chapter will look at how language functions in the District Court, not as a tool of adversarial battle but nonetheless as a tool of exclusion, a marker of difference, and an instrument of power, authority and control. However, it will also describe how the language of the District Court is both a feature of and functions to facilitate the specific features of the District Court described in this chapter, including its heavy workload, the speedy and informal nature of proceedings, the minor nature of offences processed, the role of the Garda-as-prosecutor, and the wide discretion enjoyed by judges in this highly ritualised verbal arena.

Notes

1 The Garda Síochána (literally 'guardians of the peace') is the Irish police force; the collective or plural Gardaí is also used and a single guard or police officer is a Garda. The Irish terms are usually used.

2 Most technical terms are explained in the text or the notes. Glossaries of terms and jargon used in the District Court are also available in Appendix C. For further reference on any matters of criminal procedure there are a number of recent and wonderfully detailed textbooks that either cover or deal exclusively with criminal procedure in the District Court, including Byrne & McCutcheon (2009); O'Malley (2009); Campbell, Kilcommins & O'Sullivan (2010); Conway, Daly & Schweppe (2010); Coonan & O'Toole (2011); and Law Society of Ireland (2012).

3 Throughout this discussion the terms 'accused' and 'defendant' are used almost interchangeably. However, the Law Society of Ireland (2012) explains that the correct term depends on whether the person is being prosecuted by a summons issued under the Petty Sessions (Ireland) Act, 1851 (defendant) or the Courts (Nr. 3) Act, 1986 (accused); or whether on a charge sheet for a summary offence (defendant) or an indictable offence (accused).

4 After the Supreme Court (court of final appeal), the High Court (court of first instance with full jurisdiction in all criminal and civil matters) and the Circuit Court (court of first instance with limited jurisdiction, organised regionally). At the time of writing, a new Court of Appeal is also due to be established, which will sit between the High Court and the Supreme Court and hear both civil and criminal appeals. 'Special courts' and military tribunals are also provided for by the Constitution; the Special Criminal Court – three judges, no jury – deals predominantly with criminal charges involving terrorist organisations and organised drug activities.

5 The number of District Court judges has increased a number of times over the years from the thirty-four allowed by the Courts (Supplemental Provisions) Act, 1961; it can be varied depending on need (Courts (Establishment and Constitution) Act, 1961).

6 Fines Act, 2010. There was a substantial increase in female committals in 2012, but well over half of the 2,151 female committals to prison were for defaulting on a fine (1,687; Prison Service, annual report, 2012).

7 Interpretation Act, 1923: that 'courts of summary jurisdiction' means the District Court (s. 4(5)).

8 In *Melling v Mathghamhna* (1962) four relevant factors were identified: the severity of the punishment; the moral quality of the act constituting the offence; and the state of the law and public opinion at the time the Constitution was enacted. See also *Conroy v Attorney General* (1965).

9 Fines Act, 2010 provides for different classes of maximum fines that apply to summary convictions. For Class A, the highest category of fine, the maximum fine amount is €5000.
10 Offences can also be distinguished as serious or non-serious offences (e.g. Bail Act, 1997) and arrestable and non-arrestable offences (created by the Criminal Law Act, 1997, which abolished the felony/misdemeanour classification).
11 The law on public order offences is largely found in the Criminal Justice (Public Order) Act, 1994.
12 The main provisions are set out in the various Road Traffic Acts.
13 Accused persons under the age of eighteen are an exception; they can opt for a jury trial regardless of the offence (Children Act, 2001).
14 This is the collective name for the prosecution's evidence, prepared where a case goes forward for trial on indictment. It is served on, or given to, the defendant in court.
15 Based on field observations.
16 To qualify for appointment as a judge of the District Court, a person must be a solicitor or barrister of at least ten years' standing (Courts (Supplemental Provisions) Act, 1961, as amended).
17 A bench warrant means the Gardaí can arrest that person and bring them before the court (bench) to address the warrant. Proceedings are unlikely to go ahead if the accused person is considered to be 'at risk' of a prison sentence (Law Society of Ireland, 2012).
18 These technical descriptions of legal language are based primarily on Mellinkoff (1963); Charrow & Charrow (1979); Danet (1980); Maley (1994); Gibbons (2003); and Mattila (2006).

2

Barristers, bench warrants and bail bonds

'May it please': the language of the District Court[1]

To walk into an Irish District Court for the first time is to enter an unfamiliar world of incomprehensible, organised chaos. Scores of people busily fulfil often unidentifiable roles. Silence is regularly called for yet noise levels are often such that proceedings cannot be heard, a factor compounded by solicitors/barristers addressing the court (judge) with their backs to the rest of the court and by the widespread custom of ignoring microphones and mumbling at high speed. Of that which is audible, most will make no sense. And yet things typically progress seamlessly and in an orderly fashion with a seeming minimum of confusion. The judge, registrars, solicitors, barristers, Gardaí, probation officers and so on proceed with efficiency and ease, and almost all of those present, including many defendants and their families, appear oblivious to and unfazed by the mayhem that surrounds them and that is, to the uninitiated, seemingly impenetrable.

That an outsider and someone unfamiliar with the District Court may understand very little or nothing of what is going on is perhaps unsurprising. The language used in a court of law is widely perceived as differing from that used in everyday life, and one might reasonably expect to have difficulty understanding the complex legal arguments and legal language of antagonistic lawyers as they do battle to win their case. However, as was considered in Chapter 1, the nature of District Court proceedings means that these factors alone cannot account for any comprehension difficulties experienced in the District Court. Proceedings are characterised by the minor nature of offences; the absence of legal argument ('[f]or the most part ... we don't really open law a whole lot. ... We're not getting into difficult legal terminology, we're not getting into legal argument' (Gwen)); the fact that usually only the defence involves a lawyer while prosecutions are conducted by the Gardaí; and the fact that confrontation and conflict are limited and where they exist tend to be of a minor nature. The following rare example of disputed facts illustrates the nature of District Court matters:

> SOLICITOR: The facts are as the Inspector stated, bar I'd like to say one thing: the defendant didn't 'throw' the pint at the Garda, but an accident resulted in its spilling on the Garda.
> INSPECTOR: The Garda's report intimated that the pint was thrown at him.
> SOLICITOR: ... There's no doubt that the Garda got wet, but it is the manner in which it happened that I am disagreeing with.
> JUDGE Z: [Summing up] Mr. [Solicitor] says that it happened – inadvertently or otherwise – that the Garda got wet. The Garda's report says that the pint was fired at, thrown at, poured ...
> SOLICITOR: We would say it wasn't thrown, but there is no doubt that it was spilled.

It is submitted that the question of why the language of the District Court is difficult to understand lies, instead, in the fact that while outsiders and those unfamiliar with the District Court struggle to make sense of what is happening, the 'regulars' – all those that work and spend a significant amount of time in this setting – can understand proceedings and communicate successfully despite the fact that many of them do not come from a legal background, and in spite of frequently deficient communicative conditions including poor acoustics and the sometimes breathtaking speed at which participants speak and at which things generally proceed. The defining characteristic of District Court language, and the explanation for its inaccessibility is thus not its legal characteristics but its more general 'insider' nature, or the fact that access to the language of the District Court is restricted to regulars or insiders – those with experience and who share a specific knowledge base that includes aspects of the law, District Court procedure and certain jargon. It is on the basis of this shared knowledge that insider language functions, and at the core of its functionality are two distinguishing features of the District Court: its large workload and the consequent perceived need for speed, and the repetitive nature of its workload.

The District Court being the busiest of the criminal courts, its workload is heavy and intense, and an individual District Court can have a list of up to 200 cases to deal with on any particular day. Though it may not be possible to get through a list of this length in one sitting, and accepting that courts have lists of differing lengths and sit for varying numbers of hours, a court that sits between 10.30am and 1pm and from 2 to 4pm with a list of 100, for example, has 2.7 minutes to dedicate to each of these cases. Some will be dealt with quickly, others will take longer, but the clear consequence in any event is that 'the District Court is a court of speed. I mean that's the whole essence of it' (Mark). There is a strong sense that without being able to process cases at speed the system would grind to a halt, and to achieve this speed necessitates a high level of communicative efficiency.

It is essentially the repetitive nature of District Court proceedings that facilitates this communicative efficiency; each case progresses through the system according to established procedure, as part of which a set of specific elements needs to be addressed, including, for example, the charge, the facts of the case, the mitigating circumstances of the defendant, the sentence, and so on. The same elements are addressed by the court repeatedly, which means that the same questions are asked (e.g. as to what the facts of the case are), the same information is provided (e.g. as to the defendant's social situation) and the same decisions are made (e.g. as to what the sentence will be). This routinisation means that a solicitor or barrister knows exactly what elements will need to be dealt with and what information will be required in any given case, and it explains why poor communicative conditions have much less impact on insiders with knowledge of District Court procedure than on those unfamiliar with the context. It is also in the repetitive and routinised nature of District Court proceedings that the features of insider language can be found.

Omissions and truncations

These constitute perhaps the most prominent feature of insider language in the District Court. They refer to the omission of key pieces of information in discourse, as well as the truncation of sentences and questions whereby selective grammar is used; verbs and pronouns are often omitted and even single-word sentences may suffice for successful communication as certain knowledge can be assumed and the relevant information thus omitted, both with regard to the procedures of the court and the context of the case. As an example, a judge may address the court presenter and ask 'Directions?' The question lacks the key information that the directions are those of the DPP in regard to whether the offence before the court can be tried summarily. It is a truncated, one-word question that in its more complete version might be: 'Do you have directions from the DPP in this matter?' The judge, the court presenter and the solicitor/barrister will be aware that this is an indictable offence triable summarily or a hybrid offence and that the jurisdiction of the court to deal with it must be addressed. Communication, therefore, will continue and the response of the court presenter will be given, while those unfamiliar with District

Court procedures, with the jurisdiction of the District Court and with the nature of the offence in question are unlikely to understand the meaning or import of the question.

In addition to the nature of proceedings in the District Court being repetitive, the same offences – traffic, public order, and so on – are tried by the District Court over and over again, and the same sections of the same Acts are naturally used in these prosecutions (e.g. Section 47 Road Traffic Act, Section 4 Public Order Act). It thus becomes possible to omit certain information such as the name of the Act where this knowledge can be assumed ('It's a Section 4'). Although not used in every circumstance, omissions and truncations are extremely common in District Court procedure due to the vast quantity of knowledge that can be assumed, and this feature of the language undoubtedly contributes to the speed of processing offences:

> 'Remand in custody, the 5th of November'
> 'Any previous road traffic?'
> 'Am I to put the Section 38 to him?'
> 'Any previous?'

Many more examples will be given later in the chapter.

Standardised phrases and formalities

As the District Court is essentially a formal setting as well as a setting of routine, formalities and formal, deferential language are used as standard by all official participants, principally the judge, solicitors and barristers, and the Gardaí. Terms of address are extremely important and the judge is consistently addressed as 'Judge' by most participants (though some defendants use 'Your Honour'), with some solicitors/barristers and Gardaí punctuating every sentence – often multiple times – with the term 'Judge'. The judge uses terms of address such as 'counsel', 'Superintendent', 'Inspector', and so on (e.g. 'Forgive me, counsel. In relation to Mr. C, I believe you indicated to me there were a number of outstanding charges' (Judge Q)), and will sometimes address a person using the third person ('Does the registrar have a date for Balbriggan?' (Judge Q)) as well as regularly speaking *as* the court in the third person ('The court notes that ...') and being addressed as such in return ('I submit to the court that ...'). Solicitors/barristers sometimes refer to each other as 'my friend' and inevitably refer to the client formally as Mr./Ms.

Many of the deferential expressions used to address the court are standardised formalities and phrases that are used over and again in the same context. Among these are a small number of archaisms routinely used by solicitors/barristers to address the court, often at the end of the case:

> If it please you, Judge
> May it please the court
> Much obliged

In making submissions or requests to the court the conditional tense is often used: 'I would ask the court', 'I would request that …', and the formal and respectful nature of the requests is often verbalised ('Very formally I would ask you to fix recognisance'; 'In my respectful submission'). Because of the routine nature of proceedings, many of these phrases have become standardised and are used repeatedly. Deference to the judge and consequent standardisation of phrases applies across proceedings, and not just to submissions; for example, the prosecution may verbalise the fact that it is the judge who must decide ('Judge, I'm in your hands') and, when giving evidence, will use the same formulaic descriptions relevant to the charge ('I made a lawful demand …').

District Court jargon

Here 'jargon' refers to the vocabulary or technical terms used in the District Court. These can basically be divided into three sub-categories:

1 Terms that are specific to the legal context but are in common usage and therefore familiar to the average person (examples: accused, allegation, convict, guilty plea, judge, lawyer).
2 Legally based terms that are specific to the District Court but would be unfamiliar to, or unlikely to be fully understood by, the average person (examples: bench warrant, précis, recognisance). This section may also include Latin terms, used in moderation in the District Court: 'The other matters will be remanded *simpliciter*' (Judge Q); 'I think I could accept the *bona fides* of it' (Superintendent, RC); 'What was the alleged *modus operandi*?' (Judge R).
3 Terms that are commonly used in everyday language but have either a different or a very specific meaning in the District Court context (examples: directions, instructions, application, sheets, jurisdiction, hearing, mention, take into consideration, strike out, appear, elect, plead, on her/his feet, at risk, and so on).

The latter category is the largest and the one that is potentially the most challenging for outsiders due to the confusion that may be caused by the use of familiar terms in an unknown context (see Appendix C for a more comprehensive list of District Court jargon).

It is notable that defendants are not generally expected to be familiar with this terminology ('Before lunch you mentioned the word "strike out"; where do you know that from?' (Judge Z)). However, an important feature of District Court language is that because of its repetitive nature much can be acquired through direct experience; the more time one spends in the District Court, the more likely one is to understand what is going on. Naturally, training and the provision of the relevant information are another route to this knowledge but it is of note that much can be acquired through osmosis.

'Now listen here, my good man': different actors, different language

The above features of insider language are used by all District Court participants to a greater or lesser extent. Aside from this common feature, however, the language or speech style of participants can differ significantly, with those from a legal background often using language that is not only more formal but more sophisticated, fluent and self-reflective than the Gardaí, whose less experienced members, perhaps in trying to match the sophistication and formality of the language used by legal professionals, sometimes demonstrate somewhat less linguistic control when attempting improvised formal use of language; the language of the Gardaí is also formal and technical but usually involves the use of standardised rather than improvised phrases. Finally, while some defendants (repeat offenders) master some of the jargon, their use of language is often reflective of a lower socio-economic background.

Barristers, solicitors and judges: sophisticated and conscious use of language

The adept and sophisticated use of language by judges, solicitors and barristers is striking, and their fluid, rapid and concise presentation is both notable and potentially a source of serious comprehension difficulties for those less fluent and able. In practice in court, judges and barristers/solicitors consistently demonstrate a highly sensitised consciousness of the language they use and its impact. Consciousness is sometimes displayed that the language of the court diverges from that of everyday life ('When, to use plain man's language, "he went berserk"' (Judge R)) and judges may modify speech where this causes difficulty:

> JUDGE Z: Is it your intention or aspiration to engage a legal representative?
> DEFENDANT: Sorry?!
> JUDGE Z: Do you want to pay for a solicitor?

JUDGE Z: Give me one good reason why you should not receive a custodial sentence in respect of ... the language you perpetrated on the Garda when she was executing her duty.
DEFENDANT: Eh, can you break that down for me?
JUDGE Z: Would you like two months' detention?

Judges, solicitors and barristers also commonly reflect aloud on the suitability of their words:

'I have my own suspicions, if I might use the word' (Judge Z)
'I'm going to ask Garda P. the alleged time – and I stress "alleged"' (Judge Z)
'My hands are tied. I don't mean it technically, I mean it symbolically' (Judge S)
'... if you want to use the expression, "horsed in" a payment of 2000 Euros' (solicitor/barrister, RC)
'... a failure, but with a small f, rather than a capital F. I'd like to put it that way' (solicitor/barrister, RC)
'It's an explanation rather than an excuse, and it's certainly not a defence, Judge' (solicitor/barrister, RC)

The same reflective consciousness was apparent in interviews with solicitors/barristers:

'... for want of a better word' (Thomas)
'... would be average. I wouldn't say excellent. Average, I would have thought' (Mark)
'There isn't, how shall I say, how do I put this best? ...' (James)

Solicitors/barristers also tend to measure the effect of their words and may distance themselves from what they are saying on a client's behalf:

'He instructs me that he does not suffer from any addiction' (RC)
'I told him the court might call his bluff and ask for urine analysis. Those are his firm instructions' (RC)

JUDGE: Where is his passport?
BARRISTER: He says that he lost it (CusC).

Some of the comments made by solicitors/barristers on the language they use are also interesting to consider in this context. Mark feels the public nature of the setting necessitates consciousness of how language is used – 'it's a public forum; people are listening, the press are attending' – while James feels it is important to speak clearly 'and without recourse to flowery language 'cause it's not your job and it doesn't make you better at it'. However, he recognises a tension between this and 'making sure that the way you express yourself is appropriate' and reflects that 'if we all spoke in a straight kind of way, I mean obviously we'd be done out of a job'. Gwen explains that sometimes you want to convey things to the judge about the client without offending them, and spoke of a colleague who used her fantastic command of the English language to do this; '[she] was absolutely brilliant at that ... and clients absolutely loved her because they didn't realise ... They just heard big words and thought "she's super".'

The language of the Gardaí

As we have seen, generally only the defence is represented by a legal professional while the prosecution is conducted by a member of the Garda Síochána. The difference in the professional background and training of solicitors/barristers and the Gardaí is likely to be influential in the language use and speech styles of both in court, and a distinction can also be made between the language of the court presenter (Superintendent or Inspector) and other Gardaí: the former prosecutes the bulk of cases and is a permanent fixture in the courtroom with potentially more experience of District Court language than many of the Gardaí who come to court to prosecute a particular case.

The Gardaí tend not to reflect on their use of language in the same way as legal professionals and they also tend not to use the archaisms often employed by solicitors and barristers ('may it please' etc.). In general, their speech styles could be said to be slightly less 'flowery'; instead of making requests using expressions like 'if the court was so minded' or 'I would respectfully submit', a Garda may use a more simple yet still formal style, often employing the conditional tense:

> 'I would ask you to strike that out'
> 'I would be seeking a return to trial on that'

Formalities are thus observed and much of the dialogue will involve standard phrases that a Garda will use to give evidence of an arrest or a charge: I made a lawful demand, I made a legal demand, he was handed a true copy of the charge sheet. Omissions, truncations and District Court jargon are also widely and comfortably used by members of the Gardaí. However, while the court presenter often uses formal language successfully in addressing the court ('That is effectively the case, Judge' (RC); 'No documents have been proffered to me, Judge' (CusC)), it is sometimes the case that when a Garda witness with less experience presents the evidence and facts of the case, their attempts at improvised formality fail and betray a less sophisticated grasp of the language:

'The likeliness to re-offend again would be pretty high' (CusC)
'His demeanour towards me was one of aggression' (CusC)
'I inadvertently forgot' (RC)

The language of defendants

District Court language can be difficult for defendants to understand due to its insider nature, particularly where they do not have a solicitor. In such situations judges sometimes have to spend considerably more time dealing with some elements of the case, as that which is apparent to a solicitor and can thus be truncated or omitted in communication must be made explicit to an outsider where an informed response is required.

JUDGE: Do you understand the charge before the court?
DEFENDANT: No.
JUDGE: Right. It is alleged that ... [explains charges]. So do you understand those?
DEFENDANT: I was arrested. ...
JUDGE: What?
DEFENDANT: I was arrested for being drunk.
JUDGE: Yeah. Do you intend pleading guilty or not guilty?
DEFENDANT: I plead guilty to being drunk.

As the majority of defendants are represented, the voice of the defendant is that which is heard least in proceedings and it is not unusual for a defendant to remain silent for the duration of their case. Interestingly, as the above extract suggests, it is sometimes the case that the judge also has difficulty communicating with an unrepresented defendant, though it is impossible to say whether this is due to frustration at proceedings being slowed down, to problems with the use of non-standard English, or to the judge being focused on interaction using insider language and perhaps, therefore, not attuned to language that deviates from this. However, the language used by the average defendant is clearly not insider language and often lacks formality and sophistication, and in straying from the grammar of standard correct English may suggest a lower socio-economic background:

'Once he ownded the vehicle I thought it was OK' (RC)
'I haven't got this chance before. Thanks very much' (CusC)
'That's exactly what happened. I just didn't know how to say it like that' (RC)

JUDGE P: Do you wish to apply for a legal aid solicitor?
DEFENDANT: Yes
JUDGE P: What solicitor do you want?
DEFENDANT: I don't know.
JUDGE P: You are entitled to choose your own solicitor.
DEFENDANT: [Looking around, obviously doesn't know any] Whatever you have.
JUDGE P: What?
DEFENDANT: Whatever you have.

As in the above example, judges sometimes display a degree of condescension, perhaps in believing themselves more linguistically sophisticated than the defendant:

JUDGE S: Two months ago.
DEFENDANT: No, a couple of months ago.
JUDGE S: A couple generally means two. What does it mean to you?

DEFENDANT: As far as I'm aware I never had probation.
JUDGE S: [Disparagingly] You would *be* aware if you had.

JUDGE P: *In vino veritas*, which means that when you're drunk you say what you mean.
DEFENDANT: I know what it means.

Many defendants appearing in the Irish District Court are not there for the first time and such defendants may be familiar with the system and insider language. Matthew says that repeat offenders 'would know the system very well, in terms of the procedure, and what happens when you come before the court for the first time, what a bail application is like etc.', and James agrees:

> They know the process, they know what's coming next, they know the difference between a summary and an indictable offence, ... they know what it means when a judge refuses jurisdiction, they know the kind of things that a judge will take into account in deciding whether or not to grant bail. They know the kind of things that a judge will take into account in determining the correct sentence.

The repeat offender is thus likely to be able to understand and perhaps even use insider language: 'I'm remanded on these four' (CusC).

Linguistic discretion and control: the style of individual judges

We looked in the previous chapter at judicial discretion and, in practice, the judge is 'the God of the court' (Stella), at the head of the court and at the helm of all that happens. While solicitors, barristers, the Gardaí and other official participants in the District Court must adhere to set protocol, the judge is at liberty to choose his or her own style of language and each has his or her own mannerisms, expressions and methods of conducting procedures and keeping control of the courtroom. For example, while solicitors, barristers and Gardaí consistently use formal terms of address, a judge may refer to or address the defendant formally (Mr. D), indirectly as 'the client' or 'the defendant', on a first name basis or using terms of address such as 'my dear fellow'. The judge is generally the most verbally active person in court, though some judges are more verbally active than others, and this is something that seems to equate directly to the level of intervention or control practised by the judge. It is the judge who controls proceedings and the speech of others – who can speak, when and to say what. Some do this forcefully by interrupting, contradicting, forbidding or demanding speech, while others are less intrusive and may request specific information or invite participants to speak:

> 'Would you mind answering the questions. You're continually writing instead of listening' (Judge S)
> 'Will you speak up a little so I can hear you?' (Judge S)
> 'I don't give a damn. I'm just interested in finding out whether you have been engaged in criminal activity elsewhere' (Judge Z)
> 'Would you like to say anything?' (Judge Y)
> 'Would you answer, please?' (Judge Q)

Judges also use language in different ways to control the courtroom, for example by expressing their authority or their expectations when behaviour is perceived to deviate from that which is appropriate:

> 'This is *my* court' (Judge S)
> '*I'll* decide how I'll run my list' (Judge S)
> 'I'm entitled to put the case back' (Judge S)
> 'I'm the Presiding Judge in this matter' (Judge R)
> 'I would suggest, quietly, that neither you nor the prosecution has the right to decide who should appear' (Judge Y)
> 'Were you appointed a District Court judge recently?' (Judge Y)
> 'Now listen here, my good man. This is not a public house you're in now' (Judge Z)
> 'I'm not going to be tolerating this kind of arrogance. ... I'd ask you to have some manners at the very least. It's not a lot to ask, but there you are' (Judge Z)

In addition and related to this, the judges I observed also spent time delivering monologues or lectures that only sometimes related to the case before the court on such topics as frustration with bureaucratic or court-based inefficiencies ('I really wish you'd prepare these things before you came in' (Judge S) or 'In the High Court ... if they worked any slower they'd slip into reverse' (Judge Z)); societal and moral ills ('The insidious nature of this problem in this society is not recognised' (Judge Z)); money ('Don't mess up dates. Don't waste taxpayers' money' (Judge T)); rights and duties ('The defendant is entitled to a presumption of innocence. He is entitled to use the system fully and fairly' (Judge U)); criminality, courtroom control, and so on. As these examples suggest, the linguistic discretion and control of judges is used in a variety of different ways and represents probably the most individualistic aspect of District Court dialogue.

Deviance from standard District Court language: informality, colloquialisms and humour

As has been seen, deviance from standard District Court language is largely controlled by the judge and, in some cases, judges themselves may indulge in such deviance (such as the monologues above, the use of informal and colloquial language, or humour) but not tolerate it from other court participants; solicitors and barristers appear to know, or quickly assess, what style or degree of informality is appropriate for any given judge and to adapt their language use accordingly. Deviance from standard District Court language may be an attempt to reduce the banality of proceedings ('I'm trying to debate the matter with you. I have to make decisions that are not bland or rubber-stamped' (Judge R)) or perhaps to render things less formal:

> 'What was naughty about his driving?' (Judge P)
> 'His excuse doesn't wash' (Judge S)
> 'I believe he's trying to pull the wool over this court's eyes' (Judge Z)
> 'As they say in Ireland you want jam on both sides of your bread' (Judge Z)
> 'Had you a liquid lunch or something?' (Judge Y)
> 'This man was polluted' (Judge R)

Such informality and colloquialisms are predominantly used by judges but are also employed occasionally by solicitors and barristers, and concurrent use with archaisms, formality or jargon can create a bizarre effect:

> 'Because of the turn number I told him he could go off for a cup of tea. May it please' (RC)
> 'Unless he's in the loo. [Pause] We are pleading, Judge' (CusC)

Informality, the minor nature of the court's workload and the authority of the judge are also sometimes indicated through the humour not uncommonly used by judges:

> JUDGE Y: [To Garda in bullet-proof vest] I'm just looking at your vest; are you in danger of being shot?
> GARDA: Sorry, Judge. I apologise for my attire.
>
> DEFENDANT: Not guilty.
> JUDGE P: Is it going to be one of those cases? Cut throat?
> SOLICITOR: [Smiling] It is, yes.
> GARDA: [The defendant assaulted Mr. X in Y Park]
> JUDGE P: What were they doing in the park? Were they there to feed the ducks?
> GARDA: [They were at a concert]
> JUDGE P: What was the nature of the alleged assault? ... Did he throw the duck bread at him?
>
> SOLICITOR: [Defendant pleading guilty to theft of significant amount of alcohol] This is a young man who has been in the country for two years. The plan was that he was going to have a party.
> JUDGE Z: [Laughing] They weren't going to be thirsty, I can tell you that!

'All stand in court': a District Court case in action

Here, the District Court case is broken down into a set of linguistic units. These units do not exist in reality, as in reality there are no marked divisions between the different aspects of a case that are dealt with by the court on a particular day. However, they broadly represent the stages that a case goes through when being processed and eventually disposed of. On each day, the case before the court has a Beginning, a Middle and an End, with the Middle being the most variable and that which is dependent on the type of offence in question and on the stage at which the case is at as it moves through the system. Analysis of the District Court case as a series of linguistic units allows a better understanding of the use of insider language in action.

The Beginning

> Standing in court
> All stand in court
>
> Garda X and [Defendant]
> DPP versus [Defendant]
> Defendant A followed by Defendant B

In the District Court everything starts with the registrar or court clerk, who opens each court session and calls each individual case. The voice of the registrar remains otherwise silent for the most part. There is a degree of amusement to be had when the name is foreign, as registrars inevitably struggle and judges have at least as much difficulty ('Can you pronounce that properly? Have you got that in front of you? It's number 36 on the list' (Judge Z)). District Court jargon and archaisms are prominent, and participants are established using the expression 'to appear':

> JUDGE: Who's appearing?
> Any appearance by or on behalf of [Defendant]?
> SOLICITOR/BARRISTER: Judge, I appear for Mr. N.
> If it please you, Judge, I appear for Mr. D.

In the event of a foreign-sounding name being called the presence, lack of or need for an interpreter may be addressed (see also Chapters 4 and 5) and, if one is assigned, the judge often officialises their presence verbally: 'I certify for the interpreter present'; 'I certify for a Polish interpreter'. In the case of unrepresented defendants the question of legal representation may be introduced at this point:

> JUDGE R: Do you have a solicitor?
> DEFENDANT: No.
> JUDGE R: Do you know a solicitor?
> DEFENDANT: No.

The purpose of the appearance is sometimes made explicit by the solicitor/barrister concurrently ('I appear. It's an ID matter' (CusC)), the judge may raise the context ('What's this about?' (Judge R), 'There are two prosecutions before me' (Judge Z)), or the context may remain undisclosed. If the case is in progress through the system, what happened on previous occasions may be raised ('It was conceded on the last day that ...' (RC)).

In many instances participants are not present or ready to proceed. For example, a solicitor/barrister may need to 'take instruction' from the client and will request that the matter be allowed to 'stand', be 'put back' or be put to 'second calling', all further examples of District Court jargon meaning that the case will be called again later on the same day. As with other aspects of court procedure, judges have individualised responses to and tolerance levels for such requests; some will acquiesce without question ('Of course, no problem') while others become impatient:

BARRISTER: I'd like to ask for second calling.
JUDGE R: Why?
BARRISTER: I need to take instructions
JUDGE R: You should know your business ...

The Middle

What happens in the Middle depends on the type of case and what stage of the system it is at. It usually involves a combination of the following units:

The Applications (strike out/bench warrant; legal aid; bail; disclosure; remands/adjournments)
The Charge
Jurisdiction (DPP directions; judge's decision; defendant's election)
The Plea
The Facts/Evidence
Criminal Record
Mitigation/Defence
Sentence

This analysis focuses on the guilty plea, such that while all of the units before 'the Plea' are the same, the principal difference thereafter is that on a plea of not guilty the case proceeds to a hearing which from a linguistic perspective cannot be said to differ substantially from the guilty plea at District Court level, though evidence is given and cross-examination carried out ('I put it to you that ...'), and there is more likely to be conflict and submissions as to the unlawfulness of arrest and so on ('I submit he didn't tell him in full where the power of search was from' (CusC)).

THE APPLICATIONS

An application is basically any request made to the court. They typically involve heavy use of insider language including District Court jargon.

STRIKE OUT/BENCH WARRANT

In the event of non-appearance by one party, certain applications may be made; if the defendant fails to appear the prosecution may ask for a bench warrant, which gives the Gardaí the power to bring that person before the court. A Garda will typically say 'My application would be for a bench warrant', a request which uses the characteristically formal conditional tense and District Court jargon: 'application' and 'bench warrant'. If the prosecuting Garda fails to appear and has not given the court presenter instructions, the defence may ask that the charge be struck out or dropped. 'Application to strike out' (CitC); this example uses a truncated sentence without the pronoun and the verb, and more District Court jargon. Strike outs can be made for many other reasons, such as the charges being withdrawn, and they are also regularly requested by the prosecution.

LEGAL AID

'Would you consider a certificate for legal aid?' (RC)
'There would be an application for bail and legal aid' (RC)
'Would you consider granting legal aid, Judge? He would be at risk' (RC)

Legal aid is often dealt with in tandem with assigning legal representation; for example, the judge will assign the defendant a legal aid solicitor. If the defendant is already represented, an application may be made by the solicitor/barrister for legal aid. The term 'at risk' is used to mean that there is a risk that the defendant may be given a custodial sentence and the request is often made with formal, deferential language, possibly because of the wide discretion of judges to grant or withhold the assistance. It also seems that the more stringent a judge is about legal aid, the more formal and deferential is the request; judges appear to have different criteria by which they consider granting legal aid and very different approaches to applications. Judge Z, for example, often pursued the matter of vehicle ownership at length:

JUDGE: Do you have possession or control of a vehicle?
DEFENDANT: Yes.
JUDGE: How much is it worth?
DEFENDANT: Around 1500 Euro.
JUDGE: Why don't you sell it and pay for your legal fees?
DEFENDANT: [Smiling] Nobody wants to buy it.
JUDGE: Do you drive it?
DEFENDANT: Yes.
JUDGE: Does it run on water?
DEFENDANT: No.
JUDGE: Where do you buy fuel?
DEFENDANT: In Shell.
JUDGE: It is not the intention of this court to spend the taxpayers' money. You can submit a statement of means and you should sell your vehicle to pay your legal fees.

Some judges routinely granted legal aid as it was applied for or asked basic questions, including whether the person was at risk or if the person was working. However, Judge Y, for example, would not deal with the issue of legal aid when she replaced the sitting judge for a day, saying mysteriously, 'I have introduced very strict conditions for legal aid that you mightn't like, so I'll leave it to the sitting judge.' In relation to linguistic discretion, the issue of legal aid and the related issue of taxpayers' money was a popular monologue topic for District Court judges.

Bail applications

> 'Any objection to the defendant being admitted to own bail?' (Judge Z)
> 'Is there an objection to bail?' (Judge R)
> 'There would be an objection to bail' (prosecution, CusC)
> 'No objection' (prosecution, CusC)
> 'On the basis of the evidence I'm refusing bail' (Judge W)
> 'I am refusing bail today. If you adduce medical or other evidence you can go to the High Court with it' (Judge R)

When the defence makes an application to have the defendant released on bail, the judge commonly asks the prosecution if there are objections to granting bail, whereupon any objections are outlined; these may be based on considerations such as a 'history of warrants' (where the person had not appeared for trial previously), on the person being a 'flight risk' (likely to leave the jurisdiction) or on not having proven his/her identity ('It's an identity issue' (CusC)). The judge will grant bail or otherwise. Unlike other units the judge rarely truncates this question and, although formal language is used, the terms 'objection' and 'bail' could here be considered words in common usage. However, the granting of bail often involves a number of conditions set by the prosecution and/or the judge which are considerably less easy to follow; the conditions and how they are expressed can be complex and vary considerably, and they are generally delivered at such speed that sometimes even solicitors/barristers have difficulties. Of the following, the first three are reasonably standard conditions often imposed by the Gardaí while the remainder – imposed by judges – differ notably in their complexity and the formality of their construction:

> Stay away from [Area]
> Reside at [address]
> Sign on daily at [X] Garda Station
> 'No alcohol, no unprescribed medication' (Judge S)
> 'Lead a sober and industrious life ... barred from all licensed premises in the state ... not to associate with anyone on bail ...' (Judge Z)
> 'On leaving custody he must go immediately to [Place] Residential Treatment. He must reside there and take all directions. Curfew; he must not leave [Place] at any time unless under direction, and he must take all treatment' (Judge S)

While for some judges the unit ends here, others address the defendant to warn (or threaten) about compliance and/or to ensure that the conditions have been understood before a bail bond is signed:

> 'I will review bail on [date], and if there is any suggestion that you are not in compliance you will be spending Christmas in [Prison]' (Judge Z)
> 'If you've any difficulty in understanding, consult with your solicitor. It's tremendously important that you comply. I wish you well' (Judge Q)
> 'May I ask you, before you sign the bail bond, do you understand the conditions of bail or do you seek clarification on any point?' (Judge Z)

The registrar usually recalls the case some time later, the judge asks 'Is this your signature?' and, on confirmation, a copy of the bail bond is given to the defendant.

Remands/adjournments

> 'Judge, I've been instructed to seek a remand' (barrister)
> 'I'm looking to adjourn that by consent' (solicitor)
> 'My application would be for four weeks' (prosecution)

Requests for cases to be remanded or adjourned are made very frequently and for a myriad of reasons. Common ones include for DPP directions, for reports, to engage counsel, for disclosure, and so on. Again, judges vary enormously in their tolerance of such requests: some grant them freely, some do not grant them without what they consider sufficient reason, and some are particularly concerned that any delays be consented to:

> 'It's clearly marked for hearing, so it's either on or out, I'm afraid' (Judge Y)
> 'And he's prepared to consent to custody for six weeks?' (Judge S)
> 'Is there consent, then, to remand in custody for one week?' (Judge Q)

Consent is not always forthcoming:

> JUDGE S: Is there consent?
> BARRISTER: No, there is no consent to any time at all.
> JUDGE S: We go into evidence when there's a dispute.

Disclosure

> 'We are seeking disclosure' (barrister, CusC)
> 'The application is to put it back for one week, and for a précis' (barrister, CusC)
> 'I am waiting for statements. I have them in one and not in another' (solicitor, RC)

'An order for précis and CCTV where applicable' (Judge R)
'Would you be kind enough to get a précis and send it to Ms. [Solicitor]'s office?' (Judge R)

In District Court jargon the solicitor or barrister will 'seek disclosure', make an 'application' for disclosure, or seek or make applications for a 'précis' (statement of evidence), statements, CCTV, interview memos, and so on for which the judge will make an 'order'. Applications vary slightly between solicitors/barristers and different terms are used more frequently in some courts than others.

The charge

'Allegation, please' (Judge R)
'What's being alleged?' (Judge P)
'What is the charge?' (Judge S)

The defendant has been charged with a criminal offence, which should be known to the defendant, the solicitor/barrister and the prosecution. As such, it is not surprising that insider language is generally used in referring to it, such as in the judges' enquiries in the form of truncated questions above and in the reading of the charge, which in District Court jargon is frequently abbreviated to a section number, the nature of the offence or a combination of both:

'Strike out Section 4. That leaves us with Section 49' (Judge Z)
'He's also anxious to deal with the Section 13 matter' (barrister, CusC)
'Straightforward shoplifting' (Judge S)
'Three counts of criminal damage' (court presenter, CusC)
'Section 2, public order' (Garda, CitC)

The set of charges may be more complex, as one solicitor from the Rurual Court indicates here in a typically eloquent manner: 'In addition to the new charges before the court today, there are a number of others of some antiquity.' Particularly when defendants are unrepresented, judges tend to ask them whether or not they understand the charge, though different judges concern themselves with this to varying degrees:

JUDGE Z: Do you understand the charge before this court?
DEFENDANT: I suppose, I guess. Yes.
JUDGE Z: No, I have to be absolutely clear. Do you want me to read out the charge?
DEFENDANT: No, I understand.

For charge sheet offences, evidence is required with regard to the arrest. The typical examples of one judge's questions below indicate their 'insider' nature: it is a standard request for standard information, the arresting Garda is fully anticipating the question, and the Judge (Z) can thus dispense with grammatically complete sentences.

> 'Evidence of arrest, charge and caution?'
> 'Reply after caution to the Section 13 offence?'

Much of the time the judge simply waits as the Garda is sworn in and begins to give the evidence without prompting. These excerpts demonstrate the standard and formal manner in which evidence is given about the charge; terms and expressions like 'legal demand', 'lawful demand', 'true copy of the charge sheet', 'Garda station of his/her choice' and 'conveyed to the station' are commonly used by Gardaí in providing this evidence.

> 'Judge, this morning before the court I charged defendant on charge sheets [numbers]. He was cautioned for each sheet and made no reply' (CusC)
> 'I explained in ordinary language what this meant and why I was stopping him' (CusC)
> 'He gave no reply after caution ... He was handed a true copy of the charge sheet' (CusC)
> 'The defendant was conveyed to [Town] Garda Station' (RC)
> 'I made a legal demand for him to produce his licence at a Garda Station of his choice' (RC)

Jurisdiction

This unit applies only to indictable offences triable summarily or hybrid offences. On any given day, the unit can involve one or a combination of the three elements: the 'directions' or 'instructions' of the DPP as to whether the case may be tried summarily; the judge's willingness to try it in the District Court; and the 'election' of the defendant of summary trial. The insider nature of District Court language – particularly omissions, truncations and jargon – is very apparent in this unit and the jargon can be particularly misleading or confusing; the words 'directions' and 'election', for example, though having a very specific meaning in this context, can mean very different things in other contexts. If the case is not to be tried summarily the prosecution must produce a 'book of evidence' ('the book') for the defence which is 'served' on the defendant ('All charge sheets on indictment please. ... The guard is about to serve the book' (CusC)).

DPP directions

> 'Have directions been given?' (Judge Z)
> 'The DPP consents to summary?' (Judge Z)

'Mode of trial?' (Judge Z)
'First of all do we have instructions?' (Judge S)

The judge frequently uses truncated questions to ask the prosecution about the DPP's orders. The order may not yet have been received and, if it has, the details will be given in formal language:

'We are still awaiting directions in this matter. The file is with the DPP and I've been told it's being given priority' (court presenter, CusC)
'I have directions from the Director, so it is purely an indictable matter, and I would be seeking a return to trial on that' (court presenter, RC)

The judge's decision

The judge asks for details of the alleged offence to decide whether to accept or refuse jurisdiction:

'What's the allegation, so that I can consider jurisdiction?' (Judge R)
'I refuse jurisdiction. It's not a minor offence' (Judge S)

Judge S: Nobody was intimidated?
Prosecution: No, Judge.
Judge S: I'll accept jurisdiction.

The defendant's election

The decision of the defendant may be requested or simply given. As the defendant can only waive the right to jury trial if he/she is aware of that right, judges are concerned (to very varying degrees) about whether this is the case.

Judge S: Is your client ready to elect?
Barrister: Electing District Court, Judge, aware of .... [trails off]

Judge R: Have we dealt with jurisdiction under Section 2?
Barrister: Electing for District Court. I would ask for disclosure.

Judge S: Is the client accepting this court?
Barrister: Yes.
Judge S: Knowing his rights?
Barrister: Yes.

The Plea

Judge R: Is there a plea of guilty?
Barrister: Yes, Judge.

Judge Z: Can you indicate how you're pleading; guilty or not guilty?
Defendant: Guilty.

It is probably fair to say that the notion of admitting or denying guilt is fundamental to the criminal justice system and is therefore not difficult to understand, despite this unit involving the frequent use of truncated sentences and the occasional use of more formal constructions. The solicitor/barrister may 'indicate' or 'enter' a plea on appearance, in which case language style may involve more elements of insider language:

> 'I appear. There's a plea, Judge' (RC)
> 'We are in a position to indicate a guilty plea' (RC)
> 'It's in for a plea or a date. I'll take a date, please' (CusC)

In District Court jargon a case is often described as being 'in' (before the court) or 'put back' (remanded/adjourned) for a particular purpose. These include for 'mention', 'hearing', 'a probation report', 'a book of evidence', 'a plea or a date', and so on. In the expression 'a plea or a date', 'a plea' is a guilty plea and 'a date' indicates that a date is to be set for a hearing if the plea is one of not guilty. Thus, in the last example the barrister is indicating a plea of not guilty, quite an obscure reference if one is not familiar with District Court language and procedure.

The facts/evidence

> 'Election of summary trial, a plea of guilty, I'll hear the facts' (Judge Z)
> 'Now, facts please' (Judge S)

The 'facts' of the case are basically what is alleged by the prosecution to have happened in relation to the offence before the court. Logically, therefore, the prosecution is the primary element in this unit and in the event of a guilty plea the facts will generally be furnished or established by the arresting Garda or the court presenter. As mentioned, these may also be considered in respect of jurisdiction and it is not uncommon for them to be given on a number of occasions by the prosecution and/or to be summarised or revised by the judge. The facts of each case are necessarily different but a common feature is the speed and low volume with which Gardaí tend to deliver them, often making them very difficult to follow and understand. The insider standardised phrases used by the Gardaí are also common, as similar details concerning the court are given in many cases, including about the behaviour of the defendant:

> 'I have to say that Mr. X was fully co-operative and completely truthful. Anything he was asked he answered truthfully' (RC)
> 'He hasn't come to the attention of the court' (RC)

Questions from the judge will often supplement the Garda's account:

JUDGE Z: The chinchillas, were they returned to the owner?
SOLICITOR: Well, a rabbit escaped.

JUDGE S: He abused somebody who tried to help him. Did it continue in the presence of the Gardaí?
PROSECUTION: He had to be restrained.
JUDGE S: How much damage was done?
PROSECUTION: 80 Euro.

Efficiency and relevance appear to be two important characteristics in the presentation and establishment of the facts. Consider the following questions fired quickly (and without verbs) by one judge (R) to ascertain the missing details: 'Time of evening? ... People present in the premises? ... Value, circumstance, location? ... People present, elderly, young? ... Manner of entry? ... No violence?'

The facts are rarely disputed, though occasionally an issue may be contested or questioned and the judge may give an unrepresented defendant the opportunity to do so. Otherwise facts are often affirmed by the solicitor/barrister or the judge:

'That's the position. There's just one issue I'd like to put to the Guard' (solicitor, RC)
'Have you any questions for the Garda?' (Judge Z)
'The facts are as the Inspector has fairly stated' (solicitor, RC)
'In relation to the facts you've no quibble' (Judge Q)
'The facts there speak for themselves' (Judge R)

A final possibility, which relates somewhat to Mitigation below, is that the judge may seek clarification or explanations on certain elements of the facts:

'Why was the accused not insured?' (Judge R)
'Why does he not have a passport? Where is it?' (Judge S)

CRIMINAL RECORD

JUDGE: Has he previous?
Any previous?
Previous convictions?
Previous?
Now, are there any previous convictions?
GARDA: No previous
Reading of 70. One previous conviction. Section 47 Road Traffic (RC)

In this unit, the defendant's criminal history, or lack thereof, is established and most dialogue is between the judge and the prosecution, though the solicitor/barrister sometimes provides the requisite information.

The dialogue of this unit is generally very fast and insider language is common, with truncation of questions and statements used more often than not. The details of previous offences are given and if these are numerous the judge may ask for the most recent or for a breakdown:

> 'What was the last one?' (Judge Z)
> 'What is the pattern?' (Judge Q)
> 'What is the gist of the rest?' (Judge S)

Mitigation/defence

> 'Would you tell the court what's causing this? What's causing this recidivism by Mr. C?' (Judge R)
> 'What's going on in his life? Anything in mitigation?' (Judge R)
> 'What are the financial, family and work circumstances?' (Judge Z)
> 'What do you have to say in defence?' (Judge S)
> 'What's your explanation?' (Judge Z)

The objective of this unit is for (usually) the defence solicitor/barrister to throw as positive and favourable a light as possible on the defendant, personally and/or in relation to the offence. Details will be given about the defendant's background, typically highlighting either the fact that this represents an aberration from his or her usual, upstanding self, or indicating that social background and many difficulties have contributed or led inevitably to deviance; reasons, explanations, excuses, apologies and aspirations are proffered in an effort to mitigate the severity of sentence. The unit may be opened by the judge addressing either the solicitor/barrister or the unrepresented defendant, or by the solicitor/barrister, who in either case will generally deliver a monologue that constitutes the bulk of the unit. Interestingly, the use of 'insider' language is relatively rare, which may be due to the desirability that the defendant understand what is being said on his or her behalf and thus feel fairly and truly represented. That said, Mitigation is often – like the rest of the District Court case – extremely repetitive with the same type of information being given in the same type of cases over and again. The judge and his or her known sympathies and intolerances undoubtedly influence the details given, though the following topics are commonly broached:

Age, character and employment

> 'It's hardly the work of a criminal mastermind' (RC)
> 'He's not an aggressive type' (RC)
> 'He's a young man in gainful employment. He's never been in bother before' (RC)

Family support and background

'He comes from a big family, his father died when he was [age]' (CusC)

'He is living with his father, who is behind him there' (RC)

'He is a man who has two young children. He is in a stable relationship with his wife' (CusC)

Alcohol and drug status

'He appreciates he has a very serious drug problem' (CusC)

'He is a man who would benefit from treatment' (CusC)

'He admits that a few drinks had been taken' (CitC)

'He has no addictions' (CusC)

Achievements, co-operation and guilty pleas

'He's one of the success stories' (RC)

'He has turned his life around, he's trying to improve. He drinks a lot less than before' (CitC)

'I would respectfully submit that his plea of guilty is not based on being caught red-handed' (CusC)

'He did assist the Gardaí, and when he was approached on the street he admitted the offence, thereby saving the Gardaí time and expense' (RC)

Apologies, remorse and acknowledgement of mistakes

'He wants to apologise for his behaviour' (RC)

'It was an appalling mistake' (RC)

'He greatly regrets and is embarrassed by this' (RC)

'He throws himself on the mercy of the court, Judge' (CusC)

Acknowledgement of seriousness

'He knows that he's facing a custodial sentence today' (CusC)

'He is fully aware that the court will take a very dim view' (CusC)

Request for leniency

'I would ask for leniency. He has pleaded guilty to an opportunistic offence' (CusC)

'He regrets the offence. These are his only two transgressions ever. I would ask you to be lenient, Judge' (RC)

The following illustrates a typical monologue (CusC):

> He is a Polish man of thirty-six. He has been married for two and a half years. He minds his friend's child. He was employed in warehousing for a year and a half. He is on social welfare. He knows that his behaviour was stupid. Drink is the problem, alcohol dependency. He did plead guilty.

Judges sometimes react to the points raised, for example in congratulating a person on an achievement or – more commonly – expressing disbelief or a lack of acceptance:

'It was disrespectful of the client to raise the issue of his bereavement in this court in defence of his position. If you respect the dead, this is the last place it should be resurrected' (Judge Z)
'I'm always suspicious of people who use innocent children to save their own bacon' (Judge Z)
'I wouldn't accept that. You're nothing but a blackguard' (Judge Z)
'Why was he drinking all night and all day? That doesn't show any remorse or contriteness' (Judge Z)
'It is not credible' (Judge Q)
'For him to make excuses like this is no credit to him at all' (Judge Q)
'He may have had something terrible happen to him … but it doesn't really seem to have much to do with the offences' (Judge S)
'A bad childhood? That sounds like you're blaming your parents' (Judge S)
'Excellent, well done. I congratulate you' (Judge R)
'I see that, which is very excellent news' (Judge R)
'I'm impressed by one factor only – he's been drug-free since the 18th of December' (Judge R)

Sentence

'Section 49 convict and fine 400 Euro, four months' (Judge O)
'Convict and fine 200 Euro, one month to pay, ten days in default. Recognisance on own bond fifty Euros' (Judge O)

Judge Q: I'm imposing a three month sentence. I will suspend it for twelve months. He will enter a probation bond, twelve months, in his own bond 200 Euro. He will provide compensation to the owner of the property. In what sum [Inspector]?
Prosecution: 200 Euro.
Judge Q: And he will attend counselling. The second matter, convict and take into consideration in light of the sentence imposed.

Sentence may be (or have been) adjourned for a variety of reasons such as for a pre-sentence report, probation report, community service report or substance abuse report and it is, naturally, imposed by the judge. As such it is generally only the judge who speaks in this unit, which is notable for the extreme speed and low volume with which it is customarily delivered, for the amount of jargon used, and for the complexity of sentence structure as well as the complexity of the sentence itself. This may involve numerous orders: details of fines involving the amount and how long the person has to pay; dates, length and place of custodial sentences, which may be suspended or given concurrently; the length of time of disqualification from driving; probation or community service; Probation of Offenders Act; compensation or contributions to charities or the court poor box; taking into consideration of offences, and so on. Where sentencing is in respect of multiple charges, as it often is, this unit can be utterly bewildering.

In addition, some judges offer a degree of sentencing rationale or reasoning:

> 'What I'm trying to do is keep people out of prison. I think it's in the interests of justice' (Judge Z)
> 'I've no option but to send him to jail' (Judge S)
> 'I took a dim view because this man has been twice disqualified from driving' (Judge Q)
> 'Cigarette smuggling is a serious offence. Convict, fine 400 Euro, four months in prison, suspended for two. Enter into a peace bond for twelve months on own bond of 1000 Euro' (Judge T)

Finally, in this unit the judge frequently expresses his/her views on the crime or the convicted person and monologues are not uncommon:

> 'It's crimes like this that prevent people getting help when they need it' (Judge S)
> 'It's a blatant, criminal, putting-lives-at-risk thing to do' (Judge S)
> 'This was outrageous. ... It's more than a drink problem' (Judge S)
> 'It's important for this court to understand how many people this person has contaminated' (Judge Z)
> 'It is a sad reflection of certain people in Ireland who persist in this shameful [behaviour]' (Judge Z)

The End

If the case is not being disposed of on that date but must come before the court again, a further date is given and the purpose of the new date often specified. Jargon and truncated sentences are usual:

> '28th of October for a plea or a date in all matters' (Judge S)
> 'In for hearing, 11th of July. 2pm' (Judge T)
> 'By consent to the 15th, this court, to verify ID' (Judge S)
> 'Remand in custody, 8th of April 2009' (Judge X)
> 'Remand on continuing bail until 23rd of April.' (Judge X)
> 'For directions ASAP' (Judge S)

If being disposed of, the judge may formally announce this:

> 'That completes that matter' (Judge Q)
> 'That leads me to conclude the proceedings in respect of Section 50' (Judge Z)
> 'The accused is now free to go. He's at his liberty' (Judge R)

Some judges end by thanking the participants – sometimes as a signal that it is over – and, as the solicitor/barrister did at the appearance stage at the beginning of the case, he or she will usually thank the court with formal and archaic expressions:

> Much obliged
> If it pleases the court

Breaking down the case in this manner may create a somewhat false illusion as things do not always progress in this, or any, neat sequence. There is no pause or divide between what have been labelled units here; turns are not taken slowly, one by one, as it may appear when neatly written down; and a case may come before the court on numerous occasions, and over long periods of time, before it is disposed of. The reality is that when a case is called, three or four units may be dealt with in less than a minute and the case swiftly remanded or adjourned to another date. In one breath, the solicitor or barrister, for example, can cover multiple topics, providing information and making applications, all with fast-flowing and formal articulacy, replete with District Court jargon, punctured with truncations and omissions, and wrapped in deferential archaisms.

Conclusion

In one sense, the District Court is a model of efficient and effective communication. In another sense its exclusive and exclusionary language makes it inaccessible and meaningless to outsiders. Its defining feature is its reliance on shared knowledge and experience to function as communication, and the language used in the District Court is both a product of, and facilitative of, District Court proceedings and the workload of this court; things move quickly due to the large workload, such that speech and proceedings are often rapid and difficult for outsiders to follow. The perceived need for speed is also undoubtedly a factor in some of the principal features of the 'insider' nature of District Court language: the omission of pivotal pieces of information that another participant can be assumed to identify and understand implicitly, and the grammatical truncation of sentences, whereby principally verbs and pronouns are omitted and sentences or questions may consist of only one word.

The effectiveness of such communication stems from the repetitive nature of District Court proceedings; first, the same types of cases, often with similar circumstances, are dealt with over and over again, such that those familiar with the District Court will be familiar with the cases being processed and can easily understand truncated references, such as 'It's a Section 99'. Secondly, the processing of the District Court case is essentially a ritualised, routinised procedure that consists of a combination of a limited set of elements; the elements relevant to the case depend on the offence in question and on the plea, while the elements dealt with on a particular day depend on the stage at which the case is in the system (or what the case is in for on that day) and what is being sought. On any given day a case will have a very formal Beginning and End in which standardised, deferential and often archaic expressions are used by participants to address the court. The Middle section typically consists of a combination of the following units: Applications (strike outs, warrants, legal aid, bail, remands, disclosure), The Charge, Jurisdiction, The Plea, The Facts/Evidence, Criminal Record, Mitigation/Defence and the Sentence. The more experience one has in the District Court, the easier it becomes to understand and use the language.

In addition to omissions and truncations, District Court insider language features formalities and standardised phrases as well as District Court jargon, which can be divided into three sub-categories: legally based language that is familiar and commonly used; legally based language not commonly used; and everyday words that are used in a different sense or have a specific meaning in the District Court context. The latter sub-group is the largest, the most commonly used and also that which can potentially create the most confusion for those unfamiliar with the language and proceedings.

Perhaps the final defining feature of the language used in the District Court is the difference in the speech of various participants. Judges are undoubtedly the most verbally active and in control of the speech used in the courtroom; they use all the features of insider language, but it is also the judge that controls variance or deviance from this, including the use of humour, informalities and colloquialisms. Judges also have discretion to use terms of address inappropriate for other participants and to deviate from set procedure to deliver monologues or lectures on topics that may include, for example, moral ills, societal problems or bureaucratic frustrations. Judges, in common with solicitors and barristers, not only tend to be fluent and excellent language users, but also reflective language users that demonstrate a sensitised consciousness of the language they use, and they will often reflect on or qualify a choice of words.

This tendency is not evident in the language used by the Gardaí, who nonetheless use very formal, standardised language in the course of proceedings. The difference between solicitors and barristers and the Gardaí is further underlined by the less experienced Garda who sometimes attempts to improvise with formal and sophisticated language but fails to use the formal language correctly. In general, members of the Gardaí tend not to use archaic or 'flowery' expressions to the same extent as solicitors/barristers.

Though the voice of the defendant is that which is heard least in the courtroom, there is a notable difference in the language of repeat offenders who have experience and knowledge of the language and procedures of the District Court, and the defendant who has no such experience, as the former often understands and can use insider language, specifically District Court jargon. However, the language spoken by defendants often suggests a lower socio-economic background as it lacks the correctness of standard English and the formality otherwise used in court.

District Court language thus reflects the defining features of the court itself; generally minor, repetitive matters that proceed at high speed without contest, conflict or legal argument and which are prosecuted by members of the Garda Síochána, who generally do not have a legal background, and defended and judged by members of the legal profession, who clearly do. It reflects the wide discretion of the District Court judge in deciding how offences are processed, sentences given and courtroom discourse managed; solicitors/barristers' awareness of judges' proclivities and the adaptation of their strategies accordingly; and the somewhat unusual position of the Garda as a prosecutor who will sometimes endorse the defendant or their claims. It reflects the fact that defendants are sharply divided into those that end up in court by some misfortune or aberration and those that are there in a long cycle of repeat offending, that the same types of cases are heard repeatedly by the court and that the same old stories are told and excuses given, time and again, to varying degrees of interest, belief and tolerance on the part of the sitting judge.

Until now the District Court has been considered as a monolingual institution but the next chapter introduces a new type of defendant – the LEP defendant. In addition to tracing the development of the interpreting system designed to cater for the language needs of this new defendant, it explores in detail the role of the interpreter in a criminal trial, the process of court interpreting and the right of defendants to interpreting at trial.

Note

1 Please refer to 'Guide to extracts from District Court field notes and interviews' for an explanation of how anonymised courts and judges are referred to in the text.

PART II

Immigration and the Irish District Court: changing context, new challenges

3

LEP immigrants in Irish courts

Social changes and evolving demands

From the mid 1990s and particularly after 2001, immigration levels to Ireland began to increase significantly. In 2002 the national census contained a question on nationality for the first time; 5.8 per cent of the population, or 224,261 people, reported themselves as having been born outside Ireland (CSO, 2002). The 2006 census recorded 419,733 people from 188 different countries living in Ireland, making up around 11 per cent of the population (CSO, 2006). Immigration levels peaked in 2007, after which they began to fall, and in 2009 Ireland became a country of net emigration again for the first time since 1995, as immigration levels fell substantially and non-Irish emigration rose (CSO, 2010).

The perception began to prevail that immigrants were 'going home' in ever increasing numbers, an image fuelled at least in part by media coverage of a 'huge exodus', 'sharp drops' and plunging numbers of immigrants driven away by the recession (Doyle, 2008; Black, 2009). However, although the non-Irish population has fallen slightly since its highest point and the makeup of that population may have changed, it has certainly not disappeared. At the time of the 2011 census, the percentage of those with a nationality other than Irish had actually increased to 12 per cent, or 544,357 people of 199 different nationalities, and 11 per cent reported speaking a language other than Irish or English at home (CSO, 2011). The recent EU accession states[1] have contributed most highly to the growth in immigration and to the emigration trends of non-Irish people, yet there has been a net growth in the population of this group (CSO, 2002, 2006, 2011). The Immigrant Council of Ireland (2010) has said that demand for their services has remained consistently high, and Krings *et al.* (2009), looking at the situation of Polish migrants in post-Celtic Tiger Ireland, submitted that while some migrants, particularly those hit by recession, were likely to leave, many had reasons – including employment, welfare entitlements and social networks – to stay.

Immigration and Irish courts: growing demands for language services

Attempting to quantify the number of LEP defendants that have appeared or appear on an ongoing basis in Irish courts is a difficult task as there are no available statistics; the youthful field of Irish criminology is notable for its lack of coherent data on the Irish criminal justice system, and estimates, anecdotal evidence and occasional statistics often have to suffice in analyses of the system (see e.g. O'Mahony, 2002; O'Donnell, 2005). An imprecise picture can be painted of LEP defendants using a variety of sources, including the reports of the Irish Courts and Prison Service, but this is a picture of the whole Irish court system and not just the District Court.

As the vast majority of criminal offences are tried in the District Court and almost everybody charged with a criminal offence begins their journey through the criminal process here, it is reasonable to deduce that the heaviest demand for language services will also be at this level. That language and interpreting developments have particularly impacted on the District Court is also suggested by the fact that many sources, including media sources, have focused on this court in discussing and commenting on the issues, and in 2007 one District Court judge estimated, as immigration reached its highest recorded level, that up to 20 per cent of daily appearances involved 'foreign offenders' (Riordan, 2007). Empirical research for this study involved sitting in a number of different District Courts in 2009 and 2010. Figures varied considerably, with a daily average of between nine and thirteen LEP defendants; it is difficult to say what percentage these figures would represent, but possibly between 5 and 20 per cent of defendants on any given day.

While this suggests that issues of interpreting affect the District Court more than any other court, this chapter looks at the development of language services in the Irish court system generally. Chapters 4 and 5 will then go on to present original ethnographic research specific to the District Court. As well as detailing how the Irish interpreting system has developed until now, this chapter explores many of the issues involved in providing interpreting services to criminal defendants. Drawing from literature on interpreting in the English-speaking common-law world, some EU literature and relevant legal sources,[2] it examines the interpreter's role, the process of court interpreting and the right of LEP defendants to have an interpreter in court. It also looks at how courts perceive and deal with language need and interpreters.

The principal indicator of the rising numbers of LEP defendants has been the demand for language services by the Courts Service. This has generally been measured by the amount of money spent on interpreting services, as well as by the numbers of languages being interpreted and requests for those services. The cost of those services increased dramatically from the €103,000 spent in 2000 to a peak of €3.6 million in 2008 before falling back to €1.56 million in 2012, a figure comparable with that of 2005 (see Table 5). While a fall in demand is one of the reasons for the decreased costs of services, savings were reportedly also made 'through contract negotiations with companies providing the service' (McKinley, 2013),[3] and schemes have reportedly been introduced in some areas to reduce costs by making more efficient use of the interpreters provided (Reilly & McArdle, 2010).

It is unclear exactly how many languages are and have been interpreted in Irish courts. Until 2007, when an official figure for that year was provided by the contracted interpreting agency, various articles put the number at 167 (O'Brien, 2006), 200 (Tighe, 2009) and, more often, '210 dialects and languages', a figure provided by the Courts Service and cited widely (e.g. ITIA, 2002; Donaghy, 2004, 2006). Official figures were provided by the new service provider in 2007 and were considerably lower: seventy-five in 2007; seventy-one in 2008; sixty-three in 2010 and sixty-five in 2011 (Courts Service, annual reports), though it is unclear whether this apparent drop relates to an initial over-estimation, a sudden decrease in the heterogeneity of languages/dialects, omission of dialects from latter counts, different agencies catering for particular languages and dialects, wildly inaccurate guesses, or perhaps error. Two hundred and ten languages and dialects may also represent a collective figure over time (McKinley, 2013).

Table 5 Cost of court language services

2000	€103,000
2001	€232,000
2002	€461,000
2003	€631,000
2004	€554,000
2005	€1.26 million
2007	€2+ million
2008	€3.6 million
2009	€3 million
2012	€1.56 million

Sources: 2000–2005 (Courts Service, annual report, 2005); 2007 ('Interpreters keep …', 2008); 2008/2012 (McKinley, 2013); 2009 (Phelan, 2011)

In terms of the frequency of requests, the 2008 Courts Service annual report stated that 10,000 requests had been made for interpreters that year. The 2010 report noted that interpreters had been requested in more than 10,000 cases, and the 2011 report put the figure at 6800 cases. Polish, Romanian, Lithuanian, Russian, Mandarin Chinese, Latvian, Portuguese, French, Czech and Arabic are the ten most frequently interpreted languages in Irish courts (Courts Service, 2008, 2012). The number of requests fails to tell us much in terms of defendant numbers, however, as many courts had (and have) interpreters for the most common languages present throughout all sittings. Thus interpreters requested for one case are likely to interpret for one or a number of other cases while at court, meaning that in many cases an interpreter is present without having been requested. It also fails to tell us how many LEP defendants were in court *without* interpreters.

Prison statistics can also give some indication of the extent to which non-Irish people are being processed by the Irish justice system, and the Prison Service provides information on the nationality of those committed to prison. Its statistics suggest a consistently high presence of non-Irish nationals in Irish prisons since 2001, the first year such statistics were provided. Like the immigration trend, the representation of non-Irish committals to Irish prisons rose between 2001 and 2007, when it peaked at one third of all those committed (see Table 6). This fell to just under 30 per cent in 2008 and to 18.2 per cent in 2012, but the decline is less dramatic when those committed under immigration laws are excluded, as immigration committals also declined considerably during these years, at least partly due to decreasing numbers of asylum applications (see Table 6) (Prison Service, annual reports, 2004, 2005).

Despite the decline from 2008 to the present, the percentage of non-Irish-born people committed to prison remains high, and higher than the non-Irish-born percentage of the Irish population. However, as O'Nolan (2011a:380) points out, while these statistics point to the need for additional research on how the Irish criminal justice system treats and processes non-Irish citizens, they 'do not, in themselves, provide us with any explanations' – that goes both for more substantive issues of criminality and for the procedural issues in question here; some of those committed under immigration laws, for example, are subject to administrative detention and never appear in an Irish court.[4] These statistics also fail to indicate how many of those committed would have needed or would need an interpreter in court. However, from Prison Service annual reports we can see that between 2001 and 2005 non-Irish prisoners came from between 90 (2001)

Table 6 Committals of non-Irish offenders to Irish prisons

Year	Non-Irish committals (% of all committals)	Non-Irish committals excluding immigration offences (% of all committals)
2001	18.0	**
2002	20.6	**
2003	25.7	6.8
2004	20.5	9.7
2005	25.2	15.3
2006	29.9	18.4
2007	33.6	21.8
2008	29.7	20.9
2009	24.4	18.9
2010	22.2	18.8
2011	19.3	16.4
2012	18.2	15.4

Source: Prison Service, annual reports, 2001–2012
** statistics unavailable

and 115+ (2003–2004) different countries, from which it would seem likely that quite a number of non-Irish prisoners would not be native English speakers and that there would be a significant variety of languages spoken by prisoners and, by extension, by defendants in criminal cases.

It is apparent that within a very short time, a significant change had taken place in the Irish court system as the numbers of criminal defendants whose mother tongue was neither English nor Irish had increased substantially. Up until this point, most speakers of a language other than English were using Irish, and interpreting issues tended to relate to the implications for Irish speakers in court of Article 8 of the Constitution, which provides that either Irish or English can be used for official purposes.[5] Very few LEP defendants had appeared before Irish courts and the infrastructure required to deal with the demand simply did not exist. Guerin suggested in 2004 that 'it would not be unreasonable to expect that an officially bilingual state would have had sufficient experience of the difficulties that arise in multilingual court proceedings, and would have devoted sufficient effort to resolving those difficulties, to be able to cope with the challenge of an increasingly multi-cultural and multilingual society' (Guerin, 2004). However, in reality the courts had little experience of dealing with LEP defendants, at least on this scale, and the Courts Service acknowledged that it was not immediately obvious where to find people that could act as interpreters for the increasing numbers of defendants ('From Irish to ...', 2006).

Multilingual court proceedings: the need for interpreters

Language is a vital and integral part of court procedure. Where defendants (or witnesses) do not speak the language of the court, interpreters bridge the language barrier by ensuring that both sides understand each other. To do this, they must understand and interpret court proceedings for the non-English speaker, and convey to the court what is said by that speaker. The aim is to 'convey precisely, accurately, and completely in the target language the information contained in the source language' (de Jongh, 1991:288). To avoid miscommunication and ensure nothing is 'lost in translation', the message should be conveyed 'with its entire semantic, emotional and aesthetic baggage', a task that requires attention to nuance, style, register, formality, tone and gestures (de Jongh, 1991:288). The interpreter is thus tasked with conveying both what is said and how it is said.[6]

The difficulties of realising such an aim are significant. From a broad perspective, languages are not directly equivalent; they have different grammar structures, even similar words can have very different meanings, and basic perspectives and cultural concepts vary. In the legal context, legal terms and concepts can exist in one legal system and not in another and, as such, can be 'incomprehensible for a foreigner' (Mattila, 2006:221). Dueñas González, Vasquez & Mikkelson (1991) give the example of Navajo Indians, for whom the concept of individual guilt does not exist and whose language does not have any word for 'guilty'. Attempting literal translation from one legal system to another may thus cause confusion (Edwards, 1995). In addition, legal argument can be difficult to follow, particularly as lawyers do not usually modify their speech for the benefit of laypeople (or interpreters) (Colin & Morris, 1996). Finally, court interpreting happens instantly without time for reflection or consultation, and there are often situational barriers where comprehension is affected by speech levels and the speed of participants, poor acoustics or amplification, background noise or physical barriers such as glass panels (see e.g. Colin & Morris, 1996).

For these reasons, a good interpreter needs to be highly proficient in both languages, able to hear, analyse and repeat a message, and be familiar with a variety of subject matters. The court or legal interpreter should have knowledge of legal language and the legal system as well as differences between systems (see e.g. Butler and Noaks, 1992), and should be able to use both languages at various levels, from the technical and formal speech of legal professionals and expert witnesses to non-standard or colloquial speech and slang (Edwards, 1995; Gibbons, 2003). Certain practical skills are also important for a good interpreter, including good hearing, a clear speaking voice, physical stamina, a confident manner, diplomacy and awareness of professional ethics (see e.g. Colin & Morris, 1996; Gibbons, 2003; Granger & Baker, 2003). Considering the extent of what an interpreter is expected to do, attaining fluency in two languages is only the beginning of their training and an important distinction should be made between a bilingual person and a professional court interpreter (see e.g. Hertog, 2001; Berk-Seligson, 2002).

A professional court interpreter facilitates proceedings by permitting the court to understand defendants and witnesses who are not fluent in English (de Jongh, 1991), and helps the court to maintain a certain agenda by ensuring that courtroom interaction continues (Wadensjö, 1998). It has been asserted that those working in the legal system have a right to dependable interpretation so they can work to appropriate legal and professional standards (Wadensjö, 1998; Hertog, 2001), and that the evidence of the non-English speaker must be available to the court to protect the general public's right to have crimes investigated, and perpetrators tried and convicted (Storey, 1998). In Ireland, the Courts Service has described interpreting services as assisting with 'the efficient management of cases' (Courts Service, 2005:38).

Although court interpreters are, indeed, necessary to facilitate communication for the court, greater emphasis is generally placed on the perspective of the LEP defendant attempting to access justice (Butler & Noaks, 1992). This is certainly true in Ireland, where there has been considerable focus on interpreting in the context of correctness of procedure (Coulter, 2003; O'Brien, 2010a,b) and 'the integrity and safety of the Irish criminal process' (Guerin, 2004); interpreting as an integral part of constitutional and natural justice (Riordan, 2007) and access to justice ('Concern at ...', 2005; Courts Service, annual reports, 2007; 2008); and interpreting in the context of fair trials, procedural rights and the right to interpretation (Bacik, 2007; 'Irish lead ...', 2007; 'Proposal to ...', 2010). The Courts Service has explicitly recognised that for people 'for whom English is not their first language, the court process can be difficult and sometimes unintelligible' (Courts Service, 2005:38), and the Irish Translators' and Interpreters' Association (ITIA) has stated that (2008:3):

> Interpreters are provided to ensure that the defendant with limited English will be in the same position as an English-speaking defendant. If an interpreter cannot interpret all the evidence, the defendant will be excluded from part of the proceedings. This is a breach of natural justice.

The right to an interpreter in Ireland

The above sources incorporate a joint discourse of human rights and natural justice which reflects the history of the right to an interpreter in criminal proceedings in Ireland. Until very recently the right was not explicitly provided for in Irish law, though it was nonetheless well established. The Constitution (1937) provides that anyone charged with a criminal offence must be tried in due course of law, which equates to and includes due process of law and basic principles of justice (*Conroy v Attorney General*, 1965; *State (Healy) v Donoghue*, 1976). Although debates on language and interpreting in Irish courts have traditionally related to the constitutional entitlement to conduct a case in either Irish or English, courts have also invoked reasoning in this regard that is based on broader principles of natural justice, recognising the right to understand one's trial as a fundamental principle of law and natural justice (*Attorney-General v Joyce & Walsh*, 1929; *State (Buchan) v Coyne*, 1936; *O'Monachain v An Taoiseach*, 1986).

Irish courts also draw on the case-law of other common-law jurisdictions, and the failure to provide 'translation' where needed has long been held as contrary to the 'fundamental and elemental principles of justice' (*R. v Kwok Leung & Others*, 1909), 'basic notions of justice' (*R. v Tran*, 1994) and 'simple humaneness' (*United States ex rel. Negron v the State of New York*, 1970). Common law demands that all those charged with a criminal offence be able to understand the nature of proceedings and the case against them, and have the opportunity to answer that case (*R. v Tran*, 1994).

Ireland has ratified the European Convention on Human Rights (ECHR) and the International Covenant on Civil and Political Rights (ICCPR), which provide criminal defendants with the right 'to have the free assistance of an interpreter if he cannot understand or speak the language used in court' as part of the right to a fair and public hearing when charged with a criminal offence, and the entitlement to equality before courts and tribunals.[7] The right to an interpreter is thus based on the notions of fairness, justice and equality before the law; as O'Malley points out, where a person is unable to understand or participate meaningfully due to linguistic difficulties, they 'cannot be said to be present at trial in a genuine sense' (O'Malley, 2009:113–14).

An important development in the right to an interpreter in Ireland is the 2010 EU Directive on the right to interpretation and translation in criminal proceedings ('the Directive') (Directive, 2010),[8] the provisions of which are largely based on the relevant case-law of the European Court of Human Rights (ECtHR).[9] Although Ireland opposed an early part of this process on the basis that it already had procedural rights in place that exceeded those proposed,[10] it opted into the legislation, and in December 2013 the Minister for Justice and Equality introduced regulations to give effect to the Directive (S.I. 565/2013).

The Directive is particularly interesting in having been heavily influenced by practising interpreters and translators, as it has long been a concern of linguists that courts of law too often fail to appreciate fully the challenges and the importance of the interpreting process. While judges and lawyers are sophisticated users of language, it has been found that they do not always understand the mechanics underlying language or its function in particular situations (O'Barr & Conley, 1976; Charrow, Crandall & Charrow, 1982; Solan & Tiersma, 2005), that unwarranted and unfounded linguistic assumptions are made throughout the legal system (O'Barr, 1982), and that many of the criminal justice system's 'deeply entrenched notions about language' are wrong (Solan & Tiersma, 2005:104).

The Directive, however, recognises that legitimating the necessity for and presence of interpreters, and even providing them, is just a starting point in ensuring access to justice for LEP defendants. In some of its progressive provisions, the Directive explicitly recognises that, because of a lack of knowledge, awareness or training, courts do not always maximise their facilitation of the communicative process where interpreters are involved (Art. 6); that how a court allocates or refuses to allocate interpreters is important and that there should be appropriate mechanisms in place to facilitate this process (Arts. 2(4) & (5)); that a person will be unable to understand his or her case or put forward a defence if the interpretation is not of sufficient quality (Art. 2(8) & Art. 5); and that interpreters must deal with certain ethical issues (e.g. Art. 5(3)). However, the development of the Directive also highlights the fact that courts – and the justice system – necessarily have different priorities from language professionals; through its various incarnations, certain provisions that were undoubtedly the province of language professionals have been weakened, reflecting the need for a practical balance between the needs of the justice system and the rights of the defendant, as well as respect for judicial autonomy (Waterhouse, 2010). The need for balance and autonomy is evident in the new S.I. 565/2013, as it does not embrace all the opportunities for progressiveness provided for by the Directive, for example in such areas as training of the judiciary and interpreter ethics. However, it provides that anyone appearing in criminal proceedings 'who does not speak or who does not understand the English language' has 'the right to the assistance, at no cost, of an interpreter' (Reg. 3) and it addresses, albeit briefly, such issues as quality (Reg. 7), assigning interpreters (Reg. 4) and the role of the interpreter (Reg. 6). These and other aspects of the right to an interpreter will be explored in more detail later.

Development of service provision in Ireland

The rapid increase in LEP defendants in Ireland created an urgent demand for interpreting services. An *ad hoc* system very quickly sprang up, comprising individuals and private agencies that provided language services to the courts. There was stiff competition for business and, according to accounts of interpreters that were present as the system began to develop, the battle for clients took place in crowded courtrooms where interpreters literally scrambled to be assigned to relevant cases. We know that in 2004, for example, fifty-five different companies or persons provided interpreting and translation services to the courts (Felle, 2005). The result, by those same accounts, was mayhem, an impression that is borne out by media and other reports of the time.

The *Irish Independent* (hereafter 'the Independent'), Ireland's biggest-selling broadsheet, reported on 'legal log-jams', chaos and trying times in courts caused by a shortage of 'translators' (Riegel, 2001; Donaghy, 2004). The *Irish Times* (hereafter 'the Times'), Ireland's paper of record, also noted the havoc, but took a slightly different perspective, focusing on the shortcomings of the service provision, which it variously reported as 'patchy and haphazard' ('Concern at …', 2005), 'disorganised, and lacking any real sense of planning for the future' (O'Brien, 2006) and 'partial, inadequate and lacking a sense of long-term purpose' ('Growing demand …', 2007). Despite the novelty and magnitude of the changes wrought by LEP defendants in Irish courts, relatively little attention was paid to the issue, such that media reports constitute one of the main sources of information on the development of the interpreting system, notwithstanding that the reliability of such sources cannot be considered absolute.[11] An analysis of relevant newspaper articles in Ireland's two main newspapers – the *Independent* and the *Times* – between 2001 and 2010 (Waterhouse, 2010) found that the papers had a markedly different approach to reporting on the issue. The former tended to adhere to what might be considered a more 'official' view – the same view put forth by the Courts Service and in some relevant government comments – that the language needs of LEP defendants were being responded to satisfactorily.

The *Times*, on the other hand, tended to focus on the unsatisfactory and inadequate nature of a system in urgent need of reform, a perspective supported in relevant studies, commentaries and academic articles on the topic, and most strongly advocated by the ITIA.

Accordingly, while the Courts Service acknowledges in its early reports the challenge posed by the growing demand for services, its 'official' view was simply that interpreters were being, and would continue to be, provided (Courts Service, annual reports, 2002, 2004, 2005). More generally, however, there was considerable concern that the *ad hoc* arrangements occasionally fell 'far short of the standard required to administer justice openly and fairly' (Riordan, 2007:101-2), and there was a clear need for a change in the organisation of the system.

Two options were available to the Courts Service; the first was to outsource the provision of interpreting to private agencies and the second was to create a national register of accredited interpreters and/or to establish an interpreting section within the Courts Service. Best practice favours registers as, unlike private agencies, they allow control over who is approved to interpret in courts and thus safeguard the interests of all parties (Hertog, 2001). The ITIA (2002) strongly advocated a register and an interpreting section from very early on, pointing out that private agencies were failing to test the language knowledge and ability of interpreters, and were sending interpreters to court without specialised training, a code of ethics or adequate knowledge of the law or legal terminology. There was wider support for the creation of a national register (Heffernan, 2006; National Consultative Committee on Racism and Interculturalism (NCCRI), 2007), and Bacik (2007) cautioned that privatisation could potentially jeopardise the right to a fair trial unless there were recognised national standards in place to which all agencies adhered.

While registers are considered best practice, however, 'a marked trend' towards outsourcing was developing across English-speaking jurisdictions (Morris, 2010:56), possibly part of a wider trend of 'rationalising' justice identified by criminologists as involving the increasing privatisation and altered management of criminal justice agencies to ensure that services are delivered 'in a just, efficient and cost-effective way' (see e.g. Garland, 2001:210). In its 2005 annual report, the Courts Service stated that the growing need for interpreters necessitated a 're-evaluation' and a 'rationalisation of the management of interpretation services' (Courts Service, 2005:38), echoing a growing tendency of Irish criminal justice agencies to employ such managerial language in their annual reports and plans (Kilcommins *et al.*, 2004). In spite of the recommendations to establish a register of interpreters, the Courts Service put out a request to tender for the provision of interpreting services in 2005, a single service provider was subsequently engaged, and provision began by that agency in March 2007.[12]

Organisation

Once the service provider was in place, the 'official' view was that 'quality interpretation services' continued to be provided (Courts Service, annual report, 2007:37) and that the increasing need for interpreters continued to be dealt with 'effectively' (Courts Service, annual report, 2008:34) and in a 'positive and proactive way' ('Interpreters keep ...', 2008:11). The Courts Service announced that there was a satisfaction rating of over 99.5 per cent with the new service provision, where the few existing complaints were 'due to teething issues' ('Interpreters keep ...', 2008:11). Many Courts Service reports have failed to mention the topic of court interpreting at all (Courts Service, annual reports, 2008, 2009, 2012), while others have simply noted that the Service 'continued to provide interpreters to facilitate access to justice for those for whom English is not their first language' (Courts Service, annual reports, 2010:26, 2011:17), perhaps evidencing the idea that service provision was proceeding without issue.

ITIA members observed, however, that 'the provision of interpreters is not working' and that there were still regular problems with the booking system (Phelan, 2007:4). A number of such incidents appeared in the media. In October 2007, a Donegal newspaper reported a case where no interpreter turned up to court, leading Judge Zaidan to criticise strongly 'the company who supplies interpreters to the courts service'; he noted that this was not the first time it had happened and threatened that if the interpreter did not appear on the next occasion, 'I will be asking the state to supply me with a Polish dictionary and I will go ahead with the case' ('Donegal Democrat ...', 2007). In January 2009 a murder case in Galway District Court had to be postponed as the interpreter was a 'no-show'; Judge Fahy commented that 'this is the most serious charge a District Court can have and the interpreter has not appeared' (Nee, 2009). A 2008 article in the *Independent* reported on another situation where proceedings were delayed as the court wearily awaited an interpreter for hours, and when at last the interpreter arrived it was to take the affirmation 'in hesitant English', leading barristers to 'exchang[e] glances of alarm' and to the dismissal of the jury (Anderson, 2008).

In 2010, the Courts Service announced another organisational change in the form of a new procurement process for regional contracts to replace the single national service provider.[13] The purpose of this change was 'to improve the efficiency and cost effectiveness of the service' (Courts Service, annual report, 2010:26).

The cost of services

Money has emerged as a frequent and sometimes controversial theme in discussions of the developing system. In the media, while much of what was published by the *Times* focused on the need to ensure access to justice, procedure and rights, the *Independent* tended to focus, particularly in the years of highest immigration (2004–2007), on the costs involved in providing interpreting services, conveying a sensationalised concern as to the amount of money being spent on language services in the criminal justice system:

Trying times for courts as translation costs soar	May 2004
€550,000 payout for court interpreters	August 2005
€15m is lost in translation by the courts	January 2006
Courts body to fork out €2m on interpreters as demand rises	July 2007

Although costs were certainly increasing as the numbers of LEP defendants rose, the need to provide language services to defendants without fluency in English was never denied, and the money necessary to ensure those services was provided. The issue of pay arises frequently in the literature on interpreting; the broad issue tends to be that a lack of understanding by people other than language professionals as to the skills, training and professionalism required for the job results in a failure or reluctance to pay corresponding professional rates. At least initially, the case in Ireland seemed somewhat different, and interpreters interviewed in the course of the study noted that in the 'early years' (pre-2007) the pay was excellent. After the privatisation of services, however, an issue of distribution seemed to arise and wages began to fall.

In July 2007, it was reported that the Courts Service paid €46 an hour for interpreting services (O'Brien, 2007). A few months later it was reported that while the service provider continued to receive that amount, interpreter rates had been 'slashed' to between €15 and €25 (Phelan, 2007). At that point, one commentator compared the situation to cowboys and Indians, 'where the cowboys are those who make the biggest profits at the lowest possible cost and the indians [sic] are those who facilitate the cowboys', and she questioned what kept interpreters going, reasoning that: 'It can't be the money, it certainly can't be professional recognition, never mind job security' (Fuehrer, 2008:3). In 2009, the Courts Service sought an 8 per cent reduction in fees from the service provider, but this was passed on to interpreters as a further 28 per cent cut in their hourly rate, rendering rates for interpreters among the lowest in Europe (Tighe, 2009). The *Times* reported the complaint of a Garda of the Garda Representative Association that 'while the agencies providing the interpreters are earning considerable profits the individual interpreters are "being paid buttons"' (Lally, 2009).

While the Courts Service has a clear and understandable desire for cost-effectiveness, there is a question about how cost-effective these developments have been in reality. Although the Courts Service was paying a certain amount to obtain those services, a decreasing percentage of that payment was reaching the actual interpreters, and the *de facto* wages received by interpreters created potentially negative long-term effects on the system as a whole, as decreases such as these lead to realistic fears about the ability of the sector to maintain competitiveness, attract quality interpreters, ensure cover for the courts and, ultimately, ensure justice for LEP defendants (Tighe, 2009; Gartland, 2010). Indeed, Morris, in her recent monograph on court interpreting, finds in Ireland a 'cautionary' tale as a system where because of a 'poorly designed and poorly managed outsourcing system' standards are dropping and well-qualified interpreters are likely to leave the profession on the basis that they cannot make a living, 'leaving only the inexperienced and incompetent to service the justice system' (Morris, 2010:62).

Similar results of outsourcing have been felt elsewhere. The 2009 outsourcing in Scotland reportedly led to 'a mass exodus of professional interpreters', and to poor interpreting quality, delays and abandoned trials (UK Association of Police and Court Interpreters, 2010). In the justice sector of England and Wales, despite there being a well-established and adequate system of public service interpreters, outsourcing of all language services began in early 2012. This led to boycotts by professional interpreters, due not in small part to the decreased pay and well-founded concerns for quality based on the fact that the new system would require lower levels of qualification than those already in existence (Maniar, 2013). A 2013 inquiry by the House of Commons Justice Select Committee found that the Ministry of Justice 'did not have a sufficient understanding of the complexities of court interpreting work prior to initiating the procurement of a new service' and that it pursued the new arrangements despite evidence that it would compromise the quality of court language services, effectively leading to the exclusion of professional interpreters (House of Commons Justice Committee, 2013:19). One freelance interpreter has called the result of the privatisation 'shambolic and unworkable' and explains that the privatisation is actually 'inefficient, counterproductive and lead[s] to greater costs at the public expense' (Maniar, 2013).

There is an argument to be made, therefore, that not only are language professionals and those concerned with procedural rights wary of outsourcing and privatisation on the basis of how they impact on the interpreting profession and the right to a fair trial, but that a focus on efficiency and cost-effective management can be counter-productive.

The quality of services in Irish courts

Before interpreting services in Ireland were outsourced, a court interpreting study by Pérez (2000) found that there were no interpreting standards to be met in Ireland, that there was no system to monitor interpreting quality in court, and that interpreters lacked adequate training and guidelines for their work. An EU study using data from 2002 confirmed that no qualifications were necessary to act as a legal interpreter in Irish courts (Spronken & Attinger, 2005), while the ITIA (2002:1) called the lack of testing and training for interpreters a 'fundamental flaw' in the system, and Guerin (2004) made the point that '[i]t is easier to be appointed to act as interpreter for an accused person facing a serious criminal charge than it is to get a licence to drive a taxi'. A second EU study showed that the profession in Ireland was unregulated, and most respondents indicated that there was no monitoring of quality or testing of standards, no requirement for competence or proficiency, and no guidelines (Hertog & van Gucht, 2006). Bacik (2007) also pointed to the unsatisfactory lack of guidelines, training, quality control and testing.

Major issues with the quality of interpreters appearing in Irish courts were also being reported in the media. The *Independent* reported on complaints by judges about the 'appalling' standards of translators ('Judge attacks ...', 2004), and numerous *Times* articles discussed the need to improve the system, focusing on the lack of quality standards, qualifications and training (e.g. Coulter, 2003; Holmquist, 2006; O'Brien, 2006). There were reports of dubious recruitment practices by agencies, alleged to be handing out fliers in ethnic restaurants and recruiting anybody who claimed to speak two languages (Coulter, 2003), and it was reported that agencies were telling their interpreters 'to be seen talking' at all costs in court as the judge would only notice a problem if they remained silent (Heffernan, 2006).

Interpreters were reported as having questionable knowledge of ethics; defendants sometimes asked their interpreter for guidance on how to plead and the ITIA (2002:1) pointed out that because there was no code of ethics, interpreters 'do not know how to behave if they make a mistake'. In 2003 the *Times* reported that a 'translator' who had aided the Gardaí in taking a witness statement from a Chinese man accused of two murders later went on a date with the accused after the Gardaí gave the man her phone number (Phelan, 2011). The criminal record of interpreters themselves became a source of concern; the Garda Representative Association reported that a Chinese interpreter, hired to assist in an interview, had turned out to be an illegal immigrant himself, and revealed that while interpreters are vetted for a criminal record in Ireland, the record in their country of origin is not checked (Lally, 2009).

The Media Relations Adviser of the Courts Service acknowledged that it was not always easy to find 'interpreters of suitable experience', but said that, in spite of this, few problems of understanding had arisen in court, and that any such problems had been resolved ('From Irish ...', 2006):

> Considering the number of occasions in which an interpreter is used, frequently at very short notice, there have been few issues or problems in the understanding of the court process by those involved. Where an issue of understanding arises, the dynamic of the court setting tends to make this apparent. On these rare occasions the interpreter is replaced.

Some of the reasons why the dynamic of the court setting is highly unlikely to make problematic interpreting apparent are discussed in the next section.

As the Courts Service moved towards the outsourcing of interpreting services, in addition to general reservations about privatisation, specific flaws in the tender document were highlighted, principally the system of language qualification levels. This focused on language competence to the exclusion of interpreting competence and did not guarantee that interpreters at the highest level would be available for languages other than the most commonly used (Bacik, 2007). Nonetheless, there were clear expectations, or at least hopes, that the new system would bring improvements (Bacik, 2007; Riordan, 2007), and in the years after the interpreting contract commenced, the Courts Service claimed to have continued to 'provide quality interpretation services to the courts during the year' (Courts Service, annual reports, 2007:37, 2008:34).

However, a 2008 study suggested that where interpreting services were being provided, the 'lack of quality checking, or the means to do it' was a 'key issue of concern', and other key weaknesses included the lack of coherent policy, quality control, appropriate staff training, and a lack of awareness (NCCRI, 2008:xi,xiv). A 2008 ITIA submission to the Courts Service pointed out that there was still no system in place to ensure that interpreters were 'qualified, adequately trained and competent' and suggested that the time had now come to improve the situation, stating that:

> [t]here are far too many people working as interpreters in our courts who have no background in translation or interpreting, no knowledge of legal terminology or interpreting techniques and a doubtful knowledge of ethical issues. (ITIA, 2008:5)

In one ITIA bulletin, concern was expressed that interpreters' reputations were being jeopardised by the fact that '[i]ncompetent, unqualified bilingual people (I hesitate to call them interpreters) are being employed to do work that should be reserved for professionals' (Hayes, 2007:2). In 2010, two articles in the *Times* reported nearly the same issues as were being reported as early as 2003: interpreters without qualifications, agencies not testing interpreter competence or proficiency, no quality control and interpreters with poor English (O'Brien, 2010a, b).

The Courts Service's most recent procurement process for regional contracts seems to regress in terms of quality provisions. The 2006 tender, which was criticised for overemphasising language competence to the detriment of interpreting competence, specified four levels: level one involved competence in English and the language concerned; level two, a native speaker of either language with competence in the other; level three, a native speaker of either language with a third level qualification in the other; and level four, a person qualified at level three with, in addition, qualifications specific to translating or interpreting. The subsequent tender, however, omitted the fourth level of interpreter competence, thus requiring service providers only to provide interpreters with varying levels of language competence but not requiring agencies to ensure that any interpreters have interpreting qualifications (ITIA, 2011; Courts Service, 2012). This raises serious concerns about expectations of interpreting quality in Irish courts.

The next section goes inside the courtroom itself and examines how courts deal with the presence and provision of interpreters, how interpreting impacts on court proceedings, and how courts interpret the need for quality and competence in interpreters.

Interpreting issues in the courtroom

Interpreters: violent opponents of soap and sunlight or translating machines?

Literature from across the English-speaking common-law world depicts the attitudes of courts towards interpreters as involving varying degrees of mistrust and negativity. In his 1952 interpreters' handbook, Herbert used the phrase 'necessary evil' to describe the attitude of the court to the presence of an interpreter, and it has been widely employed since then to represent a certain lack of enthusiasm around interpreter participation in trials. While much interpreting literature implicitly or explicitly accepts this negative perception of judicial attitudes, Morris offers some extreme examples, including Norman Birkett of the Nuremberg War Crimes Tribunal Bench, who reportedly called 'translators' 'touchy, vain, unaccountable, full of vagaries, puffed up with self-importance of the most explosive kind, inexpressibly egotistical, and, as a rule, violent opponents of soap and sunlight' (Hyde, 1964 IN Morris, 1999a:9).

It has been suggested that an element of distrust towards foreign language speakers generally may be found in the courtroom (Goodrich, 1987) and that this may extend to the interpreter. Indeed, distrust may simply be created by the fact that interpretation, by its nature, may involve more or fewer words than the original utterance (Tribe, 2005). The cumbersome nature of bilingual cases that can take up to twice as long as other trials can cause frustration, and other tensions are well illustrated in a report of the Australian Attorney-General, which looked at some of the beliefs about interpreters that contribute to their under-use there (Australia Attorney-General's Department, 1991 IN Gibbons, 2003:233): an interpreter will give a second-language speaker with some knowledge of the language the advantage of extra time for thinking and developing a response; it is difficult to gauge the credibility of witnesses, as non-verbal information is altered; interpreters may modify content and not interpret literally; interpreters may take an active role and intervene in interaction; and a right to an interpreter affects judicial discretion in deciding whether one is needed.

Negative attitudes have been found to impact on interpreters. In a study on interpreting in Scottish courts, interpreters reported feeling that they were not treated as professionals, that the court atmosphere was stressful, pressurised and unwelcoming, and that their work was hindered by the court's failure to understand their role (MVA Consultancy, 1996). Interpreters also sometimes report a lack of respect and appreciation, feelings of isolation and not quite fitting into the court team, intimidation through exposure to public scrutiny, a lack of training and support, difficult situational conditions, and unpredictable employment and low pay. Overall, it seems, interpreters do a difficult job that many feel is rarely acknowledged and poorly compensated.

In apparent contradiction to this negativity or suspicious attitude, there is also evidence of an assumption often made by courts that interpreters can and do perform their job perfectly (Morris, 2008), perhaps acting more like machines than humans. Courts in the US have described interpreters as 'a transmission belt; transmission wire or telephone; ... a translating machine; ... a mere cipher; ... a mouthpiece' (Morris, 1999a:8), and the view is further evidenced by a tradition in the US of instructing bilingual jury members to disregard evidence in the original language and pay attention only to the interpreted version that will appear on record, regardless of the accuracy of that version (see e.g. Edwards, 1995; Berk-Seligson, 2002; Conley & O'Barr, 2005). The assumption of accuracy or competence is tied to the expectation of courts that interpreters can and do provide literal or *verbatim* interpretations of all that is said in the courtroom, which as a standard is described as interpretation 'without editing, summarizing, deleting, or adding while conserving the language level, style, tone, and intent of the speaker' (Dueñas Gonzáles, Vasquez & Mikkelson, 1991:16). Based on what we know about the nature of language and interpreting, it is clear that the idea of interpreting 'word for word' or 'literally' is not only all but impossible in the truest sense (Dueñas Gonzáles, Vasquez & Mikkelson, 1991), but is likely to impede an interpreter from fulfilling his or her role of *communicating* across languages.

An important consequence of the assumption that an interpreter can and does perform the job of interpretation perfectly is the consequent assumption that the provision of an interpreter – any interpreter – fulfils the obligations of the court to the LEP defendant and ensures access to justice. There is evidence of this assumption in the fact that courts almost never concern themselves with the performance of interpreters in practice. In a study on interpreting in English and Welsh courts, it was found that an interpreter who is 'plainly incompetent' will be replaced, but there is otherwise no systematic quality assurance (Butler & Noaks, 1992). In Ireland, a small number of anecdotal accounts have appeared in the media where judges have taken action in the face of apparent problems with interpreting; in some, judges noted discrepancies between what was being said by the accused and that being interpreted by the interpreter, and reacted to that discrepancy (O'Brien, 2010a citing *Galway Advertiser*, 2 May 2008; Phelan, 2011), while other accounts have involved judges expressing serious doubts about the English-language skills of the interpreter ('Judge dismisses ...', 2007; Anderson, 2008). As will be seen in the chapters to come, however, this study found – like the study of courts in England and Wales – that with extremely limited exceptions (see e.g. Appendix E), no attention was paid to the quality of interpreting in practice.

The assumption of competence may also contribute to the fact that when defendants make complaints about interpreting on appeal, courts almost never find that proceedings were prejudiced by the interpretation.

Before looking at how courts deal with issues of quality and competence, however, the issue of how and when courts provide those interpreters must be addressed.

Who gets an interpreter?

A criminal defendant who cannot understand or speak the language of the court is entitled to the free assistance of an interpreter. Real linguistic necessity has been found to be a vital element of that right, which is strictly one of procedural fairness and cannot be invoked as a matter of choice, convenience or politics (Trechsel, 2005; O'Malley, 2009). Accordingly, S.I. 565/2013, giving effect to the Directive in Ireland, provides that interpreting should be provided to anyone appearing in criminal proceedings who 'does not speak or understand the English language sufficiently to enable the person to participate fully in the proceedings' (Reg. 4). The problematic aspect, from a linguistic perspective, is in determining genuine need or sufficient competence. While this is obvious where a person cannot understand or speak a single word of the language of the court, it can be less clear when the defendant has some knowledge and use of the language, but is not fluent.

Solan and Tiersma (2005) have suggested that US courts occasionally allow linguistic experts to resolve questions of proficiency and some jurisdictions have rating scales to ascertain proficiency,[14] but the decision is almost always at the discretion of and made by the judge, who is considered by the ECtHR as the 'ultimate guardian of fairness' (*Cuscani v UK*, 2002). S.I. 565/2013 also provides that the decision to assign an interpreter is at the discretion of the court in specifying that interpreting should be provided 'where it appears to the Court' that it is required (Reg. 4). In the US, it has been found that decisions on assigning interpreters are often arbitrary and based on perception; if a judge carries out an assessment of language skills, it usually involves simple questions requiring 'monosyllabic answers, which provide little insight into the comprehension or communication ability of a minimal English speaker' (Benmaman, 2000). More often, however, judges avoid assessing proficiency and, instead, wait for the defendant or counsel to request an interpreter or ask the defendant directly if they need one (Radmann, 2005). It will be seen in later chapters that the reality in the Irish District Court is similar.

Berk-Seligson (2002) has found that in the US, the failure to provide interpretation was the most common interpreting-related grounds for appeal in the 1970s and early 1980s, and that it remains a problem. In Ireland, there is some anecdotal evidence of District Court judges having refused to certify for or appoint interpreters; one judge was reported as holding, for example, that it was 'absolutely ridiculous' that a person could not speak English having lived here for five years (ITIA, 2008:11, citing *Galway Advertiser*, 11 January 2007), and for another '[a] show of being unable to understand English cut no ice' ('Judge refuses ...', 2005; see also Phelan, 2011). This study did not find that the provision of interpreters was denied in practice, however, and the absence of criminal case-law involving claims about provision supports this finding; none of the tiny number of relevant criminal appeals has involved the failure to provide an interpreter at trial.

A small number of asylum/refugee cases have involved claims that an interpreter was not used, however. In fact, the majority of cases that have dealt with language and interpreting issues in Ireland are judicial reviews of the asylum/refugee process and, increasingly, European Arrest Warrant cases. While not criminal cases and thus not requiring the same stringent procedural protections, they can nonetheless provide some insight into judicial attitudes.[15] None was successful on the issue of a failure to provide interpreters. In one, the judge (Smyth J) referred to the applicant's own profession of fluency and willingness to be questioned in English (*Fuwa Oladale Olawale v ORAC, MJELR*, 2002). In another, the judge (Clarke J) highlighted the applicant's 'comprehensive and fluent answers' and contradictory responses as to whether an interpreter had been requested (*S.O.A v MJELR & Anor*, 2009), suggesting that Irish judges might assess the need for an interpreter in a variety of ways, including through a person's assessment of their own fluency and through the judge's observations on their fluency in communicating. It also hints at a potential responsibility on the part of the person that needs an interpreter to request one.

There are a number of reasons why relying on a defendant to assess their own language ability or need for an interpreter is not the best way to make a true assessment; they may fear being judged negatively, they may be trying to co-operate, they might genuinely think one unnecessary, they may want to go home quickly, or they might not, for example, wish others from their language community to know about their court appearance (Storey, 1998; Solan & Tiersma, 2005). O'Malley (2009) correctly points out that assessment of competence can be complex, and warns that courts should proceed with care and permit waiver of the right to an interpreter only when sure that to do so will not result in an unconstitutionally run trial. In fact, the Directive contains a provision (Art. 2(4)) that Member States must have a procedure or mechanism in place to assess the need for an interpreter, though it also provides that the mechanism may include any 'appropriate' method, including consulting the suspected or accused person.

The impact of interpreting

Once an interpreter has been provided, a new set of issues arises. It was suggested earlier that courts tend to assume that interpreters function perfectly. There is a corresponding assumption that interpreters bridge a communicative gap but do not otherwise alter, impact on, or prejudice proceedings. However, as Tribe (2005:169) puts it, even 'working with an interpreter is a qualitatively different experience from working without one'. Berk-Seligson (2002:54) submits that, although in the American legal system the interpreter would ideally be 'physically invisible and vocally silent, if at all possible', attention is in fact constantly being drawn to the interpreter, who engages verbally far more than is generally realised.

Numerous studies demonstrate that interpreting *does* change and influence criminal proceedings. In particular, it has been found to affect control and power relations in the courtroom, and to impact on the adversarial nature of trials. Berk-Seligson (1990, 2002) demonstrates that interpreters manipulate language and alter the flow of courtroom discourse, albeit unconsciously, while others have shown that interpreters alter the control of lawyers over witnesses by changing the aspect of questions (Rigney, 1999) and impact the relationship between lawyer and witness by consistently reducing the politeness of the language used (Hale & Gibbons, 1999); that speakers' intentions are systematically altered by interpreters who leave out or incorrectly translate discourse markers (Hale, 2002); and that interpreters alter the flow of cross-examination, making it less adversarial and reducing the lawyer's ability to destroy witness credibility (Ellison, 2001; Berk-Seligson, 2002).

In the context of the courtroom, it is easy to imagine that complex and difficult legal jargon poses difficulties for the interpreter. However, this and other research shows that, in fact, most issues arising from the interpretation of courtroom discourse are pragmatic in nature, or stem from trying to maintain the 'how' of how a person speaks (Hale, 1999). Because *how* something is said is as important as what is said, the interpreter should ideally maintain the way the witness/defendant speaks, conveying 'the same impression in English that the witness would have given to a lawyer examining directly' (Colin & Morris, 1996:91). Berk-Seligson (2002) found interpreters to be largely unaware of pragmatics and inattentive to the relevant aspects of speech such that their interpretation inevitably skewed the meaning and tone of speakers, even where they were not conscious of this.

If qualified, competent interpreters can impact and alter criminal proceedings, the effect must naturally be far greater when the quality of interpreting is poor, and the complexity of the interpreting process and the legal setting create multiple possibilities for erroneous, incomplete or misleading interpretation (Colin & Morris, 1996). When inaccurate interpreting means either that the court or jury does not fully understand the case being made by one or both parties, or that the defendant does not fully understand the case against him or her and is not in a position to put forward a defence, the fairness of the trial must be impaired, and there is a risk of serious injustice (O'Malley, 2009). That the quality of interpreting can affect the fairness of proceedings is explicity recognised by the new S.I. 565/2013, giving effect to the Directive in Ireland (Reg. 4).

Some criminal cases successfully appealed on interpreting grounds attest to the dangers inherent in poor interpreting. Consider the US case of Juan Ramón Alfonzo, who believed that he was pleading guilty to stealing a toolbox and was shocked to find himself sentenced to fifteen years in prison for stealing a dump truck (de Jongh, 2008). Consider the English case of *Iqbal Begum* (1991), where the defendant pleaded guilty to murder without understanding or appreciating the charge, then sat silently through her trial because she did not understand the interpreter (who did not speak the same language as her), at which relevant mitigating circumstances were not raised because of the interpreter's incompetence. Mrs. Begum was convicted and, although the conviction was subsequently quashed, she killed herself.

Nonetheless, courts rarely find that interpreting problems have led to injustice. In fact, the very great improbability of appeals succeeding on the basis of incomplete or inaccurate interpreting has been identified as a feature of common-law jurisprudence (see e.g. Morris, 1999b; Berk-Seligson, 2002; Hayes & Hale, 2010), and of the case-law of the ECtHR (Trechsel, 2005). Although there has been only a tiny number of criminal appeals in Ireland based on interpreting issues, courts seem similarly reluctant to find that issues of interpreting prejudiced the fairness of the trial.

Ultimately, no Irish court has found interpreting issues to have definitively prejudiced criminal proceedings. In fact, it is notable that despite the huge rise in the numbers of cases involving LEP defendants, and despite widespread concurrence that there are serious issues of quality with the interpreting system, only a very small number of criminal appeals have dealt with language issues, even fewer have been based even in part on interpreting issues, fewer again on interpreting issues at trial, and in a single successful appeal that resulted in a reduction of the applicant's sentence, the Court of Criminal Appeal's decision, while partly based on language difficulties, was also based on the wishes expressed by the victim, making it impossible to ascertain the degree to which the language issue influenced the decision (*D.P.P. v Vasile Vardoshilli*, 2009).[16]

Firm conclusions as to how Irish courts perceive the impact of interpreting more generally are elusive. The Court of Criminal Appeal has suggested that any situation involving an interpreter involves omissions in translation (*D.P.P. v Yu Jie*, 2005) and that language difficulties should be taken into account (*D.P.P. v Stanislaus Stokowski*, 2009) and given weight by the trial judge (*D.P.P. v Vasile Vardoshilli*, 2009). However, it has also stated that the impact of interpreting amounts to no more than an inconvenience that in no way goes to the safety or reliability of conviction (*D.P.P. v Adriano Martins Costa & Jose Claudio Batista*, 2008). The High Court, on the other hand, has accepted that – in theory at least – interpreting can impact on the jury's perception of the defendant and the outcome of a criminal case (*MacCarthaigh v Ireland*, 1999).

In at least one Irish refugee case, fair procedure was found by the Supreme Court to have been breached by poor interpreting (*Petrea Stefan v MJELR, the Refugee Appeals Authority Ireland & the Attorney General*, 2002), but most claims as to language have been regarded negatively and attempts to blame interpreting quality have been found to undermine credibility (e.g. *S.I.M. v RAT & Ors*, 2009; *F. & Anor v RAT*, 2010; *C. & Ors v RAT & Ors*, 2012). Interpreting claims have commonly been rejected on the basis that credibility decisions should be considered as a whole and individual elements, including interpreting, examined in isolation only with caution (*Radzuik v MJELR & RAT*, 2009; *T.D. v RAT & Anor*, 2010; *H.S. v RAT & Ors*, 2013).

Thus, it seems that Irish courts are somewhat willing to concede that interpretation is not a perfect science, and are divided on whether or how it impacts on process or outcome. In 2011, Jarmołowska provided unique empirical evidence of the impact of the lack of policies, regulation, and quality standards and control in the system of Irish legal interpreting and translation. Studying a sexual assault case involving an unrepresented LEP Polish defendant, she was able to track and analyse the witness statements taken by the police, their Polish translations, and court transcripts from the subsequent trial in which the statements were used. In the first instance, statements were taken at the police station by Polish witnesses using interpreters. However, due to the apparent incompetence of those interpreters, the quality of English in the resulting statements was severely compromised, thereby 'hindering understanding of the statements by the English speaking participants' at trial (Jarmołowska, 2011:14). The statements should then have been translated (back) into Polish for the defendant. However, due to a 'lack of policy and explicit guidelines regarding the translation of evidence' (Jarmołowska, 2011:161), two different Polish translations of the same statements were commissioned and provided to the defendant. The quality of the resulting translations was such, or differed to such an extent that, when provided to the defendant, he believed them to be two separate statements.

During the trial, while English-speaking participants used the English version of the statements, the defendant's understanding of the case had been so significantly altered by the translations that not only did frequent miscommunications and confusion arise in the courtroom as to what the defendant was attempting to reference at any given time, but as he attempted to make out a case against one witness based on ambiguities between what he believed were two statements she had given (in reality ambiguities between both translations of her single statement), the confusion led to frequent interruptions of his cross-examination. It is unclear the extent to which these interruptions impacted on his control of the witness or his ability to put forth a defence, and, as Jarmołowska points out, it is unclear what the impact on the jury was, but due to the nature of the resulting discourse, they may very well have believed the defendant to be 'purposefully misrepresenting the statement' (Jarmołowska, 2011:186).

Taken out of the context of a rigorous academic study, the case appears almost a caricature of what can go wrong with language issues in the criminal process. However, instead of occasioning alarm as to the imperilled fairness of the trial or inciting an urgent call for reform of the system, the evidence from Jarmołowska (2011) suggests that the court treated the issue simply as one of 'inconvenience and delay experienced during the course of the trial itself', as suggested in *D.P.P. v Adriano Martins Costa & Jose Claudio Batista* (2008).

Indeed, where complaints are made about interpreting, courts tend to reject claims not raised at the time of the proceedings. This is true for the ECtHR (*Kamasinski v Austria*, 1989), and for Irish courts, where weight has been given to whether or not an objection about an interpreter was raised at the time (*D.P.P. v Yu Jie*, 2005); it has been held in asylum cases that interpreting issues should not be relied upon at 'the eleventh hour' (*M.A.W. v RAT & MJELR*, 2009), but must be flagged when they arise (e.g. *L. v RAT*, 2011; *C. & Ors v RAT & Ors*, 2012); and in a recent European Arrest Warrant case it was specifically observed that:

> the respondent is not a mere passive observer. ... If there were matters which he did not understand there was nothing which could have prevented him from bringing that fact to the attention of his legal team or indeed to the court. In my view, he cannot blame anybody but himself if

he failed to speak up in this regard. (*Albert Jarzebak v The Governor of Cloverhill Prison & MJELR*, 2010)

The responsibility of the defendant to recognise and raise any problems with interpreting has also arisen at the ECtHR (*Vrahimi v Turkey*, 2002), and the Directive provides that control over interpreting adequacy should be exercised where authorities are put on notice. S.I. 565/2013, giving effect to the Directive in Ireland, provides for the possibility of having an interpreter replaced only where a motion or application has been made (Reg. 7). This may be made by the Court or any of the parties concerned (Reg. 7). However, the likelihood of such a motion being raised is questionable for a number of reasons.

First, there is the question of how someone with genuine language difficulties might be expected to recognise interpreting problems, something that was acknowledged by Feeney J in the Irish High Court (*Daud Abdilahi Gilingil v RAT & Ors*, 2006). Berk-Seligson (2002) points out that a defendant with no or very little comprehension of English would not be able to detect even 'grossly inaccurate interpreting'. However she further notes that the court itself (which by logical extension includes the parties involved) might not be alerted or put on notice even where the interpreter is completely changing the testimony, as what is said could still make sense to the court (see also Benmaman, 2000; del Valle, 2003). An LEP defendant might also try to raise the issue of interpreting, but must rely on the same interpreter to communicate any issues to a lawyer or the court; if a sub-standard interpreter is unwilling or unable to pass on any such comments, such a motion will never actually be made (Morris, 1999a).

The trial record can also create a difficulty for those attempting to challenge proceedings on the basis of an interpreting issue. It has happened that complaints allegedly made at trial did not become part of the court record and so could not be offered as evidence (*Kamasinski v Austria*, 1989). As court records tend to be kept only in the official language of the court, there is generally no means of verifying the adequacy or otherwise of interpreting at trial. In fact, Berk-Seligson (2002) found that US appeals based on interpreting mainly failed because no concrete proof of interpreting issues could be provided as proceedings were transcribed only in English.

What is good interpreting?

Although interpreting is rarely found to have prejudiced the fairness of proceedings, the right to an interpreter has been interpreted by the ECtHR (*Brozicek v Italy*, 1989; *Kamasinski v Austria*, 1989; *Güngör v Germany*, 2001; *Hermi v Italy*, 2006) to mean, and is included in the Directive (Art. 2(8)) as meaning, that interpreting should be adequate to safeguard proceedings, or such as to enable the defendant to have knowledge of the case against him and to defend himself, notably by being able to put before the court his version of events, and that an interpreter should also be competent (*Cuscani v UK*, 2002). S.I. 565/2013 provides that interpreting should be of sufficient quality to ensure that a person can effectively exercise his or her right to a fair trial (Reg. 7). At common law, quality interpreting was most often understood simply as enabling comprehension between parties, including the interpreter (*Gradidge v Grace Bros. Pty. Ltd.* 1988; *R. v West London Youth Court*, 2000). However, the most complete definition of quality that has been provided in terms of substantiating an alleged violation of the right to an interpreter was outlined in *R. v Tran* (1994). According to this definition, interpreting need not be perfect, but it should be, at a minimum, continuous (no breaks, interruptions or summaries), precise (word for word and idea for idea, as far as possible), impartial (objective and unbiased), competent (to ensure 'justice is done and seen to be done') and contemporaneous (accurate timing: consecutive favoured over simultaneous interpreting).

This definition has considerable merit, though it has slight imperfections; while precision is desirable, for example, the problem of word-for-word interpreting has been discussed. Of the remaining features, while interpreters should be impartial, complete impartiality may not be a realistic expectation; interpreting should be continuous; its timing should be accurate but care should be taken in endorsing modes of interpreting (consecutive versus simultaneous); and while interpreting should certainly be competent, the meaning thereof remains elusive. Each of these features is now discussed in more detail.

Impartiality

The interpreter is tasked with faithfully interpreting what is said, an important part of which is that the interpreter remain impartial and neutral. An interpreter should not give legal advice or advocate to the court on behalf of the LEP defendant, and it is important that interpreters avoid introducing bias through their choice of 'language, emphasis, intonation or body language' (Hertog, 2001:28). Interpreting contexts can be complex, however, and providing interpretation means adding another *person* to the proceedings, such that complete neutrality may be difficult (Hertog, 2001).

In practice, it has been found that courts do not take a rigid view of the interpreter's role but that their view is shaped partly by the interpreter's experience and partly by the court's familiarity with, and perception of, interpreters (Butler & Noaks, 1992). Where a defendant is unrepresented, both the defendant and courtroom personnel may use language difficulties as an excuse to pass the advocate's responsibility to the interpreter (Morris, 1999a), and the court's (mis)understanding of interpreting procedures can also mean that the norms of interpreted conversation are not used, thus impacting on the interpreter's neutrality. The standard rule in interpreting is to use the first and second person as if the speakers were conversing without a third party (the interpreter) being present. However, lawyers will often address the interpreter directly with the question intended for the defendant, and defendants or witnesses commonly address the interpreter personally (Colin & Morris, 1996).

The Irish Court of Criminal Appeal, in dealing with the issue of interpreter impartiality, actually appears to approve in one case of an interpreter's perceived empathy with the accused, in finding that the interpreter acted 'professionally and in a detached way ... and, if anything, acted with a certain affinity and sympathy towards the accused' (*D.P.P. v Yu Jie*, 2005). There are also anecdotal reports of interpreters in Irish courts speaking on behalf of defendants; in one example, an interpreter informed the court that because the defendant had not understood the summons, the charge should be struck out (Phelan, 2011).

Interpreters themselves have been found to have conflicting perceptions of their role, with most considering it part of their job to be a cultural broker, technical explainer and advocate (see e.g. Granger & Baker, 2003). The relationship between the defendant and the interpreter can be complex; while defendants may feel vulnerable due to their dependence on interpreters (Tribe, 2005), they often consider the interpreter, who speaks their language and may share their background, as a kind of 'saviour' or the 'Shangri-La of communication' (Morris, 1999a:6–7, 9). Particularly when unrepresented, they may expect interpreters to be on their side and ask them questions or for advice. The resulting predicament is well described by an interpreter-turned-barrister (Morgan, 1982:51):

> there is almost inevitably a strange, transient intimacy between interpreter and defendant ... exacerbated by the fact that the interpreter stands alongside the accused in the dock and on the witness stand and repeats his words as they are uttered, using the first person singular. The result is a curious identification with the defendant ... The accused, for his part, nearly always responds warmly, regarding the interpreter more as a friend and ally than as a person paid by the prosecution to do a job. After all, in

> many cases the interpreter is the only person around with whom he can hold a direct conversation! It is sometimes hard for him to accept that the interpreter's role is other than friend and mentor.

Continuity

According to the *Aequitas* publication on best practice in the EU, interpreters are obliged to interpret everything that is said. Summarising involves prioritisation of specific details by the interpreter but decisions of how or what to summarise are not within the ambit of the interpreter's role and would compromise neutrality. As such, summaries should be given only in exceptional circumstances and where there is consent (Hertog, 2001).

Contemporaneousness

The definition in *R. v Tran* (1994) approves of the consecutive mode of interpreting (speaker pauses at intervals to allow interpretation) over the simultaneous mode (interpreter listens and speaks almost concurrently). The choice of interpreting mode is not something that arises as an area of concern in the literature on interpreting, but it has been debated at length by the High Court in Ireland in relation to which might best be used in the courtroom in the context of the Irish language (*MacCarthaigh v MJELR*, 2002). The Official Languages Act, 2003 explicitly clarifies for the Irish language that mode of interpreting is at the court's discretion. Perhaps following from this, the Courts Service's latest tender document for regional contracts (2012, Appendix A) specifically stated that the services sought were for 'consecutive interpretation only' and not simultaneous interpreting, which, it said, 'is, generally, not feasible in a courtroom for a variety of reasons including the need to install sound proof interpreters' booths'.

The very great difficulty here is that while simultaneous interpreting may in some circumstances require such booths, this fails to recognise that in the District Court most interpreting is a type of simultaneous interpreting called 'whispered interpreting' or *chuchotage*, whereby the interpreter provides interpretations of ongoing proceedings in a whisper or at a very low volume. The ITIA (2011) has rightly called this development of consecutive interpreting services only an 'alarming' one, as it implies that interpreters are required to interpret only a fraction of what actually happens during District Court proceedings. It will be seen in Chapters 4 and 5 that because most proceedings in the District Court are uncontested and proceed on a guilty plea, the dynamic requires consecutive interpreting only on the rare occasion that the court interacts directly with the defendant; the vast majority of the time the defendant remains silent and the interpreter's role is to interpret proceedings simultaneously to the defendant.

Competence

Interpreters often, including in Ireland, swear an oath or make an affirmation that they will interpret accurately and to the best of their ability. Berk-Seligson (2002:204) points out, however, that '[n]o amount of oath-swearing can guarantee high-quality interpreting from an interpreter who does not have the necessary competency'. A competent interpreter can mitigate disadvantage, correct imbalances and facilitate access to justice by putting the LEP defendant 'on a nearly identical footing with the native speaker of the language of the legal proceedings' (Morris, 1996:1310); an incompetent, unskilled or untrained person acting as an interpreter, on the other hand, equates to 'building a weak link into the legal process' (Colin & Morris, 1996:70). Competent interpreters also enhance the efficiency of proceedings, as they ensure that things progress speedily, thus saving time, resources and money, and reducing the likelihood of costly interpreting-related appeals (Colin & Morris, 1996). Incompetent interpreters can do the opposite.

In terms of what constitutes a competent interpreter, the ECtHR has held that an interpreter does not need to have a particular qualification or certification, which is reasonable when one considers that it may be impossible, for example, to locate any qualified interpreters for some rarer languages (Trechsel, 2005). However, the ECtHR has accepted the competence of people to interpret where there is some degree of bilingualism but not necessarily any training or demonstrated competence (*Baka v Romania*, 2009; *Diallo v Sweden*, 2010), and interpreter competence at common law has also most often been linked with fluency in a language (*Iqbal Begum*, 1991; *R. v West London Youth Court*, 2000), despite the fact that fluency in a language in no way equates to the ability to interpret. In Ireland, there is some evidence that courts will accept the competence of friends to act as informal interpreters (*Fitzpatrick & Anor v K. & Anor*, 2006; *Albert Jarzebak v The Governor of Cloverhill Prison & MJELR*, 2010; Phelan, 2011), but there is also evidence that where this creates apparent comprehension difficulties, proceedings will be halted (Phelan, 2011), and that judges may query friends' qualifications for the purpose of interpretation or translation (*Muhammed Saleem v MJELR*, 2011).

We have seen that to be a competent interpreter requires great skill, but also that establishing an interpreter's incompetence on appeal (or winning any appeal based on interpreting quality) is onerous and unlikely to be successful. Logically, then, if access to justice is to be guaranteed in Irish courts for those who do not speak English (or Irish), it is vital that the interpreters that are working in courts *are*, in fact, competent. There are no universal standards or qualifications by which to show or attain competence, and numerous forms of training, qualification and accreditation exist. Some countries have systems of professional accreditation, such as the US, where interpreters who wish to become federal interpreters must pass the Federal Court Interpreter Certification Exam, and the UK, where the Chartered Institute of Linguistics runs a Diploma in Public Service Interpreting that is rigorously tested at the end. In fact, the failure rate of these exams is perhaps the clearest evidence of the skill required to act as a competent court interpreter; the US exam has a failure rate of 96 per cent (Phelan, 2006) and the UK exam a pass rate of only one third ('Growing demand ...', 2007). There are no standardised or recognised levels of linguistic competence across the EU (Hertog, 2001), but under the new Directive, as per the EU best practice already outlined, Member States should endeavour to establish a register or registers of appropriately qualified translators and interpreters, who should be independent and required to observe confidentiality.

Conclusion

Things have changed in Ireland and in Irish courts. With immigrants from 199 countries making up 12 per cent of the population, and 11 per cent of the population speaking a language other than English at home, with amounts of up to and over two million Euros being spent on interpreting and translating services in the courts system, and a potential 20 per cent of daily District Court appearances involving 'foreign offenders', Irish courts have had to adapt to deal with a rapid and substantial growth in the number of defendants with no or limited English-language skills. In the absence of any relevant infrastructure, an *ad hoc* system quickly developed, and services were later outsourced to a single service provider – a move that was portrayed as a rationalisation of the management of services.

The District Court is undoubtedly the court most affected and impacted by this change as the court that processes the vast majority of criminal offences and, indeed, most anecdotal accounts on interpreting and LEP defendants have related to the District Court. While many of these have pointed to serious problems of quality, only a very tiny number of criminal appeals have been based on interpreting issues and the right to an interpreter, a right that has been explicitly recognised in Ireland since at least 1929, at common law since at least 1909, more recently by the ECHR, and now also by the EU Directive on the right to interpretation and translation in criminal proceedings and S.I. 565/2013 giving effect to the Directive in Ireland.

There is some anecdotal evidence of District Court judges being reluctant or refusing to certify for an interpreter in certain circumstances and some evidence of a reluctance to entertain complaints about the quality of interpreting or interpreters. Attitudes among judges as to the importance and impact of interpreting on criminal proceedings have also varied; there is apparent acceptance that language difficulties should be taken into account, that interpreting is an imperfect art, and that it may impact a jury's perception and the outcome of a case, but a reluctance to accept that interpreting issues could endanger the reliability of a conviction. While these attitudes are similar to those of courts outside Ireland, they nonetheless suggest a need for quality control in the provision of interpreters.

Registers of interpreters and translators are considered best practice in the EU and, under the new EU Directive, Member States should endeavour to establish such registers. Outsourcing, on the other hand, has become very popular but has been recognised as problematic and as necessitating, at the very least, assurance of independent quality controls and mechanisms. These controls and mechanisms do not exist in Ireland, where the minimum standards required to interpret in a criminal court are worryingly basic when considered in the context of what is known about how interpreting works, the skills required to interpret competently, the impact of even skilled interpreters on pragmatics in criminal trials, and the consequent potential for incompetent interpreters to compromise fair proceedings.

Despite serious concerns being expressed on an ongoing basis about the competence of interpreters in Irish courts (the poor, *ad hoc* and unpredictable quality of interpreting; the lack of codes of ethics/conduct for interpreters and guidelines for those working with them; the lack of quality standards and monitoring; and questionable recruitment practices and insufficient background checks on interpreters), interpreting in Ireland remains unregulated. The 'official' attitude seems to be that a quality service is being provided, that there is a high rate of satisfaction with that service, and that those needing interpreters rarely have any problems understanding what happens in court.

The next two chapters examine and describe what actually happens in the Irish District Court when an LEP defendant appears, including how and when interpreters are provided, the role of the interpreter, the types of interpreters working in the court, attitudes towards interpreters and the impact of interpreters on the dynamics of District Court procedure. While some of the concerns about the impact of interpreting are more relevant to higher courts – for example, the control of a witness in an adversarial trial – the nature of the District Court as a predominantly oral institution, where language plays a central role in control, power relations and the ultimate decisions of the judge, means that interpreting nonetheless has considerable potential to influence the flow and the outcome of proceedings.

Notes

1 2004: Cyprus, Czech Republic, Estonia, Hungary, Latvia, Lithuania, Malta, Poland, Slovakia, Slovenia; 2007: Bulgaria and Romania.

2 Irish and other common-law jurisprudence and the case-law of the European Court of Human Rights (ECtHR).

3 The 2011 Courts Service Annual Report (2011:17) also refers to a recent review that 'resulted in additional value for the Service in respect of the quality and cost of the interpretation service being provided'.

4 For an excellent review of the more substantive issues in the Irish context see O'Nolan (2011b).

5 The Official Languages Act, 2003 allows any person to use either of the official languages in any court.

6 'Translation' is the general process of converting words and meaning in one language into another language, but as a term of art it is the conversion of the *written* word or text between languages as executed by translators. 'Interpreting' or 'interpretation', on the other hand, refers to the oral translation of either the written or (more commonly) the spoken word. In the 'early years', accounts by non-language professionals almost always failed to differentiate between interpreters and translators. Over time, some sources began to acknowledge the distinction while other sources have continued to use the concepts interchangeably.

7 ICCPR Art. 14(3)(f); ECHR Art. 6(3)(e). Ireland takes a dualist approach to international law: unless an instrument is incorporated into Irish law it is not enforceable domestically, though it may have persuasive value (Byrne & McCutcheon, 2009). The European Convention on Human Rights Act, 2003 incorporates the EHCR at sub-constitutional level, giving it 'further effect' and requiring that judicial notice be taken of provisions and ECtHR judgments, advisory opinions and decisions. The ICCPR is not domestically incorporated.

8 The culmination of a process that began with a 2003 Green Paper on procedural safeguards, followed by a Proposal for a Framework Decision (FD) on certain Procedural rights in Criminal Proceedings in 2004. When this failed to garner unanimous approval a step-by-step approach to establishing common minimum procedural rights was taken, with the right to interpreting and translation the first step. A proposed FD adopted in July 2009 became obsolete with the entry into force of the Lisbon Treaty. A similar proposed Directive was adopted by the European Parliament in June 2010 with some amendments. The Directive was adopted by the Council of the European Union in October 2010.

9 Among other things, that the right applies to those charged with a criminal offence, which generally means as so defined by domestic law but may extend to acts otherwise categorised but that are criminal in nature and carry penal sanctions (*Öztürk v Germany*, 1984), and that interpreting must be provided free of charge by the State without regard either to the defendant's financial position or the outcome of the case (*Luedicke, Belkacem & Koç v Germany*, 1978; *Öztürk v Germany*, 1984).

10 Ireland opposed the Proposal for a Framework Decision on certain Procedural Rights in Criminal Proceedings (2004). A second reason for Ireland's opposition was its claim that the EU lacked the competence to legislate in the area of procedural safeguards. Under the Lisbon Treaty Ireland can opt in or out of any legislation that falls under Title V: Area of Freedom, Justice and Security, which includes all areas of criminal law.

11 See e.g. Appendix E for an example from this study.

12 American company, Lionbridge, won the contract to become the sole contracted service provider. However, other agencies also provided interpreters where Lionbridge was unable to fulfil a particular assignment.

13 The regional method of organisation was not in place during the research study on which this book is based and did not come into effect until March 2013. Three agencies were contracted to provide services in four regions: Translation.ie, Context and Lionbridge.

14 E.g. The International Second Language Proficiency Ratings (formerly the Australian Second Language Proficiency Ratings).

15 The Directive is intended to apply to the execution of European Arrest Warrants and S.I. 565/2013 allows for the provision of interpreters in such proceedings. The Refugee Act, 1996, as amended, provides that interpreters will be used to conduct interviews where necessary and possible, and many asylum/refugee cases accept implicitly or explicitly that interpreters should be provided where meaningful communication is otherwise impossible (e.g. *M.A.W. v RAT & MJELR*, 2009).

16 Only four criminal appeals were found that are clearly based at least in part on interpreting issues: *D.P.P. v Ismet Ceka*, 2004; *D.P.P. v Yu Jie*, 2005; *D.P.P. v Valdas Valiukas*, 2009 and *D.P.P. v Vasile Vardoshilli*, 2009. The first three were unsuccessful; in *Ismet Ceka*, the claim that insufficient weight had been given to the accused's knowledge of English was denied; in *Yu Jie*, an allegation of interpreter bias was rejected; and in *Valdas Valiukas*, a claim involving the delayed provision of an interpreter at a police station after arrest was found to be baseless. In *Vasile Vardoshilli*, Finnegan J suspended the final two years of a ten year sentence for rape, false imprisonment and assault causing harm, citing the fact that the trial judge had not taken into account the applicant's lack of fluency in English and dependence on an interpreter, and that his ethnic and cultural background would 'cause additional hardship to someone who is in prison', although the decision was also influenced by a Victim Impact Statement and the victim's wish that a lengthy period of imprisonment not be imposed.

PART III

Processing LEP defendants: bilingual cases in the Irish District Court

4

Interpreting District Court proceedings for non-Irish defendants

What is his command of the English language?[1]

The cases a District Court is set to hear on any given day are set out in the court list. 'The list' is a sheet that in some courts is distributed freely, and in others guarded carefully and accessible only to those with the right credentials. It contains details of the persons scheduled to appear and the names of the prosecuting Garda, and the registrar will call the people on that list in an order that varies from court to court. Any number of people may be scheduled to appear at the same time and, as it is not usually obvious what order the list will be called in, there is much waiting around.

One of the changes wrought by immigration to Ireland has been the variety of names on the list, which is now usually guaranteed to contain at least a few tongue twisters for the judge or the registrar. In fact, the names on the list are often used to predict or determine who might need an interpreter. Aoife explains: 'You'd know from the names that they're not Irish.' While the nature of Irish immigration means that this is often an effective method, it is not foolproof:

> 'He is an Irish national, though his name would belie that. His father is a Malaysian national' (solicitor, RC)

> JUDGE Z: Nationality?
> SOLICITOR: I don't actually know.
> JUDGE Z [to defendant] What is your nationality, Sir?
> DEFENDANT [Mohammed]: Oirish.

How and when the interpreting issue arises

The interpreting issue often arises at the start of the case, though no set procedure is followed and the issue may equally arise at a later point or not at all. One of six things usually happens:

1 no mention is made of language or interpreting but an interpreter appears
2 the court presenter/Garda raises the issue
3 the solicitor/barrister raises or is consulted on the issue
4 the judge raises the issue of nationality/language/interpreting
5 (and/or) no interpreter is present: second calling, adjournment or remand requested
6 no mention is made of language or interpreting, and no interpreter appears

No mention is made of language or interpreting but an interpreter appears

Interpreters often have access to the court list and they are generally attentive to the names being called by the registrar. It is usually easy for them, as Mark points out, to 'recognise their own nationality's names' and, once these are called, an interpreter will often appear next to a defendant without the court making any mention thereof.

The court presenter/Garda raises the issue

This is perhaps least common, but it happens occasionally that the court presenter or a Garda alerts the court to the fact that an interpreter is required:

> 'Polish interpreter, please' (CitC)
> 'It is very important that he have a Latvian interpreter' (CitC)

The solicitor/barrister raises or is consulted on the issue

> 'I appear. A Slovakian interpreter is needed' (RC)
> 'Judge, I appear in this matter. There's an interpreter here' (CitC)
> 'A Russian interpreter was assigned the last day' (CusC)

Very often a solicitor will indicate the presence, lack of or need for an interpreter at the same time as announcing their appearance. The judge also frequently consults the solicitor/barrister for their opinion on whether an interpreter is required and their opinion is often accepted.

> 'A Polish interpreter is required, I am told, so I will accept that that is the case' (Judge O)

> Judge Z: Do we need an interpreter?
> Solicitor: No, Judge.

Sometimes, however, the judge will pose further questions and may request an interpreter even where the solicitor/barrister and/or the defendant claim that none is required:

JUDGE Z: Does he need an interpreter?
SOLICITOR: He doesn't need one.
JUDGE Z: Does he have sufficient competence; can he speak English?
DEFENDANT: Yes.
JUDGE Z: Where are you from?
SOLICITOR: Pakistan.
JUDGE Z: And what language do they speak in Pakistan?
DEFENDANT: Urdu.
JUDGE Z: What?
DEFENDANT: In Pakistan? Urdu.
JUDGE Z: Go to your solicitor and write it down.
SOLICITOR: Urdu. U–R–D–U.
JUDGE Z: I request an interpreter for that date.

This case was remanded for an interpreter despite the fact that the solicitor declared the defendant's ability to speak English and that the defendant had no apparent difficulties understanding or speaking English. While Urdu is the national language of Pakistan, it is a mother tongue only for a small percentage of the population and it is not even clear that the defendant speaks it. The defendant told the judge that Urdu is spoken in Pakistan but not that it was his own language. Without further assessment there was no reason to assume that this defendant needed an interpreter, let alone an Urdu interpreter. Even claiming to be a native or fluent speaker of English is not always accepted without question:

JUDGE Z: Language?
SOLICITOR: English.
JUDGE Z: Has he proficiency in English?
SOLICITOR: Yes, Judge. He's fluent.
JUDGE Z: His response to the charge after caution was; 'you give me this tomorrow? I do not understand.' If he speaks English, why did he not understand?
SOLICITOR: [laughing] The reason he did not understand was that the charge was a 500-year-old provision. It took me a good while to find out …

As some judges address the issue of an interpreter only if it is first raised by a party to the case, and there is no guarantee that one will be provided if it is not directly requested, it would seem that it is certainly in the best interests of a defendant to have a solicitor/barrister that will request an interpreter where one is needed. It is also clear that while the ultimate decision of assigning an interpreter lies with the judge, the solicitor/barrister's opinion carries heavy weight. As well as often having the confidence of the court on this matter, solicitors/barristers portray confidence in their own judgement, rarely expressing doubts or alluding to the fallibility of their opinion. Yet there are factors that cast doubt over the solicitor/barrister's ability to make this judgement without error. Aside from not being trained to assess a person's linguistic competence, it is notable that where the opinion of a solicitor/barrister *is* challenged, the judge often reaches a different conclusion. More importantly, defendants whose solicitors have declined an interpreter often seem to struggle without one, suggesting that solicitors/barristers may sometimes over-estimate the ability of their client to speak English, possibly because consultations are possible even with limited English. It may also be that solicitors are respecting their client's instructions to 'get it over with', and that to proceed without an interpreter is more expeditious.

In any case it is notable that although solicitors/barristers regularly request interpreters for their clients, they also advise the court against their necessity with some frequency. In the following examples the court is willing to provide an interpreter but the solicitor seems more anxious to proceed without one:

JUDGE X: Does the defendant speak English?
DEFENDANT: A little bit.
JUDGE X: Is there a Polish interpreter?
[Second calling for an interpreter]
JUDGE X: It was put back for an interpreter.
SOLICITOR: Judge, his English is quite good.
JUDGE X: Well, when he was asked ...
DEFENDANT: Don't speak English very well. Can understand.
JUDGE X: Well, that's fine.

SOLICITOR: A Russian interpreter was assigned the last day.
[Second calling for another reason]
JUDGE X: Is there a Russian interpreter?
POLISH INTERPRETER: In Court [number].
SOLICITOR: I've explained to him about the CCTV. He understands what's happening.
GARDA: If an interpreter is required, he is in Court [number].
SOLICITOR: Judge [T], they do speak some English.

THE JUDGE RAISES THE ISSUE OF NATIONALITY/LANGUAGE/INTERPRETING

If a case is already in the system and the defendant's file contains a note that an interpreter has been certified for, the judge may raise the issue by asking if the interpreter is present, or by requesting their presence:

'A Polish interpreter is required' (Judge O)
'Do we have a Slovakian interpreter?' (Judge X)
'He's a Latvian-speaking Russian' (Judge Z)

Some judges may enquire at the beginning of the case as to the defendant's need for an interpreter, usually through questions on nationality, language and language ability. They may also simply ask whether or not an interpreter is needed. These questions are often directed at the solicitor/barrister:

'Does the defendant speak English?'
'What nationality do we have here?' (Judge Z)
'Is there a language difficulty?' (Judge V)
'What language are we speaking, please?' (Judge P)

When a defendant is unrepresented, or as a preference in the case of some judges, the defendant will be questioned directly. The nature of the assessment procedure is simple and usually consists solely of asking the defendant if they speak English or if they understand what is going on:

JUDGE Z: Is your command of the English language OK?
DEFENDANT: Yeah.

JUDGE X: Do we need an interpreter? [to defendant, slowly] Do you speak English?
DEFENDANT: Yes, I do.
JUDGE X: All right.

JUDGE R: Does Mr. G need an interpreter?
GARDA: [hesitantly] No.
JUDGE TO DEFENDANT: Do you understand what's going on?
DEFENDANT: I do.
JUDGE: [unsure] You do?
DEFENDANT: I do.
JUDGE R: OK.

JUDGE Z: What is your understanding of the English language? I mean, can you speak English?
DEFENDANT [French]: Yeah.
JUDGE Z: Do you want the assistance of an interpreter?
DEFENDANT: [Didn't understand, question repeated several times] No.
JUDGE Z: Comprends?
DEFENDANT: I'm all right.

JUDGE Z: Do you have sufficient English?
DEFENDANT: [Laughing] Yes, I've been speaking English for twelve years.

While there is insufficient detail in the first three extracts to gauge with any certainty the defendant's level of English, the final two extracts provide a little more information. They are particularly interesting because although this information points to two opposite conclusions about the defendant's proficiency, the outcome in both was the same: no interpreter was provided. The last extract is grammatically sophisticated, it contains factual detail to support its complexity and it was delivered with confidence and fluidity, all of which strongly support the defendant's claim of proficiency. The penultimate extract does the opposite. The first 'yeah' provides little information, but the question about the interpreter had to be repeated several times before the defendant understood. Additionally, his spoken English was laboured and heavily accented. The case proceeded with the aid of an Irish friend but it moved slowly and painstakingly, with the defendant unable to understand the court and the court equally unable to understand the defendant. A full description of the case is provided in Appendix D and it illustrates the delays and frustrations caused for both sides when an interpreter is needed but not provided.

Some interpreters have expressed concern about the methods used to assess a defendant's English. In Marta's experience, when a defendant says they understand English this is accepted without question but she does not feel that this is sufficient evidence of whether a person is proficient enough to stand trial. She says a person is probably going to say yes for a variety of reasons when asked if they speak English: it is an easy question, they may *think* they can understand, they may also be ashamed that they cannot speak English or they may want to get things finished quickly. Marta regularly sees such defendants begin to struggle and become completely lost very quickly, even where they had been able to converse with the solicitor previously. Jevgenius gave the example of a Slovak defendant who alleged that his English was good and that he didn't need an interpreter, but when the judge asked for his plea, he didn't understand and the case had to be postponed.

Judges deal with the issue of providing interpreting in their own, personalised manner but it is fair to say that if a request for an interpreter is made, it will be granted. There is a sense among interpreters and legal practitioners that interpreters should be provided in the interests of a fair trial, but also that judges 'err on the side of caution' (James) in appointing interpreters in order to protect themselves. Mark explains that the judge's orders 'stand up to better scrutiny if the defendant that he has sentenced or penalised has been legally represented and has had an interpreter', and Aoife concurs, explaining that a judge could be judicially reviewed if the hearing 'wasn't conducted pursuant to the constitutional rights of the person'. She opines that 'District Court judges would be very cautious about not exposing themselves like that.' Overall, most feel that judges routinely grant requests for interpreters, though Gerard suggests that some have issues about 'these people' getting something for nothing and grant interpreters grudgingly. He also says that the Gardaí sometimes highlight that 'this person spoke English fluently yesterday, why does he need an interpreter today', but that in the end the interpreter is always provided:

> 'I'm absolutely aghast that people have been in this country for seven years and have not one word of English. I suggest that he knows as much English as you and I. Well, that's not a matter for now. Through the interpreter can I indicate to the defendant that the matter is adjourned' (Judge Z)

> JUDGE Z: I'm getting concerned at the amount of taxpayers' money being wasted in these particular cases. ... How long have you been in the country?
> DEFENDANT: One year and a half.
> JUDGE Z: Oh, you've great English now!
> DEFENDANT: [Laughs. Then confused face]
> JUDGE Z: How many English classes have you attended in the last one and a half years?
> DEFENDANT: None.

> JUDGE Z: How long are you in Ireland?
> DEFENDANT: [Silence. Shrugs]
> JUDGE Z: I tell you, Sir, you've more English than I have. [Addressing court] He knows what's going on! [To defendant] Off you go! Write to Santy!

These extracts raise the issue of defendants pretending not to speak English or being perceived as doing so. Jevgenius is of the opinion that some Lithuanian and Latvian defendants (those he interprets for) are abusing the system by pretending not to understand English. He has heard about defendants with many previous convictions who will use 'any excuse' to avoid more penalties or to buy more time. Molly feels that while some defendants might understand and not say anything, only a very small number use the services of the interpreter in the hope that things will turn out differently. Mark considers that the strategy of pretending not to speak English is more likely to be used in the Garda station, where 'they sort of feign a lack of understanding rather than having to answer some awkward questions', but says it is less likely to be used in court. Stephen says:

> I think it's definitely a strategy ... and people will certainly sometimes pretend that they have less English than they have. Because I have had experience myself of talking to people maybe at the station, and then they're in court and they don't seem to have any English at all, all of a sudden [laughs]. Now it wouldn't happen too often, I have to say that, but it is certainly a tactic by some individuals, and generally the ones, they're a little bit more experienced.

(AND/OR) NO INTERPRETER IS PRESENT: SECOND CALLING, ADJOURNMENT OR REMAND REQUESTED

> 'It should be going ahead, but I don't think the interpreter is here yet' (CitC)
> 'The defendant is in court. I was hoping it might be put back. I think I'm going to need the assistance of an interpreter' (RC)

If an interpreter is needed but none is present, the case may be put to second calling in the case of temporary absence, or put back so an interpreter can be ordered. A second calling may also be requested by the solicitor/barrister for a consultation 'with the benefit of the interpreter' (RC). Interestingly, judges routinely grant requests for the latter, which is in contrast to the impatience sometimes caused by requests for ordinary consultations. Most solicitors in this study indicated that because the interpreter is present at court already, consultations with LEP clients take place there. Gwen says that many LEP cases are disposed of on the same day they are assigned so that there is no need to have them in the office, and most agreed that it was unusual to have interpreted consultations outside of court. Sometimes they take place in a solicitor's office where the client brings a friend or relative who can speak both languages, but if there are communication issues the consultation is postponed until the day of court. Only one solicitor regularly uses interpreters in the office.

There appears to be an expectation by the court and the solicitors that interpreters should facilitate these consultations, but in fact they have been a source of controversy and difficulty for interpreters as they were forbidden by agency policy. The reasoning was that the court, and not the solicitor/barrister, hires the interpreter, and that work done outside of the court should be paid for separately. Molly explains that at one point this led to 'murder in court', as complaints were made to judges when interpreters refused to facilitate consultations. In those cases, the judge would order that the consultation be done, and interpreters say that the agency finally agreed to consultations where the situation permits it but that the area remains a grey one. Some interpreters feel they should get the permission of the judge first, but this approach has not proven popular. Mihai describes how a judge shouted at him for telling a solicitor to ask the judge's permission: 'The person in question thought it was very cheeky of me to refuse – made quite a big fuss to the judge about it', and another solicitor told Jevgenius that he had 'just fucked up [his] case' when he refused to facilitate a consultation. Indeed, Gerard takes a cynical view of interpreters who so refuse, saying that as long as interpreters needed work, they were willing to do them, but once the contract was in place, they became less accommodating.

In practice, these consultations are frequent and they can ultimately facilitate the interpreter's job. Interpreters say their job is easier and they can work more quickly if they have some details before going into court. Solicitors and barristers agree. For Matthew it is important 'that the interpreter is briefed somewhat on what the situation is, because it helps everybody' and it means getting 'the best use of an interpreter, if I want to be as blunt as that'. James talked about a recent experience where he had explained beforehand what he would say, with the result that 'it made him twice as fast ... it just made things a lot quicker'.

No mention is made of language or interpreting and no interpreter appears

> Judge N: Who's your solicitor?
> Defendant: L.G.
> Judge N: What?
> Defendant: My name is L.G.

When the issue of interpreting is not raised by anybody in court, the case may have been before the court already and the defendant's file may note that no interpreter is required. It is not uncommon, however, for the issue to remain unaddressed even where a defendant is in court for the first time. It is not clear why this happens or under what set of circumstances but it seems that some judges prefer to wait for an interpreter to be requested rather than addressing the issue themselves. In the above example the Polish defendant had no interpreter and was not asked if he wanted or needed one, yet his English proficiency seemed questionable at best, as he did not (appear to) understand the judge's question. He was assigned a solicitor who entered a plea of guilty and explained the defendant's background to the court, resulting in a Section 1.1 of the Probation of Offenders Act, which means that no criminal conviction is recorded. At no point was the issue of interpreting raised.

An interpreter could easily have been requested had the solicitor considered it necessary, as there was a Polish interpreter present in the court. It may be that the defendant had initially pretended not to speak English to buy time but that his English was sufficient for the purposes of this case. This explanation is particularly easy to accept as the case was straightforward, the defendant had legal representation and, because it was a Section 1.1, no criminal conviction was going to be recorded. It is possible that because of the minor nature of the case no necessity was felt to address the issue of interpreting. From the time the case was called (for the second time) until L.G. left the court with no criminal record, two minutes or perhaps even less had elapsed. It is possible that had the case been more serious and a custodial sentence possible, the interpreting issue would have taken on more significance. This case can be contrasted with the case outlined below in the section on the LEP interpreter (and also in Appendix E), where an interpreter is dismissed for being incompetent, but only after the situation becomes so serious that a custodial sentence is involved.

The wrong interpreter?

> You see sometimes there are people who would say, let's say, that they are Lithuanian, but they are really not. Sometimes passports are forged in order for people from outside the European Union to be able to come here – they would ask for [a] Lithuanian interpreter, and apparently it's not Lithuanian. ... Almost always it's Russian, because this [sic] are people either from Moldova, Georgia, well from Russian-speaking states. It doesn't happen that often, but it does happen. (Anna)

It arose in the interviews that interpreters are sometimes assigned to a client whose language they do not speak. In some cases it is an administrative error. Molly was once assigned to a Polish speaker whom they thought needed a Spanish speaker and Ewa once travelled four hours to an assignment only to find that the 'Polish' defendant she had come to interpret for was Latvian. It can also be the result of false identities being claimed by defendants, as explained by Anna above. Marta had an experience where she was assigned to a 'Polish' defendant but when she started interpreting, she quickly realised that he didn't speak any Polish. She explained that Polish is not a language that has different, unintelligible dialects – either you speak Polish or you don't. However, when she tried to tell the solicitor, the solicitor disagreed, insisted that the defendant was Polish and asked her to continue. This scenario can arise, she surmises, where someone has a fake passport or papers, they get caught for drunk-driving, for example, give the fake ID to the Gardaí, and then become afraid that if they say they cannot speak the appropriate language their real identity will be discovered and there will be an investigation. In Marta's opinion, solicitors prefer not to ask too many questions. In this case the solicitor made a statement in court to the effect that the man was a Polish national that preferred to speak Russian. Marta points out that not only was this not true, it did not even make sense, but the court accepted the explanation without question. In her view some solicitors do not pay enough attention to language issues.

Solicitors and barristers show awareness of the 'big difference between basic, conversational English and understanding what goes on in a court' (Gwen), and suggest that the intimidating nature of the court setting can also create nerves and diminish a person's language ability. James points out that 'if you're panicked or in fear, there can be a block there'. Gwen maintains that 'you always have to bear in mind ... it's an intimidating scene', and Thomas has experienced many incidences where 'the person who appears to have excellent English falters when challenged in the court system'. They suggest there is a sort of collective responsibility to ensure interpreters are assigned where needed. Some submit that solicitors have a professional responsibility to ensure that clients fully understand, and that there is an onus on the solicitor or barrister to request an interpreter in court where needed, as well as a responsibility on the defendant: 'If the client doesn't understand, he must say so' (Mark). Ultimately, it is the responsibility of the judge to ensure things are fairly run and at the end of the day, whether or not an interpreter is assigned is 'not [the solicitor's] decision, it's the judge's' (Mark).

I swear by Almighty God that I shall well and truly interpret

> I swear by Almighty God that I shall well and truly interpret and explain to the court all matters and things as shall be required of me to the best of my skill and understanding.

This is the oath that is administered to the interpreters that are sworn in in Irish courts, though only some judges have interpreters sworn in while others do not. Of those that do, some have all interpreters sworn in at the beginning of the day, and some have them sworn in solely when evidence is being given by the defendant. It is thus not a consistently observed practice. Even where some interpreters take the oath at the start of the court session, others arrive too late or may simply fail to take the oath. The following extract demonstrates how the practice depends on the individual judge. In this case the interpreter's demeanour indicated that she had never been sworn in and had also never heard of such a thing:

> SOLICITOR: Having spoken with my client through the interpreter I have a plea.
>
> JUDGE Y: Very good. I'll hear the facts. Does the interpreter need to be sworn in?

> [Solicitor looks at interpreter, interpreter looks alarmed, confused. She shakes her head]
> SOLICITOR: No, Judge.
> JUDGE Y: Very well.

The solicitors and barristers interviewed agree that an interpreter is unlikely to have any legal responsibility to provide competent interpreting, and they refer both to the sporadic nature of oath-taking and the improbability of an interpreter being judicially reviewed. Stephen says, for example, that he is 'not aware of them having a legal responsibility where they could have a duty of care and be sued for breach of that duty of care for negligence'. The interpreter's oath thus seems to be little more than a formality that is observed inconsistently, perhaps to impress upon interpreters the seriousness of their undertaking or to instil confidence in the accuracy and reliability of the interpreter. It is nonetheless interesting in terms of its content. It implies that the interpreter must interpret and explain only to the court and not, for example, to the defendant; it specifies that the interpreter should interpret that required of him or her, implying that perhaps not everything said in court need be interpreted; and it suggests that the interpreter is not expected to provide *verbatim* or word-for-word interpretation, but rather to interpret and explain.

Contrasting this with the discussion in Chapter 3 on *verbatim* interpreting, it is unclear if the oath means an interpreter may be expected to provide explanations beyond what is actually said, or that where a term or concept would be incomprehensible to the court for cultural reasons, for example, the interpreter should explain this term. In practice, some District Court judges do seem to expect *verbatim* interpretation and will pause between phrases, waiting for the words to be interpreted. Due to the nature of interpreting this can complicate things for, rather than facilitate, the interpreter. Ewa explains:

> If you are fluent in both languages, you know you have to wait for the first sentence to be finished to be able to translate it. Sometimes the judge is looking at you like, 'why are you not translating?' Because he did not finish the sentence yet. I do not know what he is going to say.

In reality, however, the court almost never directs the interpreter as to what to interpret, although the new S.I. 565/2013 provides that interpreting should be carried out 'as directed by the Court'(S.6). A judge occasionally instructs an interpreter to interpret when it seems that a particular thing is not being interpreted or where something is of particular importance, but most of the interpreter's work is done quietly and without input from the court. They are simply required to stand next to the defendant and provide a whispered interpretation of what is said in court (this mode of interpreting is also called *chuchotage*). It is unclear whether the court expects this to be a *verbatim* account.

Interviewees all feel it is important that everything be interpreted. Anna says, for example, that although she was never given instructions about what to interpret by the agencies or the court, she interprets everything. Stella was told in training that she should interpret everything, but makes the point that this is not possible; something that is widely acknowledged. Thomas explains that 'they can't interpret everything that's going on, that's the reality, because the dynamics won't allow them to'. One of the main challenges, particularly for the less experienced interpreter, is the insider language of the District Court. Much of its jargon is not contained in interpreting glossaries and is almost impossible to prepare for (an original glossary is provided in Appendix C). James talks about 'the working language of the court' that all interpreters need to know: 'You can't do the job unless you know what a sentence is, and then you know you need to know what, for example, a suspended sentence is.' Gwen refers to the archaic nature of some court language: 'How do you translate "may it please the court" and some of the rubbish that we use on a daily basis? Or "I'm obliged?"' From the perspective of a non-native speaker, colloquialisms, local expressions and humour may also pose difficulties. Ewa and Jevgenius affirm that their biggest difficulty at the start was the Irish accent: 'It took me about a month before I could understand the accent. I had to ask questions over and over.'

Other serious challenges are posed by the high speed of proceedings and the often poor acoustics in courtrooms, and there are also less obvious challenges such as struggling to hear the many numbers and figures that arise throughout a District Court case: fine amounts; road traffic offences involving number plates and expiry dates; theft offences involving dates, addresses, quantities and sums; public order offences specifying times, addresses, numbers of people and more. Allowances are almost never made for the interpretation. Speakers do not slow down, speak up or use microphones, and for the most part the case continues as if nothing were different, to the point that many interpreters say they have had to learn to lip read. Some more experienced interpreters say they are sufficiently familiar with the language and procedure to anticipate dialogue and overcome this communicative interference, while others say they ask people to slow down or speak up when they have difficulties, something which was never observed happening in practice in the course of this research. Interpreters say this is easier to do with some judges than others and tends to happen more frequently in higher courts.

Judges, solicitors/barristers and defendants can also prevent the interpreter from interpreting everything. The judge, who controls what is said, by whom and when, sometimes interrupts:

JUDGE T: Is he working?
INTERPRETER – DEFENDANT – INTERPRETER: No Judge, I –.

The judge interrupted to ask a solicitor to represent the defendant and interrupted twice when the interpreter was explaining why the defendant had failed to appear previously. There are also times when the solicitor/barrister halts interpretation of what is said in court by consulting with the defendant through the interpreter as proceedings are ongoing (something that will be considered in the next chapter) and, finally, the defendant sometimes prevents the interpreter interpreting what is said in court by asking him or her questions during proceedings. Defendants also sometimes inform the interpreter that they do not need them to interpret, and interpreters react in different ways to this. Belén tells the defendant that she has to translate and, similarly, Jevgenius feels that he is there anyway and if he doesn't interpret they might later use as a defence the fact they hadn't understood. Svetlana says that sometimes she translates and sometimes 'I was just sitting there looking at them, and when they forgot some word, I said this is this word and they said "oh, OK. Thanks".' Ewa also waits until they need help: 'I just step aside and OK, I'm here anyway. If you have any question you can ask me.' Mihai says he would generally wait for the solicitor or court to confirm that it is OK to do this and Molly also says that you need to declare your position and have permission before you stop interpreting.

The Interpreters: Silent, Selective, LEP, Advocate and Competent

The main mode of interpreting used in the District Court is whispered interpreting or *chuchotage*, such that most of what the interpreter says is not heard by any other than the defendant, and the interpreter's voice is rarely heard by the court. In any case, what the interpreter says is rarely understood by any other than the defendant. It is thus difficult to assess interpreting quality linguistically but it is possible to identify how different interpreters work and *what* they interpret, rather than how they interpret. The following original typology of District Court interpreters classifies these interpreters and their work. It encompasses the Silent Interpreter, the Selective Interpreter, the LEP Interpreter, the Advocate and the Competent Interpreter.

The Silent Interpreter

> There he was in court there, the collar of his coat up a little. He looked like a gangster, a bit of an intellectual gangster. And his case was called and the defendant was produced. And he said nothing throughout maybe the seven minutes of court proceedings. And just as they were preparing to put the defendant away he uttered a few words, and that would have been fifteen seconds in total. Nobody really noticed. It was normal. I was sitting on a bench there, and I was looking at myself, potentially, because nobody cares. That doesn't mean that it's general but it does happen very often. (Mihai)

The Silent Interpreter says nothing or very little for the entire duration of a case and is thus not interpreting what happens in court for the defendant. He or she attracts the attention of the court on only the rarest of occasions. This type of interpreter is a widespread phenomenon in the District Court. It is neither confined to, nor typical of, any particular court or interpreter nationality but it is familiar to interpreters and legal professionals alike. James found it 'alarming and frightening' when the Italian interpreter for one of his cases 'really was not interpreting at all', and Thomas has seen 'inexperienced interpreters ... who apparently have not been interpreting anything, virtually, at all'. His frustration at this is shared by Gwen, who says that she has seen 'interpreters standing beside a client, completely silent for the duration'. Gerard says it is very, very common for the interpreter's mouth to remain closed while people are talking in court but notes that solicitors and barristers are unlikely to see this, as they usually stand facing the judge and with their backs to the defendant and interpreter.

The Selective Interpreter

> I've seen [a] few interpreters who are just looking at the ceiling while [the judge] is talking to the defendant. And saying nothing or just interpreting the questions he asks: 'I'm asking you through the interpreter, tell me what's your address?' So they say 'what's your address?' ... And they are quiet for half an hour and there's a talk going on. (Ewa)

Ewa considers that there are not many interpreters who are skilled enough to interpret everything that goes on in court, which is why they sit quietly without saying anything or interpreting only what they are directed to. This is the Selective Interpreter and these are more common than the Silent Interpreter. He or she may interpret only that which directly concerns the defendant, what the solicitor/barrister says directly to the defendant, when the judge asks the defendant a direct question, or when told directly by the judge to do so, though even direct instructions are not always immediately effective:

> JUDGE P: Could the interpreter interpret that I've decided to accept jurisdiction, stay in the District Court.
> INTERPRETER: [Silence]
> [The Judge looks at her expectantly and after a pause the interpreter finally nods and speaks to the defendant.]

Aoife had an experience in which a Kuwaiti interpreter would say five or six words after two or three minutes of conversation with the client, as a result of which she did not feel that she was getting to the bottom of the issue. She tried to reason the silence: 'I felt that maybe the interpreter was a man of few words, maybe my guy was a man of a lot of words; … there are cultural barriers where maybe a Kuwaiti man wouldn't be happy discussing certain things with a woman', but at the end of the day she did not know why she was getting only 'a fraction of the information from whatever chats were going on between them'. Although this concerns the preparation of an asylum application, the principle remains the same in the District Court. The Selective Interpreter routinely omits those units of the case that do not seem to involve the defendant directly, including monologues by judges, Jurisdiction, the Facts and Disclosure.

It may be that communicative interference or the nature of District Court insider language pose obstacles too great to overcome, it may be that the interpreter does not feel it necessary to interpret these units, and it is also possible that interpreters are unaware that they should interpret them. Stella, the least experienced interviewee, says at first she thought she only had to interpret what the solicitor was saying for the defendant but a solicitor reminded her she also had to interpret what the judge said and suggested that if she did not do this the judge would think it rude. It was pointed out that the intimidating nature of the courtroom can scare inexperienced interpreters. Molly says it is common for these to get nervous; many do not know what to do and may come from backgrounds that have not prepared them for their role. She gives the example of someone who used to be a farmer, can speak two languages and suddenly finds himself in a courtroom. Such a person, she says, does not have the requisite skills. In Mihai's experience most interpreters are 'very, very shy' and do not have the courage to tell the court if they cannot hear something, and Thomas agrees that young interpreters often get nervous: 'I think sometimes they can get a little star struck.'

The LEP Interpreter

> I'll give you an example. I did have, I can't remember from where, a client last week and I was speaking to him, and the – actually, I do remember where he was from. He was Asian. But the interpreter had asked me what did a 'sentence' mean. What was a sentence! And I actually, I slightly lost the rag. I said that it's an incredibly important word – learn it! (James)

Ewa describes meeting another Polish interpreter who was in court for the first time. 'The girl was shocked. She didn't understand anything. ... She was working in the court as an interpreter without actually understanding anything. She said that she learned her English in France and then she was working in Penneys. ... It's just shocking.' Poor levels of English among interpreters are widely noted. Eleanor has often been frustrated by interpreters 'that clearly don't have a good enough command of the English language to interpret properly' and Stephen has often 'had serious doubts as to whether the interpreter was understanding what was being said'. Stella talks about one person for whom she interpreted and who actually corrected her: 'He said "no, she didn't mean that"', and Gwen does not consider it unusual for the client to have better English than the interpreter. As the interpreter's voice often remains silent it can be easy for a lack of proficiency to remain undetected, but when the interpreter's voice is heard, the frequency of basic grammar and vocabulary mistakes is notable:

> 'The ID was true' (interpreter, CusC)
> 'Yeah. He agree with that. Thank you Judge' (interpreter, RC)

> JUDGE: Does he want to consult with a solicitor?
> INTERPRETER: Yes, I would like. (CitC)

The following is an account from the Rural District Court where an interpreter was dismissed on account of his poor English and interpreting incompetence. The extract demonstrates that he lacks basic vocabulary, including the word for solicitor, and that his grammar is very poor, but while the judge notices this immediately, he allows the interpreter to continue. As the case progresses, a member of the Gardaí comes to help the struggling interpreter as it is becoming obvious that, without representation, the defendant is unknowingly setting up the circumstances under which the judge (Z) will be obliged to impose a custodial sentence. It is at this point that a real sense of concern and almost outrage arises in the court and leads a solicitor to behave in a way that is later censured by the judge. This leads to the dismissal of the interpreter (see Appendix D for full account).

> JUDGE: Would you tell Mr. L that after he was charged and cautioned he replied 'no reply' to the criminal charge.
> [The interpreter hesitates. The Judge becomes suspicious]
> JUDGE: What competency do you have in interpreting?

The interpreter said he was a level three interpreter and the judge continued.

> JUDGE: Can he afford to pay for legal representation?
> INTERPRETER: He won't be waiting for legal advice. ...
> JUDGE: My dear man, your English isn't great. And I'm talking to the interpreter. ...
> INTERPRETER: He doesn't want the legal advice.
> JUDGE: What?
> INTERPRETER: He doesn't want the legal [pause] representation. ...
> JUDGE: I have difficulty, Sir, in understanding your English. It is my obligation –
> Waits for interpretation. Interpreter remains silent. Judge, extremely agitated:
> JUDGE: Translate as I'm speaking!

The case continued haltingly through the Plea of guilty, Facts and Mitigation. The penalty was to be a fine and when the defendant said that he was homeless, the judge stated that the penalty had to be paid immediately or he would have to serve a sentence. The interpreter, instructed by the defendant, asked if the penalty could be less or if he could pay in instalments, and a Garda came to stand beside the interpreter and explain that unless the defendant could pay he would have to serve a jail sentence because he had no address.[2] Finally, the judge announced:

> JUDGE: All right, payment forthwith. In default, prison sentence of thirty days. I certify with some reluctance for the interpreter present.

The Garda explained this to the interpreter, and the judge, in an unusual move, adjourned court. In the judge's absence a number of people approached the defendant and the interpreter in seeming concern at the custodial sentence, and on the judge's return a solicitor voiced concern about whether the defendant had fully understood what had happened. Although the judge took 'grave umbrage and exception' to the implication that he had not discharged his duties fully, he recalled defendant and interpreter, and he asked the interpreter what the solicitor had said to the defendant in his absence:

INTERPRETER: He can have the solicitor with no money.
JUDGE: And when I was explaining that to him in the most simple way possible, through you the interpreter, did he not understand?
INTERPRETER: He says he didn't understand.

The judge again asked the interpreter what his competence was to interpret:

INTERPRETER: It is just a translating word to word.

The judge reiterated that he had explained in great detail about the defendant's right to a solicitor and to apply for legal aid, and the interpreter said that he had interpreted this:

JUDGE: I am not fluent in the Polish language. I am reliant on you, the interpreter, to translate.
INTERPRETER: He said he couldn't understand the legal terms.
JUDGE: Well 'free' is very simple. What did he not understand about 'free'?
INTERPRETER: He only understand –
JUDGE: [Interrupting] Now listen! I expressed my dissatisfaction with you earlier on. … It appears to me, Sir, that you are incompetent … in the field of interpretation for the purposes of the administration of justice. Please leave the court.

Court was again adjourned and when the judge returned he vacated the earlier order 'based on the lack of competence of the interpreter'. He told the defendant: 'I don't have one word of Polish. The assigned interpreter was totally incompetent to deal with the sensitive issues before this court', and he invited him to re-appear the following week.

The interpreter's English was, indeed, very poor and certainly inadequate but although the case resulted in the dismissal of the interpreter on this basis, the interpreter was not dismissed until the issue had evolved into a significant one. It seemed, in fact, that everybody in court, the judge included, was looking for a way to ensure that the defendant did *not* have to serve a custodial sentence, and it also seems from the way the case progressed that the real problem lay in the lack of representation. A solicitor would not have allowed the defendant to declare himself homeless unless there was absolutely no option. In this case, the defendant *did* have a home with his father but they had quarrelled. It seems unlikely that things would have become so serious if a custodial sentence had not been imposed, and it is useful to compare this with the example given earlier in the chapter where no interpreter was assigned to a defendant with poor English but where the case was straightforward, lasted two minutes and ended with no conviction recorded. This suggests a strong connection between the seriousness of the case or penalty, the provision of interpreters and concern for interpreting quality.

The situation did not end on this date, largely due to the fact that the local papers printed an account of the case that portrayed a miscarriage of justice to which the judge reacted very strongly when the defendant re-appeared the following week. The judge called the arresting Garda as a witness and some time was spent establishing that not only had the judge discharged his duty fully and fairly but that the defendant had deceived the court. The Garda testified that the defendant did, in fact, understand and have some proficiency in English. In an interesting submission the solicitor tried to mitigate the effect of this testimony by explaining that while the defendant had some English, it was not sufficient for a criminal case. An interpreter was present throughout.

> JUDGE: We're trying to ascertain if he had any understanding of English at all. You may or may not be aware of why the court is seeking this information. I'll take you back to [date], [street] at midnight. What happened? Why did you come into contact with this [man]?

The Garda testified that she had observed him driving, stopped him and spoken with him. She told the court: 'He understood', 'he understood me', 'he understand [sic] what I wanted. He didn't have a problem.'

> JUDGE: Did he understand why you had stopped him?
> GARDA: I asked him to put out his cigarette, he put it out. I explained that I wanted him to take a deep breath and blow into the bag, he did it. …
> JUDGE: And arising from that [breath] test, something happened.
> GARDA: He was arrested and conveyed to [town] Garda Station. And I had requested an interpreter for him.

The judge asked if they had spoken during this journey.

> GARDA: Yes. He said that he was a Polish national and that he'd eaten too many apples. …
> JUDGE: I am absolutely satisfied that he proceeded in a methodical and premeditated fashion to mislead the court. … I was watching the interpreter and, while I wasn't satisfied with his competence, I was satisfied that the defendant understood what was going on.

He went on to discuss the behaviour of the solicitor and the article in the paper, which he described as 'grossly offensive and misleading'. The defendant's solicitor, as the defendant was now represented, addressed the court:

> SOLICITOR: Yes, Judge. … There is just one issue I would like to address. The defendant did have some English that he had learned in school. He has

> what you might call 'survivor English'. He understood what the Garda was saying and he certainly understood the process.

The defendant had appeared in court with his father, his address was given and the judge convicted and fined the defendant. This case is noteworthy for the variety of interpreting-related issues that arise: the LEP Interpreter, the defendant allegedly pretending not to speak English, assessment of language proficiency and interpreting quality; and the dynamic of the interpreted case with and without representation, something that will be considered in Chapter 5.

The Advocate

> I remember the very first time we ever had an interpreter in court – a marvellous character, a Polish man came to court, and he ran his own show. He was larger than life. He told us that he was a photographer by profession and that he had come to Ireland with the Pope but stayed. So he turned up. It was about ten years ago or more, and I'll always remember that the interpretation of the remarks of myself – I think I was the advocate at the time – moved well beyond what I was saying. Quite. And he was beginning to address the judge *himself* in relation to what the Polish client was saying. And he also had started very successfully in calling the judge 'Your Honour', but he had moved quickly on to calling the judge 'Your Majesty', and it was really one of the funniest times! I'll always remember in court this Polish interpreter. So I suppose that was an extreme example [laughs] of an interpreter running his own show completely. (Thomas)

It is generally accepted that an interpreter's job is to render what the speaker says into the listener's language as accurately and impartially as possible, and that this should not involve the interpreter adding personal views, opinions or thoughts as to what is said, or leaving anything out. The dynamics of the District Court, however, oblige interpreters to make decisions about what to omit and include, as they are not able to interpret everything. While Thomas thinks interpreters should 'use their judgement' as to what is important, the question arises as to the point at which, in so doing, the interpreter ceases to be a language mediator and becomes an advocate of sorts. Gwen highlights this dilemma:

> Who's to say what's important and not? You're relying on an extremely efficient and able interpreter if they're able to say 'well, you know, I needn't give you Judge X's one-hour-long lecture on Coillte', you know, 'I'll tell you what's relevant to your case.' How much faith do you put in the interpreter? If they're not going to interpret everything?

While outsiders to the District Court, including defendants, are not expected to understand its proceedings and discourse, interpreters are. The question thus arises as to whether interpreters should facilitate proceedings by changing what is said by the court to make it comprehensible to the defendant and changing what is said by the defendant to match the formalities of the court. It is possible that the interpreter is implicitly expected to do so as, if they did not, proceedings could become very lengthy. Observations suggest that judges can become frustrated when interpreters attempt to interpret the response of the defendant rather than answering the question put by the judge:

JUDGE S: [Repeats] Did you sign this?
INTERPRETER: [Holds up hands in despair] He's telling me something else; his friends –
JUDGE S: [Interrupting] Never mind that. Is this his signature?

INTERPRETER: I had an argument with my wife –
JUDGE Z: [Interrupting] And that was on the 21st?
INTERPRETER: Yes. [Continues interpreting]
JUDGE Z: [Interrupting] Agh now, hang on, I'm not interested in any fights he had.

Some interpreters also change what is said. In this example, the interpreter adds a level of formality to the defendant's answer:

JUDGE T: Is he working?
DEFENDANT: No. [In English]
INTERPRETER: No, Judge.

Some interpreters even speak on behalf of the defendant. In the following, the interpreter answers the judge *before* interpreting his questions:

JUDGE Z: And may I ask if he has any objection to the case being put back because ... [Four reasons at extremely high speed] Does the defendant have any objection to that?
INTERPRETER: [Immediately] No objection.

JUDGE X: 19th June. Is that by consent?
SOLICITOR AND INTERPRETER: [simultaneously] Yes, Judge.

JUDGE X: Does he understand the bail conditions?
INTERPRETER: [Immediately] Yes, Judge.

In most cases the interpreter seemed to explain what had been said afterwards, but it is not clear what or how much was explained. District Court cases are often routine and predictable, and it seems that interpreters sometimes slip into the role of answering on the defendant's behalf, whether or not they are represented. It also happens not infrequently that when a defendant is asked a question in court, instead of simply asking it and interpreting the answer, a private conversation ensues between the interpreter and the defendant. If this is short the judge is unlikely to intervene, but as it becomes lengthy the judge can become frustrated:

> 'It's taking forever to get simple answers' (Judge S)
> 'There's a lot of muttering going on there' (Judge Z)
> 'I want a straight answer to a straight question' (Judge Z)
> [Shouting] 'STOP! JUST TELL ME EXACTLY WHAT HE SAID!' (Judge S)

> JUDGE P: Guilty or not guilty?
> [Defendant and interpreter consult at length]
> JUDGE P: It's a simple question.
> INTERPRETER: Guilty.
> [Another lengthy consultation]
> JUDGE P: What is he saying, please?

It is impossible to know what is being discussed in the consultation but in answering for the defendant, in embellishing the defendant's answer and in consulting with the defendant about his or her answer, instead of simply interpreting it, the interpreter appears to go beyond the role of language mediator, blurring the boundary between this and the role of legal advocate.

Another challenge arises for the interpreter where the defendant or arrested person sees them, as Thomas describes it, as 'a beacon of light' because they speak the same language or are from the same place. Interpreters agree that defendants regularly view them as allies; as one defendant said to Stella: 'You are Chinese, you must help me.' Interpreters and defendants are often left alone together and it is common to see them talking during proceedings. Interpreters reveal that they are regularly asked questions like 'What should I do now?', 'What is going to happen next?', 'Can I do this, can I do that, can I call, can I pay?'(Svetlana). Defendants want to know how things work, and about things like bail or prison. Solicitors/barristers agree that interpreters should avoid giving legal advice but also acknowledge that defendants are sure to ask such questions, and Aoife says that interpreters, having acquired a certain amount of experience from sitting in court, may 'find themselves giving semi, pseudo-legal advice'. Thomas insists that although they may have a good knowledge of procedure 'they can make mistakes on the legal issues' and are not in a good position to give advice.

He has nonetheless seen interpreters 'give preliminary advices to a client', though he considers that in general interpreters are careful not to do so. In reality, solicitors/barristers themselves often ask the interpreter to explain things, such as a bail bond, to the defendant at the end of a case if they have another client to represent and must stay on their feet.

It would be very difficult to say to what extent interpreters give legal advice or semi-legal information but the interpreters interviewed say that, while they often sympathise with defendants, their role is still a communicative one. Marta says that defendants' questions in court are annoying and put her in a difficult position, and Molly finds that because some defendants 'are desperate' she wants to be able to help them but 'you have to draw a line'. Most interpreters say that they refer the defendant to their solicitor when asked such questions, as they do not feel qualified to answer them or offer advice. They also do not believe it is their place. When a defendant does not have a representative, Anna says she might give him some general information 'like that he is entitled to a solicitor, let's say, or that he is allowed to plead guilty or not guilty, and if he pleads not guilty his case will be adjourned to some other date, just this general information'.

However, Gwen's experiences suggest that not all interpreters confine their role to one of language mediation. In one case, the interpreter commissioned by the defence examined videos of the police questioning and found that the original interpreter had told the accused what answers to give. 'The interpreter said "No, no, no, you don't want to say this. What you want to say is – actually just leave it to me and I'll give the answer for you."' In another of her cases, the interpreter was a former priest: 'I think his pastoral duties got in the way of his interpretive duties. The interpreter was trying to convince the client to confess to a murder.' The following is another rather extreme example of an interpreter going beyond the role of language mediator, this time in court (CitC). A Romanian defendant was charged with providing a fake driver's licence, and a Garda expert witness testified that the document was a fake and was cross-examined by the defence solicitor, who accepted this. The Romanian interpreter then fumbled in his wallet, tapped the solicitor on his shoulder and handed him a card. He explained something, looking bemused.

SOLICITOR: The interpreter has come to my assistance.

The solicitor told the court that the interpreter had given him a copy of his own driving licence and asked if the expert witness could examine it to see if it looked real. The Garda expert witness appeared somewhat uncomfortable but took the licence, explaining that she did not have the correct equipment to make a definitive pronouncement. She confirmed that it seemed genuine and it was only at this point that the judge intervened, stating that the interpreter was there to assist the court and could the solicitor please ask the interpreter not to interfere:

> JUDGE N: It's not the interpreter's job to come to the assistance of the defence.

The case continued and the defendant was asked through the interpreter about how he had come by the licence and what explanation he had for being in possession of a fake one. While the defendant mumbled no more than a few words, the interpreter responded:

> INTERPRETER: What can I say? It never occurred to me to consider that it might be a fake document or something.

Here the court has a relatively strong, albeit slow, reaction when the interpreter visibly involves himself in the case and this is verbalised by the solicitor, but when the interpreter embellishes the defendant's reply in explanation of the offence, this is accepted. Similarly in the earlier examples, the court does not remark upon the interpreter's formalising of the defendant's reply or the fact that the interpreter has answered on behalf of the defendant. This suggests that the court's objection to an interpreter acting on the defendant's behalf is limited to when intervention is blatant; where this is subtle it is likely to go unchecked. It may be that it is simply unnoticed but it is also possible that, because such intervention facilitates proceedings and the speed of proceedings, it is actually welcomed, particularly when the defendant is unrepresented.

The Competent Interpreter

> You don't know the language but these two seem to be quite professional. And they certainly seem to communicate with the clients what the judge is saying and back. (Gwen)

An interpreter is likely to be considered competent by the court if they are experienced and familiar with the language and procedure of court, if they can speak English reasonably, and if their dress and behaviour are professional. Such an interpreter may appear without being called and will seem to interpret everything that is said, such that the defendant will not look lost or baffled; they will be easily understood by the court when they speak in English; and they will interact confidently with the court. Essentially, as the interpreter is rarely heard and almost never understood except when speaking English, their competence is necessarily gauged by appearances: successful participation in the court case and appropriate behaviour and dress.

Solicitor/barrister interviewees equate the quality of interpreters with their level of experience and whether they appear professional. For James, the more experienced the interpreter, the higher the standard of interpreting, and Stephen is of the same opinion. He says that once an interpreter has worked for a couple of years in the District Court and done some Circuit Court trials, 'they tend to know all of the issues that are going to crop up'. Matthew also points out that interpreters who have spent a lot of time in court 'know the score' and he believes that 'experience is key and ... if they have a knowledge of the way that the court system works, it makes life a lot easier'. Gwen comments that judges have a much more positive attitude towards interpreters 'even if they're not particularly good at what they're doing, if they seem to be doing their best', and in her positive appraisal of two interpreters she says they 'seem' professional and 'seem' to be communicating what is said.

Gwen also makes the point that she does not understand the language, and interpreters are aware of this. Molly says that nobody actually knows what the interpreter says when they are interpreting or whether they are saying it right, and Mihai feels that as nobody ever checks on what is said, he could 'tell a little story about Snow White while everybody's talking' if he so chose. In fact, Belén makes the disquieting claim that the agency instructed interpreters to continue 'interpreting' even where they could not hear or did not know what was going on: 'That was the first instructions we were given from the agency, like the most important thing is not only that you interpret, is that they see you are saying something.' What is perceived as competence, therefore, does not necessarily mean that the person is interpreting accurately or well, and good quality interpreting may or may not be an additional attribute of the Competent Interpreter.

Perceived standards

> I think generally it's like the standards of anything else; ... you're going to have some brilliant [interpreters] and you're going to have not-so-good ones. ... But for the most part I've found them professional and I've found them experienced and I've found them approachable. (Matthew)

Some solicitors/barristers proclaim themselves satisfied with interpreting services. James finds that while 'the standard isn't always great', overall it is quite good. Stephen says standards have improved since the less competent interpreters more or less disappeared off the scene and Eleanor also believes things have improved in recent years: 'I think it was very poor when interpretation services started to come on board' when 'anyone who could speak any language was able to work as an interpreter without any real training, any real regulation'. The interpreters are less convinced. Ewa believes standards to be very low and Molly feels that because of the relentless recruitment campaigns by agencies over the years, standards have dropped massively. She says that while there used to be a preference for experience when assigning interpreters to a case, now it is not even a consideration. Interpreters confirm that the court interpreting training provided by their agency involves no more than a half-day spent outlining the basic functioning of the courts system and giving some general guidelines as to what the job entails.

The feeling overall is that standards are mixed and can vary greatly. 'Sometimes it can leave a little to be desired,' Marks says: 'They could be better.' He is concerned, among other things, about the calibre of interpreters: 'I'm not sure how they're recruited, from where they're recruited, whether they're Garda-vetted, whether they have previous convictions themselves. I don't know how these interpreters are appointed, … whether they are suitable to be interpreters.' Thomas avers that he 'wouldn't like to criticise, I certainly wouldn't, I mean I think that it's quite good', which is interesting in light of Gwen's point:

> I think courts tend to facilitate interpreters. And I think if judges weren't that facilitating – it sounds awful – we might have a better standard, because if they were to say more often 'I'm stopping this trial until somebody comes in who can properly interpret'. I think it's a fine line, you don't want to be rude to people, but at the end of the day it's about the accused's constitutional right to a fair trial. Without being over-dramatic about it, a lot of them aren't getting a fair trial; you're entitled to know what's being said, and a lot of them [don't].

She feels that quality varies but 'a lot of it is substandard'.

The idea was discussed in Chapter 3 that there is an almost paradoxical assumption among legal professionals, at least in the English-speaking common-law world, that interpreters are qualified and competent, and that interpreting is monitored to ensure adequate standards. This assumption seems to exist in Ireland also. 'I presume, again without knowing, that there are safeguards put in place,' says Matthew, while Thomas muses that 'the Court Service probably do keep an eye, do they not, on what's going on?' James supposes that agencies providing interpreters to the court have a responsibility to ensure proper standards: 'I mean they have no business receiving the taxpayers' money otherwise.' Mihai confirms that 'the courts would never doubt, or if they do they do it in a silent way, but they would never doubt your abilities or your competence'. The fact that he appears on behalf of an agency is proof enough for the court that he is sufficiently qualified to be there. This assumption was occasionally evident in court:

> 'There's no need to repeat everything; it's all been interpreted, so he's heard it before' (Judge S)
> 'Would you just translate what he says. If you're an interpreter you know what to do. ... Speak up and tell me what he is saying' (Judge S)

Matthew wonders whether the issue of interpreting in courts may be 'one of these accidents waiting to happen', but he and others tend to focus on cases involving serious offences. He considers that 'somebody could be convicted for a very serious offence on the basis of a difficulty where something is literally lost in translation', and Gwen emphasises cases of murder and rape where the interpretation 'could be the difference between somebody getting a life sentence and not'. She goes so far as to say that not having an efficient interpreter at District Court level 'is more frustrating than anything else, but I don't know that it hugely impacts on the outcome', while Gerard also considers that interpretation at trial level is of the utmost importance, but does not have the same urgency at District Court level. In his view there are so many other issues of concern that one has to pick one's battles, and interpreting in the District Court does not seem to be one of them. An interesting point was raised by two solicitors about whether it is in the best interests of some solicitors *not* to complain about interpreting standards, which Mark explains here:

> For the hungrier solicitors, interpreters can be a source of work. ... Some solicitors would make it their business to establish relations with an interpreter so that the interpreter would contact them or bring the business to them. ... It's not in the solicitors' interests to be raising difficulties about interpreters ..., so it's not likely that there'd be complaints about interpreting.

Gwen further feels strongly that 'judges would be very, very reluctant to allow an appeal on the basis of poor interpretation' as it would get a lot of media attention and 'the whole system would then be called into question'. She spoke of her experience with a case in the Court of Criminal Appeal. The legal team had planned to make interpreting one of the grounds of the appeal, but:

> It was quite apparent to us ... that the Court of Appeal did not want to know about us saying it was down to the interpreter. ... They froze, said

'the interpreters are doing the best they can.' ... In other words, forget that point and move on to something else because you're wasting your time on that one.

Conclusion

Among those practising in the District Court there is acknowledgement that the provision of interpreters is important to ensure the LEP defendant's right to a fair trial, but perhaps greater emphasis is laid on the importance of providing an interpreter to protect the judge against the possibility of judicial review. Although there is a sense of collective responsibility for ensuring that defendants can understand what is going on, and in practice anyone involved in the proceedings can request an interpreter, how the issue is dealt with in court depends entirely on the judge, who makes the ultimate decision about assigning an interpreter and bears ultimate responsibility for the fairness of proceedings.

In common with what has been found elsewhere, as discussed in Chapter 3, this study found that some judges wait until an interpreter is requested while some raise the issue themselves, and in assessing proficiency judges sometimes question the defendant directly as to his or her fluency or comprehension and are sometimes guided by the solicitor/barrister. Both approaches have flaws; there is some evidence that solicitors/barristers can over-estimate the language proficiency of their clients, and there is also evidence to support the idea outlined in Chapter 3 that defendants may claim to speak English for a number of reasons, but when their English is not as good as they claim, they have difficulties understanding proceedings. A number of people also made the point that – perhaps contrary to or in spite of its somewhat informal image – the District Court can be an intimidating setting, causing even those with good English to falter and become nervous, such that there can be a genuine need for interpreters even where defendants have a reasonable grasp of the English language. LEP defendants without interpreters were observed leaving the court in obvious confusion, or approaching the registrar or a member of the Gardaí for help. Although apparently rare, interpreters for the wrong language are sometimes assigned as a result of administrative error or because of a false identity provided by the defendant.

Decisions as to the provision of interpreters are difficult to predict. Some defendants with clear communication difficulties say they do not need an interpreter and are accepted at their word, some defendants who neither want nor seem to need them are assigned interpreters, and some defendants are not asked if they want one even when they appear to struggle. What emerged strongly, however, is that if an interpreter is requested one will not be denied, however grudgingly granted, but without a direct request there are no guarantees. There is nothing to suggest that judges and solicitors/barristers in court are other than satisfied with the current system of assessment and assignment despite its flaws, or that doubts are held as to the competence of the court and practitioners to make accurate linguistic assessments, despite evidence to the contrary. What seems clear, however, is that the more serious the case, the more concern and urgency there will be about ensuring that an interpreter is provided.

Interpreters are sometimes administered an oath that they will interpret to the best of their ability but this is a sporadic practice that seems unlikely to be more than a formality. The wording of the oath suggests that an interpreter should interpret and explain to the court anything that is required of them, but in practice the interpreter is not instructed what to interpret. While there is consensus that everything should be interpreted, it is acknowledged that the dynamics of the District Court make this impossible. Insider language, high speed proceedings, often poor acoustics and the fact that allowances are rarely made for interpretation are some of the most obvious obstacles, but barriers to interpreting also arise through a judge's interruptions, a defendant asking questions privately, or the solicitor/barrister using the interpreter for consultation with the defendant during proceedings.

A number of different interpreting styles were observed in the District Court, few of which inspire confidence. The Silent Interpreter stands beside the defendant and says nothing or very little but goes largely unremarked in court; the Selective Interpreter, perhaps more common, omits those parts of the case not directly involving the defendant; the LEP interpreter speaks English poorly and sometimes not as well as the defendant; the Advocate, on an extreme level, might give LEP defendants legal advice, tell them what to say, or speak or answer on their behalf and, on a less extreme level, may embellish the defendant's speech to reflect District Court formalities; and the Competent Interpreter is perceived as such by the court when he or she behaves professionally, appears to interpret most of what happens and is understood by the court when he or she speaks English.

It is impossible to say whether the Competent Interpreter is, in fact, competent, but it is likely that he or she is experienced, familiar with the language and procedure of court, and reasonably proficient in English, and possible that he or she is highly qualified, experienced and competent. It is possible that some Selective Interpreters may have a degree of competence and even familiarity with the court but do not consider it necessary or part of their job to interpret more, though they may also lack competence and experience. Some Advocates may be the victim of their sympathy for an accused who asks for or expects help and advice but they may also be unaware of ethics and neutrality requirements, while others may be the product of their experience in the District Court where subtle intervention, honouring courtroom formalities and facilitating expeditiousness are favoured. There is no justification for the presence of the Silent or the LEP Interpreter but every expectation of their continued presence as standards, interpreters say, are dropping due to mass recruitment and a system that has no requirement of, or preference for, ability, experience or training.

Thus, although it is agreed that interpreters are necessary for LEP defendants and these are supplied in practice, there is little evidence of discernment as to what or how they interpret and a high tolerance of poor standards, or obliviousness to quality. It may be a case of courts displaying 'woeful disregard for how language operates in real life situations' (Tiersma, 1993) and/or blindly assuming that the interpreters provided are competent, monitored and quality-controlled. It was also suggested that solicitors might be reluctant to complain when the interpreter is a source of business for them. Perhaps most fundamentally, however, there is a strong sense among practitioners that the cases tried in the District Court are of such a minor nature that poor interpreting quality, while perhaps a source of frustration, is unlikely to change how the case is decided, or present any real danger to the liberty of the defendant. There are bigger and more pressing battles in the District Court, they say.

Notes

1 Please refer to 'Guide to extracts from District Court field notes and interviews' for an explanation of how anonymised courts and judges are referred to in the text.

2 Where a defendant has no address any fine imposed in the District Court must be paid immediately.

5

The case of the immigrant: dynamics and discourse

'Translators', tools and tensions

While interpreters are not entirely new to Irish courts, neither have they been a traditional fixture in the courtroom. However, the presence of one or a number of interpreters is now commonplace and they have become standard participants in District Court proceedings in the same way as solicitors, the Gardaí, probation officers, and so on. This becomes immediately apparent upon entering court in the morning before it is in session – the time when solicitors, barristers and Gardaí informally consult each other and the registrar for information and clarifications, to make arrangements, come to agreements, and so on. The subject of interpreting, principally the language needs of clients and the availability of interpreters, has become an intrinsic part of this interaction:[1]

> 'What language is he?' (CusC)
> 'The translator isn't here yet' (RC)
> 'We have a lot of interpreters today' (RC)
> 'Is there any interpreter here for G.B.?' (CusC)
> 'There is no Chinese interpreter' (CusC)

Sometimes light-hearted jokes are made:

> PROSECUTION: What nationality is he?
> BARRISTER: We think Egyptian.
> PROSECUTION: So he walks like an Egyptian?! (CusC)

Some courts reserve an area for interpreters but otherwise they might sit with solicitors/barristers, the Gardaí or even in the public benches and, as with other participants, may not always be easy to identify. Typically interpreters are sent by an agency and wear identifying badges but these are not always visible and most interpreters dress professionally such that cases of mistaken identity can occur. Such mistakes are not always appreciated. On one occasion a young Garda approached and asked a solicitor if she was a Polish interpreter; she said no, but afterwards muttered to another solicitor, 'Do I look like a fucking interpreter?' (CusC). In general, the relationship between interpreters and others in court is somewhere between amiable conviviality and tolerant detachedness, with an apparently harmonious working rapport. Court participants chat and joke with interpreters, thank and praise them for their work ('Good job, it's not easy' (CitC)), and some even try a few words in the interpreter's language ('Do cvidanya' (CitC)).

Interpreters describe working in the District Court as a positive experience overall. They feel they are treated with respect and that their help is needed and appreciated, though some more experienced interpreters say attitudes were not as positive before interpreting was contracted out. Pre-2007, some interpreters felt that registrars hated interpreters and 'nasty things were happening in court, because different translation agencies would be fighting for new cases' (Anna). Things have changed, however, and while Molly still feels that they are treated as outsiders because they are not directly employed by the Courts Service, most criticisms were aimed at their employing agency.[2] Interpreters working in the area for a number of years report that treatment has become more anonymous and less attentive over time and that it is marked by a lack of appreciation, flexibility and personalised management.

Most interpreters find the attitudes of judges to be positive towards them, and they describe them as neutral, fair and polite, but some highlighted that it really depends on the judge. Some judges are conscious of the interpreter and keen to ensure they do a good job while others do not even notice their presence. There was a little more reservation about the relationship with solicitors/barristers based on a sense that, while interpreters are respected because they facilitate communication, there is also an element of utility; solicitors approach interpreters when they need them, expect co-operation and want the job done quickly. Mihai says, for example: 'They treat you the same way you would treat a tool that you think you might need tomorrow – half nice, half polite, and half kind of neutral.' The issue was also raised that solicitors and barristers can sometimes fail to appreciate the difficult nature of the job and that they often make demands beyond those which can reasonably be expected.

A corresponding tension exists from the perspective of solicitors/barristers. It is broadly considered that attitudes on both sides are positive, respectful and appreciative. Solicitors and barristers recognise the importance of good working relationships and professionalism, and they consider that people working in the courts have become used to interpreters such that things generally run smoothly. At the same time, interpreting is seen as 'yet another layer of expense added to the criminal justice system' (Thomas) and concerns are raised as to whether money is being well spent. A number of legal professionals expressed the belief that interpreters make more money than lawyers and that it is an extremely lucrative profession, and a number also expressed their impression that interpreters are overly concerned with their time sheets and certification. Gwen, for example, empathises with judges' increasing frustration when interpreters fail to do their job competently and 'the only thing they do efficiently is produce their cert. for a signature to make sure they're paid'. She mentions a case she was involved in where the 'company made more out of the substandard interpreting facilities than the solicitor and the junior counsel'.

While there is some recognition that it is, in fact, the agency that receives the payment rather than the interpreter, the predominant attitude is that interpreters are well paid and often too well paid, as their work is not up to the desired standard. Interpreters, on the other hand, confirmed the media reports mentioned in Chapter 3 about ongoing pay cuts and say that pay was excellent before services were contracted out but that wages have fallen progressively since then. The current rates are considered poor and uncompetitive, particularly as interpreters work on a freelance basis, pay their own taxes and are given only sporadic assignments that might amount to no more than a couple of hours per week. Additionally, they said, the minimum time for which one must be paid on an assignment is consistently dropping. For interpreters this means that every time they are offered an assignment they have to calculate if it is worth doing at all, particularly when short notice is given or travel is required, as transport rates are poor. One of the interpreters in this study had given up interpreting in the courts as she was unable to make a living from it and others suggested that they struggled on because they liked the work but said that the rates made it difficult. As Ewa says: 'Usually after working for a few years you get a raise and our wages were slashed.'

It seems that the second large pay cut (the 28 per cent cut referenced in Chapter 3) caused many interpreters to leave and caused the remainder to lose heart. The interpreters interviewed for this study were almost all well qualified and experienced, and they attribute part of the pay issue to the fact that 'qualifications are never checked by anyone' (Anna), such that there is no basis from which to demand higher rates for better and more qualified interpreters.

Delays and the lengthening of proceedings

It was suggested in Chapter 3 that scepticism about, and therefore reluctance to use, interpreters can stem from the perception that proceedings will take considerably longer when they are involved. This does not seem to apply generally in the District Court. First, delays that involve interpreters are usually attributable to the administrative inefficiencies of District Court procedure rather than to the interpreting process. In practice, the need for an interpreter can cause delays when none is present in court; there may be a second calling if the interpreter is temporarily absent, or a remand or adjournment if one needs to be ordered. These are usually beyond the control of the individual interpreter and more matters of organisation. In fact, Gerard makes the point that delays caused by interpreting are negligible in the greater scheme of things. It was highlighted in Chapter 1 that much delay in the District Court is caused by frequent adjournments and remands. The result in practice is that a lot of court time is spent re-establishing what happened previously:

> 'Refresh my memory' (Judge S)
> 'There was damage to a series of cars … isn't that right?' (Judge P)

This process is exacerbated by the lack of a unified system of record-keeping, which means that participants rely on their handwritten notes; files have to be located and deciphered ('I'm guessing this says Lithuanian interpreter, I can't really read it' (Judge Y)); and information must be pieced together and disputes, gaps and enigmas resolved before the case can proceed. Some courts have little continuity as judges, solicitors and barristers change and move around a lot, which further complicates the process of piecing the evidence back together:

> 'There is conflicting evidence, because nobody actually recalls what the evidence is' (Judge S)
> 'There seems to be a sheet missing here. It was for ID to be established' (Judge S)

> JUDGE P: The defendant was in custody by consent.
> BARRISTER: There was never any consent.

The second reason why interpreting at District Court level does not create undue delay is that in most cases there is no direct communication between the defendant and the court. Interpreting lengthens proceedings when the court seeks information from the defendant and must wait while its questions or comments are interpreted, then wait again while the response is interpreted for the court. In a typical District Court case there is only direct communication when the defendant is giving evidence, generally at a hearing, or when the judge asks the defendant a direct question, which might happen, for example, during the Plea or the Facts. As was discussed in Chapter 3, the vast majority of interpreting at District Court level involves whispered interpreting, or *chuchotage* – a non-disruptive mode of interpreting where the interpreter stands beside the defendant and whispers a simultaneous interpretation of proceedings. Solicitors and barristers confirm that interpreting does not tend to slow things down in the District Court, 'where most business is done more quickly' (Mark) and most cases 'are just being remanded back for something else' and rarely involve dialogue unless somebody is giving evidence (James). It is generally only when there is a hearing that 'it adds a lot to it because everything has to be interpreted; each witness that gets up, it all has to be interpreted' (Stephen). As the majority of cases in the District Court are not contested, this happens relatively infrequently.

The dynamic of the interpreted situation and the impact it has on proceedings in terms of delay also depend very much on the competence of the interpreter, whether or not the defendant is represented and how well prepared the solicitor/barrister is, all of which are considered in greater detail now.

The assumption of representation

A number of factors suggest that the court largely functions on the premise that defendants will be legally represented. First, the right to representation is taken very seriously. Much time is spent in court ensuring defendants are aware of the right and ample opportunity is given to defendants to procure representation. Secondly, on a practical basis the language of the District Court is not designed to be, nor is it easily, understood by outsiders, and an unrepresented defendant can cause delays and frustration in court. While some judges are prepared to spend time with unrepresented defendants, the preference for legal representation is sometimes manifested in an unwillingness to explain things:

> JUDGE Y: Convict, fine 170 Euros, one month, five days.
> DEFENDANT: Sorry?!
> JUDGE Y: Convict, fine 170 Euros, one month, five days.
> DEFENDANT: [Clearly doesn't understand, shrugs shoulders and leaves]

Another indication of the preference for the voice of the legal representative in court is that judges sometimes overtly silence defendants:

> JUDGE Z: What is her drug status?
> DEFENDANT: I have the letter –
> JUDGE Z: [Interrupting] Listen, I'm asking your solicitor to ask you.

> 'You are not placed to say anything, Sir. I'm waiting for your solicitor' (Judge Z)

> INTERPRETER: The defendant would like to speak.
> JUDGE S: He has a solicitor for that.

Judges also verbalise the dependence of defendants on their solicitor to explain what has happened in court:

> 'Mr. [Solicitor], who is present today, will fully inform you of the import and meaning of ...' (Judge Z)
> 'Your solicitor will advise you what the consent of the DPP means' (Judge Z)
> 'If you've any difficulty in understanding, consult with your solicitor. It's tremendously important that you comply' (Judge Q)

The solicitor facilitates communication between the court and the defendant, a role comparable to that of the interpreter in that it often involves 'translating' the words of the court for the defendant and *vice versa*:

> JUDGE Z: What ages are the children?
> SOLICITOR: [To defendant] What ages are the children?
>
> DEFENDANT: Where am I supposed to get 500 Euros?
> JUDGE Z: What?
> SOLICITOR: Where is he going to get 500 Euros?
>
> JUDGE Z: It says here you find prison a challenging environment, Mr. D.
> DEFENDANT: No.
> JUDGE Z: Hmmmm?
> DEFENDANT: NO.
> SOLICITOR: He's saying that he doesn't want to go back to prison.
>
> JUDGE Z: What is your connection with the motor vehicle ... that you were illegally driving on that day?
> SOLICITOR: It was a friend's car, Judge.

As portrayed in these examples, the solicitor often answers on behalf of the client or intervenes to give the appropriate response, and there is sometimes a sense that the solicitor prevents the defendant from damaging the case by saying something inappropriate. This notion resonates with the words of one judge (S), who declared that when she gives the defendant an opportunity to speak without their solicitor 'saving them from themselves', she will never hold what they say against them. From another perspective the solicitor/barrister expedites proceedings. Without their presence, insider language cannot be successfully used in communication, and proceedings can be delayed where the court takes the time to explain things to defendants. Thomas suggests that the solicitor has an 'important role to play in court in speeding things up' and that if the defendant does not want a solicitor 'it's going to take longer with more judicial time'. If the court is not prepared to take this time there is no guarantee that a defendant will leave the court understanding what has happened.

As such, it is desirable from the court's perspective that a defendant be represented. Not only do solicitors make proceedings more reliable in terms of avoiding judicial review, they also facilitate smooth and quick proceedings, a logistical advantage without which the court would be unable to process the sheer volume of cases it is listed to hear. For defendants, legal representatives are desirable as they can generally represent the interests of the client to the court with greater effect than a layperson and they can ensure that the defendant understands what has happened in court. An LEP defendant is undoubtedly even more reliant on the solicitor/barrister to speak on their behalf and to explain what happens in court, particularly when they do not have an interpreter.

The unrepresented and represented LEP defendant

It has been suggested in previous chapters that Irish defendants in the District Court are usually represented. However, some solicitors/barristers in this study expressed a concern that LEP individuals may not always be fully informed of their rights in Garda stations, including the right to a solicitor. Aoife is confident that LEP defendants are less inclined than Irish defendants to have a solicitor in court; in her opinion 'whereas 90 per cent of Irish people have solicitors' many non-Irish defendants charged with offences, particularly minor ones, 'just want them out of the way'. Although in court all defendants are given the opportunity to engage representation, it was observed that LEP defendants decline representation relatively often, perhaps anxious, as Aoife suggested, to have things dealt with quickly:

> 'He doesn't want a solicitor. He wants to deal with it today' (friend of defendant, RC)

> JUDGE Z: Is it your wish or aspiration to be legally represented?
> DEFENDANT: I know I was in the wrong.

Where an LEP defendant is unrepresented and has an interpreter, communication is usually uncomplicated from a procedural perspective as the interpreter simply mediates between judge and defendant; with a competent interpreter, this may not take any longer than it would if a solicitor/barrister were involved, though it may take longer than the case of a similarly unrepresented English-speaking defendant. In fact, having an interpreter in this situation may be advantageous for the LEP defendant. As demonstrated with the Advocate Interpreter in Chapter 4, the interpreter may act as a buffer, making the judge's questions more comprehensible and/or rendering the defendant's responses more formal and court-friendly in the same way as a solicitor/barrister. It is unclear at what point such an interpreter may be considered to have crossed the boundary to unacceptable levels of advocacy. It is also true that the Advocate Interpreter may disadvantage the defendant. As discussed in Chapter 4, if this type of interpreter consents to remand on behalf of the defendant, the defendant may unexpectedly find her- or himself in custody for another two weeks, as the court will assume that any consent given is informed and voluntary. Nonetheless, as this role expedites – or at least does not delay – proceedings, the court appears at worst to tolerate and at best to welcome and expect this level of intervention by the interpreter.

An incompetent interpreter can also greatly disadvantage the unrepresented LEP defendant: the Silent, Selective or LEP Interpreter may not interpret or even understand proceedings. Yet the court, having provided an interpreter, is likely to assume that the defendant has understood proceedings and there will be a clear expectation that the defendant comply with court orders. This raises the question of what the implications are, for example, where the interpreter fails to interpret the bail conditions and the defendant therefore fails to comply with them. It also raises the question of how the words spoken by the interpreter on behalf of the defendant might influence the attitude of the court towards the defendant. Due to the high level of judicial discretion in all aspects of District Court procedure, the interpreter's choice of, or omission of, words has the potential to influence the judge's opinion of the defendant profoundly and, thus, the outcome of the case.

The LEP defendant with neither a lawyer nor an interpreter is relatively rare but it was seen in the last chapter that communication can become extremely unwieldy where this is the case (see Appendix D). Where an LEP defendant is represented but has no interpreter, there is generally no impact on proceedings but the defendant may struggle to understand, being reliant solely on the solicitor/barrister for explanations. The most complex situation involves the defendant that has both representation and an interpreter as there are now four people involved in communication between the court and the defendant: judge, solicitor/barrister, defendant and interpreter (see figure 1).

When the defendant is represented, the preference is often to communicate with and through the representative. Many, if not most, of the questions asked by the judge are routine and predictable and the solicitor/barrister will have the necessary information to answer them. When the solicitor/barrister does not have the requisite information and must consult the defendant during proceedings, communication becomes more complicated:

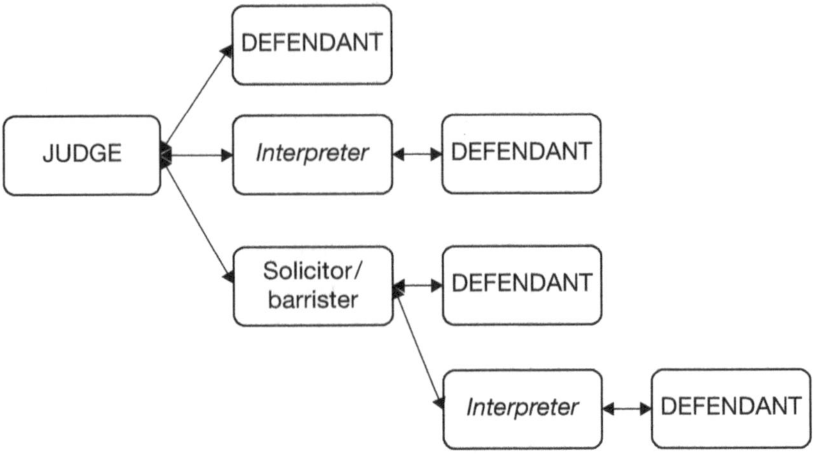

Figure 1 Communication structure in the District Court

- the judge puts a question to the solicitor/barrister
- if the interpreter has been listening and understands, the question may be simultaneously interpreted for the defendant
- that reply will be interpreted for the solicitor/barrister
- the solicitor/barrister will answer the judge

Very often, the solicitor/barrister will first have to 'translate' what the judge says for the (possibly LEP) interpreter, who will then interpret it for the defendant. The Selective or Advocate Interpreter may then engage in a private conversation before giving a reply to the solicitor/barrister, who can eventually reply to the judge. When the solicitor/barrister is not standing next to the defendant, he or she may be literally running back and forth during the exchange.

This scenario frequently occurs even when standard, basic information is requested that anybody familiar with District Court proceedings could have anticipated. It seems in such situations that the solicitor/barrister has either not consulted with the client in advance or that the instructions taken were insufficient. The practice of taking instructions 'on the hoof', as Judge Z calls it, is very common and is often commented on as a concern of judges:

> 'It's a disgrace that a person's first meeting with their counsel should be at the window [of the custody box]; it is a practice that must be stamped out. ... Imagine if it was your own brother or sister' (Judge R)
> 'You haven't even spoken to him?! This is outrageous, this man is in custody; you are consenting to a week in custody without even consulting him' (Judge S)

When the defendant is English-speaking, such consultations can generally be done with relative speed and discretion where necessary. In the interpreted case, this is impossible as consultation necessarily involves the interpreter; particularly where the interpreter is not competent, proceedings can become extremely cumbersome. James and Matthew agree that delays are caused by the unprepared solicitor/barrister in an interpreted case: 'I'm up there and if I'm doing my job right, I have all of their details and I don't need to say anything; I should only maybe clarify something. But I know what we're consenting to or not consenting to or what we're asking the court to do' (James). Mihai questions whether even the interpreted consultations that do take place are sufficient, as they are generally conducted in the space of a few minutes before the case is heard.

The preference for communication via the solicitor/barrister thus impacts more on the interpreted case than on the monolingual case when communication with the defendant is necessary. Lengthened proceedings in the interpreted case are often the result of this preference and can be compounded by a solicitor/barrister's lack of preparation and/or by an incompetent interpreter (see figures 2 and 3).

There is another, less obvious consequence of the unprepared solicitor/barrister in the interpreted case, which, instead of inconveniencing the court, may disadvantage the LEP defendant. Solicitors/barristers frequently take instructions from their client quietly as proceedings are ongoing and such consultations are particularly common in advance of Mitigation (when the solicitor must provide the court with specific details about their client) and during the Facts unit. The Facts unit generally precedes Mitigation and readily facilitates such consultations, as it usually involves only the prosecution and the judge. When an English-speaking defendant and solicitor/barrister consult as the Garda

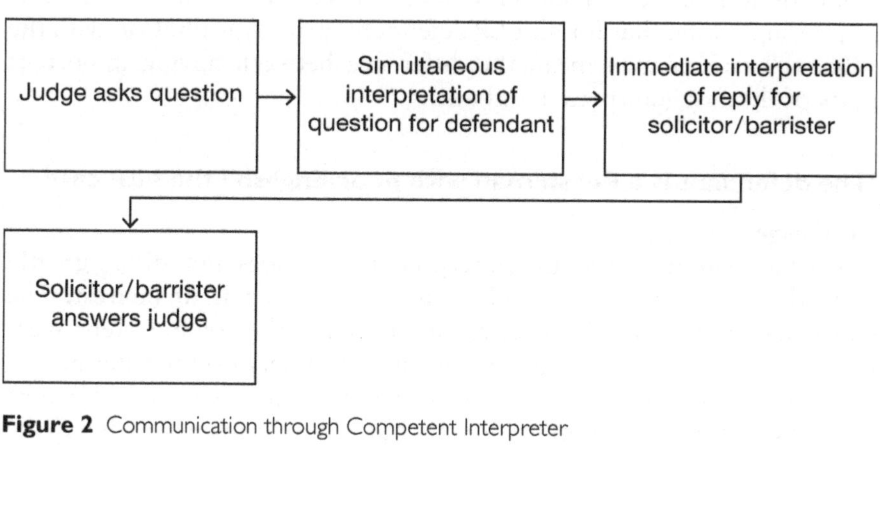

Figure 2 Communication through Competent Interpreter

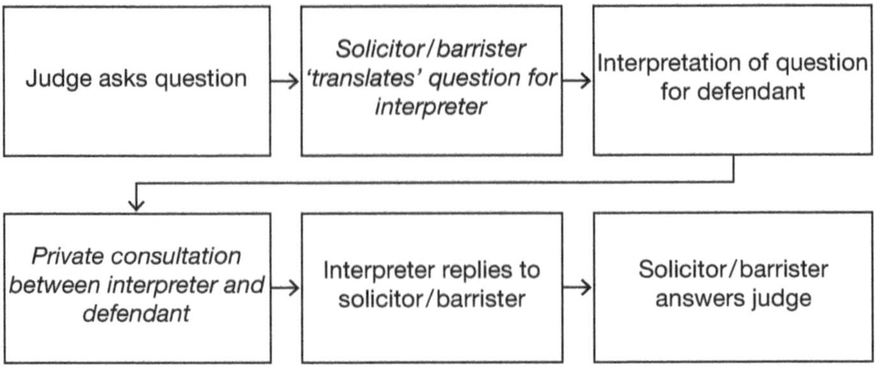

Figure 3 Communication through LEP/Selective Interpreter

is furnishing the court with the Facts, it is conceivable that the defendant can hear what the Garda is saying and answer the solicitor's/barrister's questions at the same time; in this scenario the defendant would be in a position to challenge something the prosecution alleges if necessary. The LEP defendant who is reliant on the services of an interpreter would not be in such a position; while the interpreter is facilitating the consultation, it is impossible for him or her to interpret the Facts at the same time. Observations suggest that this scenario occurs regularly in court and that it may therefore be common for the Facts in an interpreted case to remain uninterpreted, something which essentially deprives the LEP defendant of the opportunity to contest the prosecution's version of events. Although contesting or disputing the Facts on a plea of guilty is rare, it is nonetheless possible for an error to be made, and observations suggest that there are frequent errors and omissions in case files resulting from administrative inefficiencies and poor record-keeping. It is a short step to suggesting that for an LEP defendant, prior consultation with the solicitor/barrister may mean the difference between having important parts of the case interpreted and not.

'The defendant is a Polish man with poor English': the LEP case

The Charge

The Charge unit in the LEP/interpreted case does not differ greatly from the monolingual case, which in and of itself is of interest. The court does not generally seem to question whether or not steps were taken on arrest to ensure the LEP defendant understood the charge, for example by providing an interpreter. The issue arises outside of court and concerns the Gardaí more directly but is of relevance here due to the fact that an integral part of a charge sheet case is the evidence of arrest, and it is of interest because a pattern emerged from the evidence given by Gardaí of replies made by LEP defendants after caution. In case after case the prosecution stated that no reply was made to the charge:

> 'The defendant is a Polish man with poor English. ... The defendant made no reply to the charges' (Garda, CitC)
>
> SOLICITOR: He has a certain amount of English. ...
> GARDA: There was no reply after caution. (RC)
>
> JUDGE Z: The evidence is that he made no reply after caution.
> INTERPRETER: [Silent]
>
> GARDA: He was charged over the telephone by an interpreter.
> JUDGE Z: The evidence is that he made no reply after caution.
> INTERPRETER: [Not interpreting]

It wasn't until after the observation period of the research and during the analysis of data that this pattern was noted, however, such that little can be said other than to question whether it may be significant and what the implications may be. First, there is the question of whether or not a defendant must be fully informed in detail of the charge against him/her. It arose in court that if the reason for arrest is obvious there may be no need to verbalise the charge, raising the question of whether there are circumstances where that which is obvious to an Irish person may not be obvious to someone unfamiliar with Irish culture and the criminal justice system. Another issue concerns the consequences of making no reply after caution. If a defendant who does not respond is considered to be availing of the right to silence and this silence is not identified as the result of incomprehension, will this silence carry negative consequences?[3]

In terms of the type of charges answered by LEP defendants, while it is difficult to generalise and the research study did not attempt to quantify the offences being observed, comments of solicitors/barristers largely support observations in the court that LEP defendants come before Irish District Courts on the full range of possible offences and their offences tend to be less serious matters at the lower end of the criminal structure such as public order and driving offences. Many of the solicitors have noted particular trends in offences among certain nationalities, particularly young Eastern European men being charged with driving offences such as drunk-driving. Gwen offers a generalised categorisation:

> They seem to fit into niches for some reason. The Eastern Europeans seem to be predominantly road traffic cases, and you know after serious nights out on the town assaults and manslaughter, murder cases. I think there was some

> staggering statistic about a Lithuanian would be more likely to be killed by his own in Ireland than at home. … [S]ome of the readings of the drunk-driving cases are just phenomenal when you see the level of alcohol in their system when they're driving around, … they're scarily high readings. So they seem to fit into that category. … The Romanis would be mostly begging and those kind of cases, and the Romanians would be predominantly credit card fraud, ATM-related theft and fraud stuff. … The Nigerians you'd get a fair bit of minor theft and fraud, coming in pinching groceries … So they tend to fit into categories; I'm not saying that you'd obviously apply that rigidly.

The experiences of solicitors and barristers naturally differed and depended among other things on where they were based. For example, in certain courts in Dublin a huge number of LEP cases involve individuals arrested under what was then Section 12 of the Immigration Act,[4] while such cases are less likely to come before more rural courts. Under this provision a person can be arrested and detained if they do not satisfactorily prove their identity. Such cases are often remanded for very lengthy periods for verification of ID and some judges show concern for whether the defendant understood why he/she was being held:

> JUDGE R: And has it been explained to Mr. Y why he's being held in custody?
> BARRISTER: It has.
> JUDGE R: And he understands why he is being held?
> BARRISTER: He does, Judge, completely.

Identity cases are striking in that most require interpreters; the Chinese interpreters that I interviewed, for example, said that ID cases constituted the majority of their work. The Custody Court observed dealt with a huge number of such cases, which involve much discussion about receiving and not receiving ID, verifying ID and so on:

> 'We have not received any ID yet'
> 'The Egyptian embassy is trying to establish his identity'
> 'We are still awaiting verification of ID'
> 'I'm not satisfied with the ID; it's a military card'

Such discussions also frequently involve the questioning of defendants to try and resolve identity issues; interrogations almost inevitably require interpreters and communication can become complex when the interpreter is not competent. The following extract is from the Custody Court. The three Chinese co-accused had been in custody for around two months at this point:

> PROSECUTION: This ID issue is ongoing since the 13th of August, and no progress has been made.

He explained that the defendants had provided Chinese national ID cards, the Chinese Embassy had been contacted and they had been awaiting a response since 29 August. No response was forthcoming; e-mails were not replied to and phone calls were not returned.

> PROSECUTION: The Irish Embassy in Beijing has also been on to the authorities there to try to get a sample ID; they were given a lot of different sample documents, but not the Chinese identity card. These are for use only within China.
> JUDGE: So they are not prepared to give a sample ID?
> PROSECUTION: No.

The prosecution told the court he believed the defendants had access to passports. He said they had travelled from China to an EU country, possibly Spain, but that they had to have a passport getting on to the plane. He said that organised crime gangs are smuggling people into Ireland.

> JUDGE: It is not disputed that they had the passports getting on to the plane. The passports were allegedly taken by traffickers. ... The usual story ... I am not accepting it.
> PROSECUTION: I believe they still have their genuine passports.
> JUDGE: You think they got fake documents to get in? But you are only surmising; it's what usually happens.

She then asked the barrister what the defendants said to this, and the barrister, interpreter and defendant consulted as the prosecution continued to talk.

> JUDGE: [To defendants] Where is your genuine passport, each one of you?
> INTERPRETER: My passport was taken by –
> JUDGE: [Interrupting] I can't hear you. Where did each one of them come from? Where did you get a flight from?
> INTERPRETER: No idea.
> JUDGE: No idea?!

The barrister said they had taken a number of flights, and the prosecution expressed doubts about whether they were telling the truth.

> JUDGE: Who delivered the documents?
> [Barrister, defendant and interpreter continue to consult]
> JUDGE: It's a simple question. I don't know why it's taking so long ... and why the blank faces.
> INTERPRETER: One friend.
> JUDGE: [Shouting] WHAT FRIEND?

The judge then decided to hear them one at a time: 'It goes to credibility'. The first defendant was called as a witness and went to take the oath.

REGISTRAR: I swear by Almighty God –
INTERPRETER: I swear by Almighty God –
REGISTRAR: No; repeat it to him in Chinese.

The interpreter is speaking in whispers, and the judge repeatedly asks her to speak up.

BARRISTER: Now, if you could just address your answers to the Judge.
INTERPRETER: [Nothing]
BARRISTER: Tell him to address his answers to the Judge.

The interpreter is clearly confused. She had no idea that she had to interpret the oath and does not seem to understand what is going on. Even when instructed to, she fails to interpret what the barrister says. In addition, the judge is interrupting frequently as well as asking multiple questions at high speed without waiting for these to be interpreted, or waiting for an answer:

BARRISTER: He gave an answer there, Judge, you interrupted.
JUDGE: Where is his real passport? He's saying' … [that he has no idea, that a foreigner took it before he came to Ireland]. Where was he when the foreigner took it?
INTERPRETER: I was on the flight.
JUDGE: What flight? A minute ago he said it was in the airport. Is he saying it was stolen from him?

The case continues at length in the same vein and is eventually remanded for another two weeks. At the end of October the three defendants, still in custody, are brought before the court again. ID has still not been verified, but the defendants have applied for asylum. The judge comments:

JUDGE: This is a straightforward charge, but if they are convicted, complications arise with regard to how well they co-operated in establishing their identity.
BARRISTER: I would submit that they have.
JUDGE: I am not pre-judging them. They may well be innocent, but people forget that this is very important in mitigation.

The judge puts the case back for a hearing four weeks later and asks if this remand is by consent. The barrister writes down the date for the interpreter and asks her to ask them if is that date is OK.

JUDGE: There is liberty to reapply should they wish to change their plea or if they find other ID. [To prosecution] If you verify their identification earlier, please apply. There is an onus to reapply.

The barrister seems to be listening to the interpreted reply of the defendants with regard to consent but the judge has moved on to the next case without waiting for a response. The Chinese interpreter turns to sit down and sighs heavily.

The interpreter on this date is not the same as the interpreter on the first date. She gives the impression of being extremely competent, and she later revealed that she has been in Ireland for twenty years and working as an interpreter for six. The interpreter from the first date was also later interviewed. Her English in the interview was poor, but essentially she described her participation in the case as follows:

> She was asking questions, and I didn't hear them but somehow I kept interpreting to the defendant anyway. He had no idea what I'm talking about. When the Judge asked 'what did the defendant say?,' I just say 'yeah' to the Judge. I said he couldn't hear me but that was just an excuse. I don't know if the Judge knew or not, but she said OK, and repeated the question.

The first part of this case demonstrates an inexperienced and incompetent LEP interpreter but although it was obvious that she did not know what she was doing and that her English was poor, no remark was passed on this. In addition, throughout the case the court did little to accommodate interpretation. Even an experienced interpreter could not realistically have interpreted all of the judge's questions, and any answers being given were continuously interrupted or ignored. The norms of interpreted communication require that, when using an interpreter, the first and second person (i.e. 'I', 'you') should be used and the person addressed directly as if there were no intermediary; the interpreter should speak in the first person as if the words were his or her own. Observations suggest that while the majority of interpreters in the District Court do this, judges alternate between addressing the defendant directly, using the third person (i.e. 'he' or 'she') and asking the interpreter to say something:

> 'Can I ascertain through the Lithuanian interpreter, how long are you in the country?' (Judge Z)

> JUDGE P: Does he have a solicitor?
> INTERPRETER: No, I don't
> JUDGE P: Does he want an opportunity to speak with a solicitor?
> INTERPRETER: No.
> JUDGE P: Does he understand?
> INTERPRETER: Yes, I understand.

In the case of the three Chinese co-accused the judge moves frequently between the second and third person ('Where is your genuine passport, each one of you?'; 'Where is his real passport?'), and the barrister begins his examination of the witness using the second person ('If you could just address your answers to the Judge') but is then forced to address the interpreter directly as she has not understood ('Tell him to address his answers to the Judge'). Judges commonly move between using the second and third person in all cases, usually alternating between addressing the defendant directly and talking to the solicitor/barrister about the defendant, and it is to be expected that the same should happen in interpreted cases. However, judges also use the third person when there is no solicitor/barrister present and some address the interpreter directly, both of which contravene the norms of interpreted communication. While Chapter 2 revealed that the District Court judge has full linguistic discretion in the courtroom, this nonetheless suggests a lack of awareness about how to work with interpreters, though Mihai considers it more a lack of interest:

> You're not talking to the interpreter, I'm not there. I'm not on trial, you cannot ask me. You ask the defendant. I will ask him and he will answer and I'll give you the answer. ... I don't think it takes very, very much, really, to understand what a triangular communication means, but I do believe there's no interest, really, rather than understanding.

Bail applications

The Bail unit of the LEP case is distinctive in that many objections to bail commonly apply to LEP defendants, such as being a flight risk:

> 'He has no ties to the jurisdiction. Straightforward unlikely to appear' (Judge S)
> 'He is a flight risk. He has no ties here, no family, no job. He is from Poland. He lives here, but doesn't own any property' (court presenter, CusC)

The other principal issue affecting bail for many LEP defendants is identity; aside from the former Section 12s, bail is unlikely to be granted in any case where identity is an issue, such as where a defendant has given a false name or address to the Gardaí:

> PROSECUTING GUARD: There is an objection to bail for both defendants.
> JUDGE O: On what grounds?
> PROSECUTING GUARD: [They both gave false names, dates of birth and addresses in the past. They gave false details on arrest yesterday, and have produced no identification.]

Some LEP defendants may also have difficulties understanding the concept of bail; some interpreters reported that because bail does not necessarily exist in the legal system of the LEP defendant, or exist in the same form, when bail is set at 200 Euros they think they have to pay that sum and the case is over. Additionally, the unit itself is particularly fast-moving, to the point that a defendant with limited English would not be in a position to understand the conditions of their bail without having them interpreted or explained. There is, therefore, heavy reliance on the interpreter or representative in this unit. Even a competent interpreter may find it difficult to keep up and solicitors/barristers do not always have the time to explain the conditions before the bail bond is signed, as many remain 'on their feet' throughout the following cases. It sometimes happens in this scenario that the solicitor/barrister instructs the interpreter to 'explain' the bail bond to the defendant, which seems inevitably to lead to confusion; the bail bond is a legal document which the interpreter is not trained to understand or explain, and without the relevant experience an interpreter may not themselves understand the concept of bail, the bail bond or the conditions:

> JUDGE S: Is this your signature?
> INTERPRETER: [Confused] Me?
> JUDGE S: [Impatient] Would you ask him if this is his signature?
> INTERPRETER: Yes, I signed it just now.
> JUDGE S: Yes, he did.
> [Defendant is released, looks confused, asks interpreter something]
> INTERPRETER: [Whispers to barrister] Is he free?
> BARRISTER: I appear for ... [Doesn't answer, next case begins]
> [Interpreter points to door, defendant leaves. Later she approaches barrister again]
> INTERPRETER: [Whispers] Sorry, is he free?

It is clear here that the interpreter has difficulties understanding the bail process (and the basics of interpreted dialogue) and on a number of occasions interpreters were observed spending quite some time trying to decipher bail bonds, sometimes engaging the help of a Garda or solicitor/barrister, before the defendant left the courtroom holding the document and looking very confused.

Jurisdiction, Plea and Facts

The Jurisdiction and Plea units do not differ greatly in the LEP/interpreted case, if at all; sometimes reference is made to the interpreter or comprehension of what is going on: 'Having spoken with my client through the interpreter, I have a plea' (RC); 'Through the interpreter can I ascertain whether Mr. S understands that his solicitor is indicating a plea of guilty?' (Judge Z).

It is during the Facts that the voice of the interpreter is most likely to be heard by the court at any length as the judge may wish to clarify things or put questions to the defendant. As it more frequently consists of the

Garda citing facts at high speed and very often in a low, unclear voice, it is a particularly challenging unit for the interpreter, and allowances are rarely made for interpretation. It is also during the Facts that, as we have seen, the solicitor/barrister uses the interpreter to consult with the client, leaving the facts uninterpreted. The combination of these factors may make the Facts unit the least likely to be interpreted for the defendant.

LEP defendants are sometimes called to give evidence during the Facts or in the case of a hearing and, as with all witnesses, they must take an oath or affirmation. The issue of religion may arise and courts provide defendants with the appropriate Holy Book, though more commonly a language issue arises and an interpreter is involved. Perhaps because it happens so seldom that an LEP defendant is sworn in to give evidence, there is often uncertainty as to the protocol: whether the interpreter should also be sworn in, whether the oath should be taken in English or in the defendant's own language and whether the interpreter should confirm that the oath has been properly taken. Some judges seem to take for granted that the oath must be taken in the defendant's language:

> 'Explain if you are going to give evidence you must repeat the oath in your own language after the interpreter, and the interpreter must confirm that it has been fully taken' (Judge S)

In the following extract, on the other hand, it is the reaction of the defendant that leads to the oath being taken in Romanian:

> REGISTRAR: I swear by Almighty God – [Defendant turns and addresses interpreter at length]
> JUDGE P: What is he saying, please?
> INTERPRETER: He doesn't understand.
> SOLICITOR: I think he's saying he wants to take the oath in his own language. [To interpreter] Roma?
> INTERPRETER: Romanian.
> JUDGE P: [The registrar will announce the oath to the interpreter, the interpreter will translate it and the defendant will repeat it.]

Criminal Record, Mitigation and Sentence

The Criminal Record unit rarely differs in the LEP/interpreted case as the record of the defendant is generally confined to the Irish one and does not involve, for example, any record of crimes committed in an immigrant's country of origin. Judge S on rare occasions asked about criminal history outside Ireland:

> 'Does he have previous in this or any other jurisdiction?'
> 'Can you tell me more about the charges in other countries?'

Stephen submits that where the case is more serious, checks would be more detailed but that this happens more in the higher courts; 'certainly for District Court matters they don't seem to pursue that line; they check the Irish system and if there's nothing there they don't tend to go further. Maybe if there is something on the Irish system they may check with Interpol.'

The Mitigation unit always includes details related to the fact that the defendant is not Irish; monologues usually begin by addressing the nationality of the defendant and, if it has not already been stated, the judge may ask how long the person has been in Ireland or request that they tell the court the purpose of their stay:

> 'He is a Slovakian national' (Solicitor, RC)
> 'This is a Lithuanian man who has been in Ireland for five years' (Solicitor, CitC)
> 'How long has he been living in this country?' (Judge P)

That the defendant was foreign and therefore not familiar with Irish law was raised a couple of times by solicitors/barristers in Mitigation. In one case a barrister submitted that if a foreign national is being asked for his name and address he should be cautioned that not to give this information would be an offence, but Judge R replied that the same principle applied as would to an Irish person: that the circumstances of the event were so obvious that this was not necessary. In another case, a twenty-seven-year-old Lithuanian defendant was charged with possession of a knife. His solicitor told the court that he worked in a garage and had left work with the knife still in his pocket, but that he 'didn't realise the seriousness of having a knife in his pocket'. He was convicted and fined 200 Euros by Judge T. On another occasion a Polish defendant was charged with failing to produce a National Car Test and his solicitor suggested that, despite a pattern of driving offences, he had not been aware until consultation how serious these were; he had four young children, needed the car for his family and work, was 'extremely contrite' and undertook to abide by the traffic laws in future. He was convicted and fined 250 Euros by Judge P. These three judges did not seem to consider foreignness a mitigating factor and Judge Z seemed to support this ideology:

> 'If you wish to remain in the State you must abide by the law like other citizens'
> 'You're very welcome in this country, but you must comply, as any resident, with the laws of the land'

Mihai expressed concern that no consideration is given to the probable cultural element of many minor offences, where someone moves to a new country, assumes everything works the same as in their own country and only after inadvertently committing an offence realises that what they did is unacceptable. This concern was not voiced by other interviewees, a number of whom said that non-Irish defendants generally realise that they have committed an offence and they get on with it. Thomas says that while systems differ, the basis is the same: the allegation is heard and accepted, 'then they like to have an opportunity to give an excuse, and they take and respect the sanction when it's applied'.

Hamilton (2005) was certainly not wrong when she pointed out that familiarity with 'the unspoken language of the District Court' was a pre-requisite to understanding a judge's sentence. The judge reads the sentence at such high speed and it is often so complex that it is inevitably difficult to follow and understand – and to interpret. It is not usual for the judge to check that the defendant has understood, but by doing so in the following example the judge reveals that even the interpreter may not have understood him and that the defendant certainly has not:

> JUDGE Z: And I trust the defendant understands the order.
> [Interpreter looks at the solicitor then at Judge]
> INTERPRETER: Sorry?
> JUDGE Z: I trust the defendant understands the order.
> [Interpreter addresses defendant, who shakes head. Interpreter continues to talk]
> JUDGE Z: [Sighs] Well anyway [The court giggles]. We're talking about Christmas cards.

Discerning whether or not judges differentiate between Irish and non-Irish defendants in sentencing was not an aim of the research but it was noted that on relatively rare occasions conditions are imposed that would not be relevant to the Irish defendant, specifically conditions requiring departure from the jurisdiction. One judge (S) wanted to know if a Polish defendant would be going home, saying: 'It's not because he's not from the jurisdiction. It's not about that. It would be the same if he were from Donegal.' He was given a peace bond for one year, the terms of which included a return to Poland if he had no other means of surviving in Ireland and the obligation to notify the Gardaí of flight dates. In a similar case with the same judge, a Romanian defendant was given a peace bond, which included an undertaking to return to Romania, to show the Gardaí his travel tickets and the condition that 'If he is not gone in two weeks he will be picked up, brought back to me and put in prison.' A further charge was dismissed on condition that the defendant leave the State by a particular date and not return for twelve months. Finally, some judges, in these examples Judge Z, comment on criminality in the context of immigration:

> JUDGE Z: Can I ascertain through the Lithuanian interpreter, how long are you in the country?
> INTERPRETER: One and half years.
> JUDGE Z: You've found your criminal feet very quickly.

> 'I'm reluctant to give Mr. X any more leeway. He has not just worn out his welcome in this country ... He seems to have come to this country [to commit crimes]. ... This is a difficult time for every person in this State; you are making a total mockery of those who are unemployed' (Judge Z)
> 'You were made very welcome in this country; you were treated with dignity and respect. ... I'm not going to see this country abused' (Judge Z)

Conclusion

According to the accounts of solicitors/barristers and interpreters, things changed after interpreting was outsourced. Before this, the provision of interpreters was messy and unorganised which, for solicitors/barristers, was indicative of poor standards. Interpreters found, correspondingly, that they were not well treated or respected. Post-contract, some solicitors/barristers consider that services have improved and interpreters say treatment in court is much better, but interpreters also say that the attitudes of agencies have worsened and that not only have pay rates been slashed but interpreting standards have fallen. Professional interpreters are disheartened by the situation and are leaving the profession. The attitude of solicitors/barristers to interpreters, while generally positive, is less so when it comes to money and there is a perception that interpreters pay more attention to time sheets than interpreting yet earn more than solicitors or barristers in some cases.

Delays caused by interpreting are negligible in the greater scheme of things. Sometimes cases are put back for an interpreter but this is an administrative issue. As the voice of the defendant is rarely heard in the District Court, most interpreting is whispered and has no effect on proceedings. Where there is interaction between court and defendant, dialogue may take twice as long but incompetent interpreters like the LEP or Selective Interpreter can impact considerably more on proceedings, causing delays through a lack of understanding or inappropriate private dialogue with the defendant. Due to the dynamic of the District Court, delays may equally be the responsibility of the unprepared solicitor/barrister who has not taken (full) instruction, as this is likely to lead to unnecessary and unwieldy four-way dialogues. The lack of protocol in interpreted events also creates confusion and delay, as roles and expectations are unclear: the norms of interpreted interaction, oath-taking and the line between interpreting and advocacy are three obvious examples.

The LEP defendant relies on the solicitor/barrister and/or interpreter to explain what happens in court and to address the court on their behalf. Where unprepared solicitors/barristers need to consult the defendant during proceedings, important parts of the case, usually the Facts, may not be interpreted for the defendant, thus depriving him or her of the opportunity to contest the prosecution's version of events. District Court proceedings do not slow down or make allowances for the interpreter and some units of the case, including the Facts and the Sentence, pose particular difficulties due to their high speed and complexity, making them less likely to be properly interpreted for the LEP defendant. In addition, once an interpreter is provided there is an expectation that the defendant will understand proceedings and any orders made. However, the Silent or Selective Interpreter, for example, may fail to interpret or selectively interpret important parts of the case, including bail conditions and the sentence, potentially putting the defendant in a precarious position for non-compliance. The Advocate Interpreter may also, for example, consent to remands on the defendant's behalf without consultation, or may change or otherwise misrepresent the defendant's words to his potential detriment, as making an unfavourable impression on a District Court judge can have unpleasant consequences.

LEP defendants appear before the District Court on the full range of offences, though there is some evidence that young Eastern European men appear particularly often on driving offences and that certain courts deal with a large number of ID-related immigration offences, which are notable in almost always involving interpreters. The court does not seem to differentiate between English speakers and LEP defendants when hearing evidence of arrest in the Charge unit, but a possible pattern was identified of LEP individuals failing to make any reply when cautioned by a Garda, potentially indicating language difficulties. During the bail process, some prosecution objections to bail seemed to affect non-Irish defendants in particular, including failure to provide ID or providing false details to the Gardaí and being a flight risk, while some court orders were also specific to non-Irish people in requiring the offender to leave the country. The Mitigation unit always involves reference to the fact that a defendant is not Irish, as well as details of place of origin and length of time and reasons for being in Ireland. However, not being Irish and therefore being unfamiliar with the law does not seem to mitigate culpability in the eyes of Irish District Court judges.

LEP defendants and interpreters have become a fixture in the Irish District Court. Their presence impacts on court proceedings both quantitatively and qualitatively, altering the workload of the court, introducing new participants and presenting communication challenges that may appear to be overcome by the provision of interpreters but that are actually considerably more complex, not only because of the nature of the court interpreting system in Ireland and concerns about the quality of some of the interpreters provided, but because of the nature of District Court proceedings themselves.

Notes

1 Please refer to 'Guide to extracts from District Court field notes and interviews' for an explanation of how anonymised courts and judges are referred to in the text.

2 Almost all interpreters work for multiple agencies. Although one agency was contracted officially by the Courts Service, there were and are still multiple agencies in operation in Ireland. Even once a single agency was contracted in 2007, there were occasions where other companies provided interpreters when the contracted agency was unable to (Phelan, 2011). According to a 2013 article, three agencies provide most of the interpretation services (McKinley, 2013). Many court interpreters also work through the same and other agencies in other public or community settings such as hospitals, Garda stations and refugee/asylum services.

3 The right to silence has suffered a 'series of statutory encroachments' in recent years (Law Society of Ireland, 2004:125), such that adverse inferences may be drawn from the silence of suspects in increasingly wide circumstances (Ryan, 1997; Coen, 2008).

4 Observation was carried out in 2009 and 2010. S.12 was found to be unconstitutional in 2011 and replaced by the provisions of The Civil Law (Miscellaneous Provisions) Act 2011. However, these provisions do not differ greatly from the previous S.12. While this discussion pertains specifically to charges under S.12, it thus appears still to have relevance under the new provisions. Immigration provisions in relation to the District Court are discussed by O'Nolan (2011a, b).

Conclusion

To walk into an Irish District Court is, for the uninitiated, to enter a world of incomprehensible mayhem where mysterious things happen at lightning speed and actors follow a hidden script using words and phrases that often seem familiar but do not seem to make any sense. At times one feels as in a Medieval drama, such is the pageantry and so formal and archaic the words, but this can give way just as quickly to a sense of banality, as a lengthy debate ensues as to the exact manner in which a pint came to be thrown, spilled, fired or poured on the prosecuting Garda. Blink, and you miss bail being denied; cough, and you drown out the high speed mumble establishing the Facts; arrive without a word of English to answer a charge of drunk-driving, and leave without quite understanding what has happened.

The Irish District Court is a busy place that deals with a huge number of criminal offences and processes an endless stream of people charged with those offences. Almost everyone answering a criminal charge will start their journey in the District Court, and for the majority the District Court will also decide the outcome of their case. Some courts have lists with over a hundred matters to deal with in a single day. That such a quantity is even conceivable (though not always achievable) relates to the speed with which cases are processed. This can be attributed in part to the fact that for many of the names on the list, that day will involve nothing more than consenting or getting consent to an adjournment or remand. Proceedings might occur at high speed but cases can move through the system at a snail's pace, with multiple appearances required to deal with the various elements of the case: Applications, Charge, Jurisdiction, Plea, Facts/Evidence, Criminal Record, Mitigation/Defence and, finally, Sentencing.

The other facilitator of speed is the 'insider' nature of District Court language, which uses a reliance on shared knowledge and experience to allow speakers to communicate with minimum words and maximum efficiency. While in one sense a model of effective communication, it is also an exclusionary one, as much of what is said is inaccessible and meaningless to outsiders. A key feature of its functionality is the repetitive nature of District Court proceedings, where the same cases, often with the same circumstances, are dealt with repeatedly. Most of these cases are uncontested and proceed on a guilty plea, with the prosecuting Garda giving his or her facts and the solicitor or barrister doing their best to offer something by way of mitigating their client's guilt and the sentence. The voice of the defendant is rarely heard, both because there is little to say beyond 'guilty' and because most have legal representatives through whom communication with the court is conducted.

District Court defendants are typically divided into what might be termed 'aberrations', or those who appear for the first and probably last time as a result of a mistake or moment of madness, and the 'regulars', or repeat offenders, who will often have accrued criminal histories spanning years. Because the insider language and discourse of the District Court can be grasped through repetition and familiarity, repeat offenders sometimes partake in its use of jargon, while defendants more generally seem to struggle with the complex and formal language often employed by judges and solicitors/barristers.

A new type of defendant in the District Court is the result of significant changes in Ireland's population. With 12 per cent of the population born outside the country and 11 per cent speaking a language other than English at home, the numbers of defendants with no, or limited, English appearing before the criminal courts have risen significantly, and both LEP defendants and interpreters have become a fixture of the District Court.

The processing of the LEP defendant can differ from the generic case of the Irish person or English speaker in a few ways, but in many instances it will not differ at all. The type of offences are similar, if not the same, though there may be a preponderance of young Eastern European men charged with driving offences and in certain courts a large number of LEP cases are ID-related. The LEP cases largely proceed at the same speed as monolingual cases, particularly where no mention is made of an interpreter or an interpreter appears automatically, and/or where the LEP defendant is represented. Administrative delays can be the result of needing an interpreter who is not there or was not ordered, but proceedings can be slowed down to varying degrees in certain other situations, including where the court wishes to communicate directly with the defendant and there is interpreted communication, and where the court requires information and the legal representative, who does not have the information, needs to consult the defendant through an interpreter. Delays in these scenarios can be tempered by Competent or Advocate Interpreters and exacerbated by the Silent, Selective or LEP Interpreter.

Substantively, LEP cases can contain aspects not relevant or less relevant to the Irish defendant, including court orders to leave the country, and objections to bail due to perceived flight risks, failure to provide ID or providing false details to the Gardaí. Providing false details can also be a factor in interpreters for the wrong language being assigned. If at no other time in the case, the fact that a defendant is not Irish will be raised and sometimes explored during Mitigation, but Irish judges seem reluctant to mitigate culpability for reasons of not being Irish.

Although Irish courts are no strangers to language issues, historically these have involved Irish speakers either unable or unwilling to use the English language in courts under British rule and, later, the constitutional right to conduct a case in either Irish or English. This experience was insufficient, however, to ensure that an infrastructure was in place to deal with the swift, expansive and diverse rise in the numbers of defendants experiencing language barriers. A swift rise calls for a rapid response, and this came first as an *ad hoc* and later as an outsourced system of interpreting, devised to cater for the growing demand. During the 'early years', large numbers of agencies and interpreters battled for business in court, and scenes of mayhem and wild disorganisation ensued. From the outset, problems of quality were identified and, drawing on the vast experience of other countries in dealing with bilingualism in courts, numerous recommendations were made with regard to such issues as establishing a register of interpreters, quality standards, testing and monitoring, regulation and competence requirements.

However, the focus seemed to be, instead, on the rationalisation of services, or the efficient and effective management of LEP cases, which ultimately led to the privatisation of services, outsourced in 2007 to a single agency. There was an improvement in organisation that certainly seemed to make the situation more manageable, but the same complaints continued to be made with regard to broad issues of quality. Concerns were exacerbated by reports of dubious recruitment practices, scares about the lack of criminal vetting and newspaper anecdotes, such as the one where a judge in Donegal threatened to start conducting cases with a State-supplied dictionary.

There is a real difficulty in reconciling the lack of attention to quality with the fact that the Courts Service spends millions of Euros every year on interpreting services and seems committed to ensuring that interpreters are available to those who need them, and with the fact that

District Court judges routinely concede to requests for interpreters, even if concession is sometimes tempered with doubt, distaste or grudging reluctance. The failure of courts to provide interpreters has been found to be a significant issue elsewhere. In Ireland, by contrast, there is commitment to providing them, the funds to pay for them are made available (albeit in the face of some sensationalised reporting in the early years and some cuts in later ones), and in practice judges have been seen to insist on interpreters even where this was manifestly unnecessary. The right to an interpreter in Ireland is thus implicitly acknowledged in both policy and practice. How, then, to reconcile the commitment to providing interpreters with the failure to ensure that those interpreters fulfil any specific function? It is suggested that some possible reasons are the assumption of competence and the effectiveness of improved management, the primacy of provision and the minor nature of District Court offences.

First, where a system is in place that is ostensibly designed to provide qualified and competent interpreters, it is unsurprising that there is an implicit assumption among judges and practitioners, and possibly among policy-makers, that the interpreters so provided are competent. This is especially so where the focus on efficient and effective management has created a perception of improved quality. However, the assumption of competence has also been identified in courts elsewhere and contrasted with the mistrust with which interpreters are otherwise treated; while there was some evidence here that practitioners have a level of cynicism about how much interpreters are paid in relation to the quality of interpreting they provide, overall attitudes towards interpreters as part of the court process seemed at worst tolerant and at best very positive. No violent opponents of soap and sunlight in Irish courts.

The second possible explanation is the primacy of provision. Recognition of the right to an interpreter has a long history in Ireland, but appeals based on interpreting, in Ireland and elsewhere, are difficult to win and are rarely successful. Proving an alleged breach based on interpreting presents a considerable burden and the likelihood of success is probably diminished if a court, like the Court of Criminal Appeal in *DPP v Adriano Martins Costa & Jose Claudio Batista* (2008), takes the view that difficulties with interpreting go not to the safety or reliability of a conviction, but to inconvenience and delay during proceedings. As long as an interpreter has been provided, the chances of success seem low, except in egregious circumstances. If no interpreter was provided, a very high standard must be met to show that one had genuinely been necessary.

In practice, unless there is a direct request for an interpreter, there is no guarantee that one will be provided, and how the issue of language ability is assessed very much depends on the approach of the individual judge and is at his or her discretion, like most aspects of District Court procedure. There is much evidence to suggest that in Ireland, as elsewhere, there is a significant responsibility on the accused person to request the services of an interpreter where this is necessary and to pinpoint any difficulties with interpretation where these exist (although the new S.I. 565/2013 provides that the court or any party to the case may make an application to have the interpreter replaced where interpreting is not considered to be of sufficent quality (Reg. 7)). This is despite the fact that LEP defendants are likely to, and do, over-estimate their fluency and may thus not request interpretation, and the fact that if a defendant has genuine difficulties with the language of the court, they are unlikely to know whether or not the interpreting is faulty. The questions that seem to matter most in a retrospective situation are: Did you have an interpreter? Did you tell anyone that there were problems with the interpreter?

The third possible explanation in as far as it relates to the District Court is the minor nature of the offences it hears. The *Costa & Batista* attitude resonates particularly with this. Being a court of limited jurisdiction empowered to hear 'minor' offences, much of its criminal business involves what might be considered relatively trifling matters such as traffic and public order offences, and there is a sense among District Court practitioners that defendants on such charges are not as vulnerable as those in more serious cases like rape or murder. In practice, the more serious a charge, the more attention is paid by the trial judge to the provision *and* to the quality of interpreters, particularly where potential custodial sentences are involved. This fits with the principle that judges of the District Court are required to ensure fairness and natural justice, but these requirements are relative to the seriousness of the charge and its potential consequences.

It was also suggested that there are bigger battles to fight in the District Court than that of interpreting, and indeed the District Court has significant issues to contend with, not least of which is its enormous caseload.

The difficulty is that while many and most cases tried at District Court level are minor and trivial in nature, the stakes even at this level can be quite high; it cannot realistically be said that proceedings that may potentially lead to the imposition of an aggregate two year prison sentence, for example, do not warrant the highest possible level of procedural protection. In fact, the potential for a prison sentence of *any* length should be considered with the utmost gravity, not only because of the seriousness *per se* of the deprivation of liberty, but because there is evidence that those serving even short prison sentences suffer the same negative impacts as those serving longer ones: stigmatisation, and disrupted ties with families, employers and their community (O'Donnell, 1998). Importantly, a recent prior prison committal and being held on remand as part of confinement are strong indicators of recidivism (O'Donnell, Baumer & Hughes, 2008). Committals to Irish prisons from the District Court are continually increasing, particularly shorter sentences.

In addition, the outcome of a case in the District Court is the result of a process, each stage of which can potentially impact on the nature of proceedings and contribute to the judge's final decision. Judicial discretion at District Court level is extremely broad across each segment of that process, including whether or not to grant bail or legal aid. In fact, the latter issues will often be dealt with by the District Court even where more serious offences are involved and the defendant is to be sent forward for trial, such that the District Court judge has discretion as to important elements of cases tried in higher courts. The Book of Evidence is also served in the District Court in such cases, and Jarmołowska's (2011) analysis of an unrepresented LEP defendant's cross-examination difficulties must certainly serve to flag the cumulative and lingering effects that poor interpreting and translation at lower levels can have at a later stage of proceedings.

More generally in terms of language, not all courts, or all Irish courts, take the view that interpreting is incapable of compromising the outcome of a case. In fact, the somewhat extreme view in *Costa & Batista* does not seem to be representative of Irish courts overall and many Irish judges have acknowledged the potential impact of interpreting. The High Court in *MacCarthaigh v Ireland*, for example, accepted that interpreting can affect the jury's perception of the defendant and the outcome of a case. In addition, the new regulations giving effect to the Directive in Ireland (S.I. 565/2013) recognise that the quality of interpreting can affect access to a fair trial (Reg. 7), and more generally empirical studies show that even proficient interpreters can have a greater influence on proceedings than is generally realised.

In fact, the very nature of District Court proceedings creates obstacles to the interpretation of proceedings. Speed, high noise levels, witnesses failing to speak up or slow down, failure to use microphones, interruptions by judges and solicitor/barrister consultations taking place 'on the hoof' during proceedings are some significant factors. Interpreting ethics and best practice can also be compromised. A lack of awareness by some court participants may mean, for example, that the norms of interpreted conversation are not used properly and the interpreter may be addressed more in the style of an advocate than a facilitator of communication. Remaining neutral is likely to be difficult where the dynamics of the court make it impossible to interpret everything, such that the interpreter must decide what to interpret and what to omit. The formulaic and ritual structure of procedure, designed for expeditiousness, favours – or at the very least tolerates – an interpreter who facilitates this structure, possibly by embellishing the defendant's words in deference to the court's use of formalities, or even by answering on a defendant's behalf – particularly where the defendant is unrepresented.

The advent of the LEP defendant has altered the District Court as an institution, and the ability of the LEP defendant to access the justice of the District Court is inevitably shaped by that institution. The problem of the Irish defendant thus becomes that of the LEP defendant, and accessing justice involves more than simply bridging a language barrier. Bridging the language barrier, on the other hand, necessitates navigation of the District Court, and understanding and interpreting its characteristics and contradictions – the verbality and the silence; the ceremony and the informality; the speed and the delays; the chaos and the order; the mystery and the mundane. If it pleases the court.

Appendix A

Methodology

Terminology: 'LEP'

The term 'limited English-Proficient' (LEP), intended to depict limited or no English-language skills, is used in preference to other terms currently in use, including 'non-English speaker' (omits those who may have basic English but would not be sufficiently fluent to participate fully in court); linguistic or ethnic minorities (most LEPs in Irish courts are immigrants); 'non-nationals' (controversial due to connotations of lacking any nationality); 'non Irish nationals' (LEP defendants may hold Irish nationality); and 'foreign offenders' or 'foreign suspects' (concern here is with those *accused* of crimes, and 'foreign' people may be fluent English speakers).

Ethics

The study required and was given ethical approval by the School of Social Work and Social Policy in Trinity College, Dublin.

Information and consent form for interview participants
A satisfactory version of this form was mandatory for ethical approval. The final version contained: contact details; research purpose and aims; suggested length and location for interviews; voluntary nature of interviews; how the interview would be recorded (digitally with consent, otherwise hand-written) and the fact that it would be made available; anonymity, data protection and assurance of confidentiality.

Informed consent and permission to attend court
Ethical approval was delayed over an issue with informed consent and the fact that those observed in the District Court would not be giving it. Ultimately, however, anyone is free to sit in an Irish court, as long as it is not sitting *in camera*; the public administration of justice is constitutionally mandated and defendants have the right to have their

case heard in an open and transparent system. There are no privacy restrictions on what is publicly said in public court sittings, there is no expectation of privacy by those involved in court, and there is no requirement to inform those attending court or working in courtrooms of the presence of any member of the public, journalist or researcher. Nonetheless, permission to attend court as an observer was sought from and granted by the President of the District Court, and the President's Office assisted in contacting every court I wished to visit, thereby greatly facilitating the research process.

Research design

Interviews

Eighteen semi-structured interviews were undertaken with members of two key groups: solicitors/barristers that work/have worked with interpreters and LEP immigrants, and interpreters who work/have worked with LEP immigrants in court. Although I aimed for a reasonable gender mix, the majority of interpreters observed were female, and there were far more male criminal solicitors than female in certain courts. Additionally, I observed more solicitors than barristers, and because I spent more time in Dublin courts I recruited more interpreters and legal professionals there.

Solicitors/barristers

Legal professionals were recruited through networking and personal contacts, but mostly through approaching individuals after a period of observation in a particular court. Everyone I approached agreed immediately to be interviewed, and one solicitor even recruited himself. Nine legal professionals were interviewed (see Appendix B).

Interpreters

Interpreters were recruited mainly through direct contact in court, and a small number through a request for participation in an ITIA bulletin. It was important that interpreters be unaware of my purpose in court; aside from influencing behaviour, some court interpreters were particularly young, inexperienced and intimidated by the court setting, and feeling observed may have caused them to feel uncomfortable or threatened. I therefore approached interpreters towards the end of my time in a particular court; this was made easier by the fact that I was usually seated with the interpreters, and although my approach initially made some nervous, most were very keen to participate. Criteria in selecting interpreters included representation of the most commonly interpreted languages and a mix of training and experience levels. Nine interpreters were interviewed (see Appendix B). Most had a good level of experience, with only one very inexperienced interpreter, and most also had a high level of relevant education and training. From my observations, I consider that the level of experience and knowledge of these interpreters is not representative of interpreters overall.

Writing the interview schedules (legal professionals; interpreters) was a challenge due to the exploratory methodology; initial drafts reflected topics from the literature that transpired to have little or no relevance in the Irish context. Interviewees were encouraged to talk freely and add subjects, but pre-determined questions centred on core topics including the right to an interpreter, payment, fair procedure, what is interpreted and interpreting quality.

Ethnographic observation

This involved sitting in the District Court and observing proceedings. Observation was carried out in three courts and a number of factors influenced selection thereof, including the geographical location of immigrant groups, pilot observations, recommendations, logistics, presence of duty interpreters and type of court.

The first court was a busy, Dublin city centre criminal court with duty interpreters and significant numbers of LEP defendants (City Centre Court). Here, judges anonymised as N, R, T, U, W and X were observed.

The second was a custody court outside Dublin city centre with high numbers of LEP defendants (Custody Court). Here, judges anonymised as O, P, Q and S were observed.

The third was a set of three courts in medium to large towns outside of Dublin, which the same judge moves between on different days (collectively, Rural Court). These dealt with both civil and criminal matters, but because sittings were considerably longer than in Dublin courts, at least as many criminal cases were heard as in the Dublin courts. Here, judges anonymised as Y and Z were observed.

Over seven months, I spent forty-five days or approximately 183.5 hours as an observer in a total of seven courts (including the three rural, and one for a short period of time curtailed by a possible compromise of the research setting). I observed twelve different judges dealing with approximately 376 relevant LEP cases – though this is difficult to quantify acurately as it was not always clear whether defendants were LEP. There was an average of thirteen LEP defendants per day in the City Centre Court, seven in the Custody Court and nine in the Rural Court.

I contacted the registrar of each court before arrival and made myself known on arrival. The sitting judge was informed of my presence;

some expressed a considerable amount of interest while others did not engage. Staff members always offered help, and I was given advantageous seating out of the public gallery (with interpreters, solicitors or press).

Each District Court has a court list for the cases to be heard on a particular day and these are processed in different ways in different courts. However, it is generally impossible to know in advance whether or when interpreted cases will be heard (even access to the list is at the discretion of the court). As such, while I set out initially to observe cases involving language issues and interpreting, by virtue of having to be present in the courtroom throughout the entire day's sitting, I inevitably observed *all* cases and realised as I became accustomed to the courtroom discourse that these data were far more relevant than I could have anticipated, as many interpreting issues were more closely linked to the language and dialogue of the court than the literature suggested. Thus, the data collection was widened.

Limitations

A potential limitation of the methodology was the influence of subjectivity on data collection and interpretation. Another was that of note-taking, as this could only be done by hand; while I consider my note-taking to reflect accurately what I observed, quotations used are not transcripts of proceedings and should be understood as such. Generally I have distinguished between when I felt sure of having cited a person *verbatim*, or as close to that as possible, by using square brackets to indicate when the essence of what was said was captured, rather than a precise quotation. Square brackets are also used in dialogue for explanatory notes.

A third concern was how to measure interpreting quality as it was never going to be possible to analyse technical, linguistic quality. To enhance observational capacity I began studying Polish (the language most frequently interpreted in Irish courts), and while my standard was far from fluent, having some understanding added an extra dimension to observations. My background in languages more generally (B.A. Applied Languages) also helped, mainly with a theoretical understanding about the functioning of language and having had some interpreting training and translation experience. However, because interpreting in the District Court is almost always whispered, any assessment had to be based on observing the behaviour and participation/non-participation of interpreters, as well as on the opinions of interviewees. It is acknowledged, therefore, that discussions of quality are limited in their lack of technical linguistic assessment.

Finally, a qualitative approach creates the risk that samples – here courts, solicitors/barristers and interpreters – are not representative of the wider picture. The limitations of the interpreter sample in this study have been mentioned, though at the conclusion of interviews, it seemed that no new or relevant data were emerging and that the information gathered through the process was cohesive among and between the two groups of interviewees. It was also possible only to include a relatively small number of District Courts; while the diversity in those chosen, the number of judges represented (twelve of the sixty-two serving as at 31 December 2009), and the repetitive and substantively similar nature of District Court proceedings alleviate some of those limitations, it is acknowledged that other courts and judges may take different approaches to those observed during this research.

Recording, analysing and assessing the data

Recorded interviews were transcribed, and hand-written notes written up in the case of unrecorded interviews, both as soon as possible after their conclusion. Courtroom observations often involved many pages of notes, and being in court up to four times a week made it particularly important to write up notes as soon as possible.

Analysis of data was an ongoing process involving reflection as part of transcribing and writing up, frequent review of data, development and verification of thematic areas, and the creation and revision of codes. In the post data-collection phase, the interviews of interpreters and legal professionals were analysed separately at first, then concurrently, with codes modified to correspond to each other. The data from courtroom observation were more copious and diverse; while the interviews represented over twenty hours of dialogue, the observations ran to over 183 hours of observations. These data were divided into three basic categories; language, proceedings and interpreting, with numerous sub-categories that evolved over the course of coding. Once all data had been reviewed repeatedly, and the conceptual categories refined and cross-referenced with those of the interviews, the writing up phase began.

As a final stage in the methodology, discussion chapters were sent to interviewees who had indicated an interest in receiving them: all solicitors/barristers and two interpreters. One interpreter and two solicitors provided feedback. One solicitor noted the absence of direct input by judges and LEP defendants – a possibility that had been considered and rejected during the research design for ethical and methodological reasons. With regard to judges, it seemed that the majority of their relevant interaction was observable in the courtroom, while for LEP defendants, their lack of English was a fundamental barrier that would in almost all cases necessitate the use of interpreters; aside from funding issues, using an interpreter to investigate the adequacy of interpreting carried philosophical and ethical issues too great to overcome for the purposes of this study. The interpreter observed that as it was a monolingual study, its linguistic analysis could not go any further than it did. Although feedback was limited, the descriptions of District Court language and the interpreting process, as well as the substantive issues addressed in the chapters, were otherwise validated by these participants.

Appendix B

Participants

Interpreters

Name	Gender	Nationality	Years in Ireland	Languages (besides English)	Qualifications	Years of interpreting experience
Svetlana	F	Ukrainian	3	Ukrainian, Russian, German	B.A. English & German philology/ linguistics	3
Anna	F	Lithuanian	5	Lithuanian, Polish, Russian (native), Arabic & Turkish	Linguistics; Dublin City University (DCU) Graduate Cert. Community Interpreting	5
Marta	F	Polish	4	Polish	English degree (including interpreting)	3
Mihai	M	Romanian	11	Romanian & French	B.A. English; Masters French Literature	6/7
Belén	F	Spanish	7	Spanish & Portuguese	School English; DCU Graduate Cert. Community Interpreting	4.5

(Continued)

Name	Gender	Nationality	Years in Ireland	Languages (besides English)	Qualifications	Years of interpreting experience
Molly	F	Chinese	20	Cantonese & Mandarin Chinese	Business & administration, London	6
Stella	F	Chinese	0.6	Mandarin Chinese	Graphic design; school English	0.6
Jevgenius	M	Latvian	2	Latvian, Russian, Lithuanian	US exchange; works as security guard and interpreter	1.25
Ewa	F	Polish	2	Polish	English degree	10 (interpreter) 7 (court interpreter)

Legal professionals

Name	Gender	Profession	Location	Years practising	Frequency of work with LEP defendants/ interpreters
Aoife	F	Barrister (asylum focus: criminal experience)	Dublin	4	Good experience
Matthew	M	Criminal solicitor	Dublin	10	Daily
Eleanor	F	Barrister (asylum focus: criminal experience)	Dublin	10	Daily
Gerard	M	Criminal solicitor	Dublin	6	Frequent: c.10% of clients non-Irish

Name	Gender	Profession	Location	Years practising	Frequency of work with LEP defendants/ interpreters
James	M	Barrister	Dublin	4	Daily (criminal matters); also asylum experience; worked in ORAC; taught asylum law
Thomas	M	Solicitor	Rural	30+	Regular: c.20% of criminal caseload non-Irish
Gwen	F	Solicitor	Rural	1	Regular: at District Court level 25–30% of workload LEP defendants
Stephen	M	Solicitor	Rural	15	Regular: large criminal workload
Mark	M	Solicitor	Rural	20+	Regular: 1–2 days per week as part of criminal workload

Appendix C

Glossaries of District Court language and jargon

Table A.1 Archaisms used in addressing the court

Expression	Meaning	Context
If it please you, Judge If it please the court May it please, Judge May it please the Judge May it please the court May it please	Flexibly used in numerous contexts, usually by solicitors/ barristers; expression of deference to the court; also used to indicate acceptance of a judge's order	Barrister: If it please you, Judge, I appear for Mr. X Judge: I am refusing bail Barrister: If it please the court Solicitor: Would you consider legal aid Judge: Not on the basis – he's not at risk Solicitor: May it please
Obliged Much obliged	Thank you. Used by solicitors/barristers and the Gardaí, usually the court presenter. Usually marks the end of a case	Obliged Much obliged I'm obliged I'm very much obliged to the court

Table A.2 Words not used in everyday language

Term	Meaning	Context
Bench warrant	Often issued when someone fails to turn up; the Gardaí can arrest that person and bring them before the court (bench) to address the warrant	Prosecution: My application would be for a bench warrant
Bond, Bail bond, Peace bond, Probation bond	Sworn undertaking by sureties in respect of a defendant's adjudged liability in proceedings. May include numerous conditions	Judge: Convict, 200 Euro, one month to pay, ten days in default. Recognisance on own bond, 50 Euros

Term	Meaning	Context
		You are now discharged from the conditions of your bail bond Judge: Enter into a peace bond for twelve months on own bond of 1000 Euro. The terms of the bond include ... Judge: He will enter a Probation bond, twelve months, in his own bond 200 Euro
Book of evidence ('the Book')	Prepared where a case goes forward for trial on indictment; contains prosecution's evidence; served on defendant in court	Judge: Consent to remand, [date], for book of evidence Judge: How are you getting on with the book? Prosecution: The guard is about to serve the book
Indictable, indictment	Triable/tried by jury	Prosecution: It is purely an indictable matter, and I would be seeking a return to trial on that Prosecution: The DPP now consents to trial by indictment
Peremptory	No excuse for non-compliance	Judge: 4 August, 2.30, peremptory hearing
Précis	Statement of evidence	Barrister: The application is to put it back for one week, and for a précis
Recognisance	A bond, with or without sureties, to secure performance of some act by the person bound: e.g. appear in court, keep peace, be of good behaviour	Judge: I'll fix recognisance in his own bond
Remand	When the hearing is adjourned to a future date, the defendant is either admitted to bail or kept in custody	Judge: Remand on continuing bail to [date] for election, plea or date Prosecution: Application to remand in custody

Table A.2 *(Continued)*

Term	Meaning	Context
Second calling	Case is called later the same day for a second time. Third callings are less common	Solicitor: I'd like to ask for second calling
Summary disposal, summary justice, summary trial	Offence tried in District Court without a jury	Prosecution: There is consent to summary disposal Prosecution: The DPP has agreed to summary justice Prosecution: Consent to summary trial in all matters
Summons	Document that requires the person in question to attend court	Barrister: No summons has been received

Table A.3 Words specific to a legal environment but also in common usage

	Term
Accused	Judge
Allegation	Judgment
Bail	Lawyer
Barrister	Legal aid
Convict	(Not) guilty plea
Custody	Oath
Detain (detention)	Probation
Evidence	Sentence
Guilty plea	Solicitor

Table A.4 Everyday words used in a different sense or having a specific meaning in the District Court context

Term	Meaning	Context
Adjourn (adjournment)	Suspend or put off until a future date	Solicitor: I'm looking to adjourn that by consent Solicitor: I am seeking an adjournment Judge: I'll adjourn sentence for a pre-sentence report Judge: We'll adjourn for five minutes
Appear (appearance)	To appear: to be before the court To appear for: to represent	Judge: Any appearance by or on behalf of Mr. X? Barrister: I appear for the defendant/Mr. X

Term	Meaning	Context
Application (apply)	Requests made to the court	Prosecution: My application would be for a bench warrant/remand Advocate: There is an application for bail/ counsel/disclosure/a précis/ to put it back
Caution	Inform someone of their legal rights or obligations; a Garda cautions a person on arrest; when a case is sent for trial to a higher court, a caution is made about using an alibi	Garda: He made no reply after caution Judge: The court is obliged to caution you that if you intend to use an alibi for your defence you must furnish this in writing to the prosecution within fourteen days
Consent	Defendant's consent to be remanded, or DPP's consent to summary trial	Judge: Is that by consent?/ Is there consent? Prosecution: The DPP consents to summary disposal
Consult (consultation)	Usually the meeting between lawyer and client	Judge: Did you have a consultation with your solicitor? Solicitor: I haven't had a chance to consult with my client
Conviction (convict)	Usually previous convictions, or announcing sentence	Judge: Any previous convictions? Judge: Convict, fine 100 Euro Judge: Convict, two months from 13 September
Directions	Instructions from DPP as to whether offence is to be tried summarily or sent forward for trial on indictment	Judge: Do you have directions from the DPP? Prosecution: The DPP has directed trial on indictment
Disclosure	Whereby the prosecution reveals or discloses its evidence	Barrister: We are seeking disclosure
Elect	Where defendant has the right to trial by jury but chooses/ elects summary trial in the District Court	Solicitor: He is electing this court
Facts	The facts or circumstances of the alleged offence	Judge: I will hear the facts

Table A.4 *(Continued)*

Term	Meaning	Context
Flight risk	Danger that the person will leave the jurisdiction while on bail and not turn up to trial	Prosecution: There would be an objection to bail; he is a flight risk. He has no ties here: no family, no job
Go back	A case can 'go back' to another judge (or court) to deal with certain issues, or be remanded or adjourned to another date	Prosecution: If it could go back to [Court] in two weeks, time Judge: Your case has to go back for a week
Hearing	On a not guilty plea the case proceeds to a hearing	Judge: The hearing is set for 10 June at 2pm Solicitor: I'm seeking a date for hearing
Instruction(s)	Depending on context, 'instructions' may be those of the DPP with regard to summary trial (jurisdiction), or instructions by defendant to solicitor/barrister	Judge: Do we have instructions? Solicitor: I haven't had a chance to take instruction from Mr. B
Jurisdiction	Whether or not a hybrid offence or an indictable offence triable summarily is fit to be tried summarily	Judge: I accept jurisdiction on all sheets Judge: Have we dealt with jurisdiction under Section 2?
Liberty to reapply	The next court date is fixed, but should the reason for the remand be resolved earlier, an earlier court date can be requested	Judge: For mention with liberty to reapply
(The) List	Actual court list with names of defendants; usually also names of prosecuting Garda and number of offences. More abstractly, order in which cases are heard or a person's record of appearing before the court	Judge: Put it to the end of the list for proper consultation Solicitor: It's his first time on the list
Mention	First stage of a case in the system – it is mentioned	Judge: Remand, [date] at 10.30 for mention. All sheets Judge: Is that for hearing or for mention?

Term	Meaning	Context
Mitigation	Provision of factors that may mitigate severity of offence/ sentence	Judge: What's going on in his life? Anything in mitigation?
On her/his feet	Actively participating in court	Judge: Would you go and see if he's on his feet?
Order	Anything the court orders to be done; the court may order the prosecution to furnish evidence or make orders in sentencing an offender: fines, custodial sentences, community service order, probation order, and so on. A judge may make, conclude or vacate an order (which annuls it). May refer to one specific thing (a High Court order, indictment order, exclusion order, safety order); or more generally, what the court orders. Also other senses, perhaps most notably order in court, public order and order an interpreter	Judge: An order for précis and CCTV where applicable Judge: I have a number of orders. First, the sentence is adjourned to this court on [date] for a community service report. Second, there is an order for compensation ...: €49,840 to be discharged by monthly instalments of €500. In respect of the second offence, five months consecutive, adjourned for community service report. A compensation order will be served on you. There are consequences regarding non-compliance with this order
Plead (plea)	Say that you are guilty or not guilty; a plea is 'entered' Also, to plead law, though generally refers to pleading guilty or not guilty at District Court level	Judge: How do you plead? Advocate: We are pleading, Judge Advocate: The application is to plead Advocate: There is a plea of guilty
Represent (represented)	Acting on behalf of, acting as legal advocate for	Judge: The court notes that the defendant is not legally represented Advocate: I'm representing Mr. X
Return (to trial)	Send forward for trial on indictment in a higher court	Judge: Mr. X, this court is now returning you for trial to the present sittings of the Circuit Court
Serve (a sentence)	Spend time in prison	Judge: If he doesn't have the money he will have to serve twenty-one days

Table A.4 *(Continued)*

Term	Meaning	Context
Serve (the book)	If proceeding to trial on indictment, a book of evidence must officially be given (served) to defendant by prosecution in court. Other orders such as a summons may also be served on the defendant	Judge: Has the book been served? Prosecution: All charges on indictment please, the Guard is about to serve the book
Sheet(s)	Charge sheet: piece of paper where Gardaí detail person being charged/the offence	Prosecution: One sheet – strike out Judge: It's not noted on that sheet
Stand	If the case is called and a party is not ready to go ahead it may be allowed to stand, and called again later	Judge: If you want to take instructions I can let it stand Advocate: If you could let it stand to permit me to consult with the defendant
Strike (out)	If an offence is struck out, the prosecution is dropped. Often happens where prosecuting Garda fails to turn up and has not instructed court presenter to proceed; the Gardaí ask for strike outs for various reasons	Judge: Strike out Section 4. That leaves us with a Section 49 Prosecution: Strike out please, Judge Solicitor: Application to strike out
Submission (submit)	In District Court, often what the solicitor/barrister submits in defence or explanation of client's actions; also, legal submissions; also, forms or documents (such as statement of means or passport) can be submitted to the court	Judge: I'm making my judgment; have you any more submissions or are you going to interrupt as I go along? Advocate: In my respectful submission, he is a man with two young children Advocate: I submit the Garda didn't tell him in full where the power of search was from
Take into account/take into consideration	On conviction of an offence, a person can plead guilty to another offence and ask to have it taken into consideration; in this case it	Judge: Convict and take into account

Term	Meaning	Context
	is noted with the record of sentence, and the accused cannot be prosecuted for that offence unless the conviction is reversed in an appeal	
Travel	If more than one offence is before the court, and one is sent back to another District Court judge, the offences may be kept together, or allowed to 'travel' together	Judge: Garda X's case can travel with that order
Warrant	Written authority to execute process; e.g. a warrant may be issued for a person's arrest to have them brought before the court	Garda: Application to remand in custody; he has eight previous warrants

Appendix D

Vignette: unrepresented French defendant

Judge Z sitting in the Rural Court. The defendant, a young French man working in the town, has been called and arrives without a solicitor.

> JUDGE: What is your understanding of the English language? I mean, can you speak English?
> DEFENDANT: Yeah.
> JUDGE: Do you want the assistance of an interpreter?
> DEFENDANT: [Doesn't understand; question repeated several times] No.
> JUDGE: Comprends?
> DEFENDANT: I'm all right.
> ...
> JUDGE: May I ask you whether it is your wish or aspiration to have legal representation?
> DEFENDANT: [Looks at Judge in confusion; clearly doesn't understand]
> JUDGE: Do you want to pay for the professional services of a lawyer?
> DEFENDANT: Yeah.
> JUDGE: [Making a note] Yes.
> DEFENDANT: [Suddenly unsure] I already do. I already pay the fine.
> JUDGE: [Sighs] Let's start again. [Asks in an equally complex manner if he wants a solicitor]
> DEFENDANT: [Silence. Doesn't seem to understand]
> JUDGE: Well, your English isn't that good, and my French is disastrous. Can you come back at 2.15?
> DEFENDANT: Yeah.
> JUDGE: I'll try to get a French interpreter for then.

The judge is about to adjourn the case when another young man appears.

> JUDGE: You've a Dublin accent, good man! What's your competence in the French language?
> FRIEND: I don't speak French. I'm here to help him to understand. He has good English but with the mic he couldn't hear.
> JUDGE: [Laughing] Agh now, if you have complaints about the P.A. system,

direct them to [the Courts Service]. It has nothing to do with me – I just do my best!
[Court laughs]
FRIEND: He doesn't want a solicitor. He wants to deal with it today.
JUDGE: I have obligations …
[Asks if he wants to apply for assistance of solicitor under Criminal Justice Legal Aid Act]
DEFENDANT: No.
JUDGE: [Noting] Legal Aid declined. … Inspector X will go slowly.
INSPECTOR: [Facts: the accused had been in town on the date in question. He was drunk; he had told three Gardaí to fuck off and called two female Gardaí bitches. Cannabis was found on his person]
JUDGE: What work do you do here?
DEFENDANT: I am a pestrry chiff.
[Defendant has extremely heavy accent – very difficult to understand]
JUDGE: [Flummoxed] You're a what?!!
DEFENDANT: Pest-rry chiff [pause] Chiff.
JUDGE: You're a chef! You've heard the facts. In my experience this usually happens when people are intoxicated of one of a number of substances. … Give me one good reason why you shouldn't go to prison for two months …
DEFENDANT: I was drunk …
[Defendant's English extremely difficult to understand; Judge Z asks him to repeat himself several times after each answer]
…
JUDGE: Why didn't you have manners? Why didn't you give your correct name?
DEFENDANT: I was drunk …
JUDGE: Where do you work?
[Repeats at least four times; cannot hear or understand defendant's answer. The friend names the place of work, but the judge still can't understand. Finally a solicitor calls out the hotel name where the defendant works]
JUDGE: [To the friend] Tell me, my good man, how do you fit into this?
FRIEND: I work with him. He asked me to come up with him in case he didn't understand something.
…
JUDGE: [To the defendant] Like everybody else you're very welcome in this country, but I won't tolerate abuse of our police service. If you want to abuse [it] you can go back to the Eiffel Tower, stand on top, and abuse to your heart's content, but it won't be tolerated here. … It would be a good idea to go up and apologise to those two female guards.
DEFENDANT: I already did.
[Or something similar – very difficult to understand what he is saying]
JUDGE: What?
DEFENDANT: [Repeats]
JUDGE: What?
FRIEND: ['Interpreting'] He already went and apologised the next day.

JUDGE: Good. [To defendant] Aren't you lucky you have him!
[Adds something about defendant learning English now; goes on to read sentence at high speed. Defendant and friend look completely bewildered]
FRIEND: Does he have to sign a bail bond or anything?
JUDGE: [Seems not to hear; no response]
Court adjourns for lunch. Defendant and friend go to the registrar, apparently to ask for information and/or explanations.

Appendix E

Vignette: dismissal of Polish interpreter

Judge Z sitting in the Rural Court. This is the case of a young, male Polish LEP defendant prosecuted for drunk-driving. The defendant is unrepresented.

The case is first called

JUDGE: What is your nationality, Sir?
DEFENDANT: [Silence]
JUDGE: Polish, is it?
DEFENDANT: Yes.
JUDGE: What is your command of the English language?
DEFENDANT: [Silence]
JUDGE: Right. My Polish is great but I've forgotten most of it. We'll try and get an interpreter for 2. [Aside] That doesn't mean anything to you. How are you supposed to run a court under these conditions? Mr. L, will you take a seat, suí síos.

The case resumes after lunch

A young, male Polish interpreter has arrived.

JUDGE: Would you tell Mr. L that after he was charged and cautioned he replied 'no reply' to the criminal charge.

The interpreter hesitates and the judge becomes suspicious.

JUDGE: What competency do you have in interpreting?
INTERPRETER: Level 3.
JUDGE: Would you inform Mr. L that the court knows that he is not legally represented.
INTERPRETER: Yes.
JUDGE: Can he afford to pay for legal representation?
INTERPRETER: He won't be waiting for legal advice.
...

JUDGE: My dear man, your English isn't great ... and I'm talking to the interpreter.
...
INTERPRETER: He doesn't want the legal advice.
JUDGE: What?
INTERPRETER: He doesn't want the legal [pause] representation.
JUDGE: Could you please inform him [that he is entitled to be represented].
INTERPRETER: He said he's just one month here ...
...
JUDGE: I have difficulty, Sir, in understanding your English. It is my obligation –

The judge pauses for the interpreter, but the interpreter remains silent. The judge becomes agitated and shouts:

JUDGE: Translate as I'm speaking! My obligation ... is to inform ... of his right [to a solicitor].
INTERPRETER: He says he can't afford a solicitor.
JUDGE: That's the point I'm coming to. If he can't afford a solicitor ... he is entitled to apply for free legal aid. Does he want a solicitor?
INTERPRETER: He doesn't know.
JUDGE: Would you inform Mr. L that it is my obligation to inform him of his rights. I don't know if he has the capacity to watch 'Who wants to be a Millionaire' but he doesn't have the option of phone a friend, ask the audience, or do 50:50.

At this point, everybody is laughing.

JUDGE: Does he understand the charge?
INTERPRETER: Yes. Yes, he does.
JUDGE: Is he pleading guilty or not guilty?
INTERPRETER: Guilty.
JUDGE: Guilty.
INTERPRETER: Yes, he pleads guilty, Judge.
JUDGE: To the best of your competency translate the evidence.
GARDA: [Gives evidence very slowly, watching interpreter to see if he is ready for him to continue. This is very unusual] ... the defendant was conveyed to [Town] Garda Station ...
JUDGE: Would you ask Mr. L if he wishes to say anything to the court by way of explanation.

The defendant looks extremely uncomfortable.

INTERPRETER: He has no excuses, he said.
...
INTERPRETER: He is a single. ... money from part time work.
JUDGE: Can I confirm if his address is [address]?
INTERPRETER: Not any more.

JUDGE: What is his present address?
INTERPRETER: He is homeless.
JUDGE: And who is living at that address?
INTERPRETER: His father.
JUDGE: [Asking why he wasn't living with his father] Has there been some sort of disagreement?
INTERPRETER: Yes.
JUDGE: Considering his lack of address ... the penalty must be paid forthwith. If he doesn't have money ... he will have to serve twenty-one days.
INTERPRETER: He's asking if that could be less.

The judge leans forward as if unsure as to what the interpreter has said.

INTERPRETER: If you could drop the price ... less amount.

He explains that the defendant is asking to pay in instalments; the judge says that unfortunately he does not make the laws.

JUDGE: How much money does he have on him today?
INTERPRETER: He doesn't have any money, Judge.
JUDGE: He doesn't look like he's homeless.
INTERPRETER: He says he looks after himself.
JUDGE: I can see that.
JUDGE: [As he has no address and cannot pay the fine forthwith] He has to go to prison.
INTERPRETER: There's nothing he can do, Judge, he said. ...
JUDGE: Who lives at home with his father? [Accepting, he says, that it is true about the dispute]
DEFENDANT: He's living on his own.

By now a young female Garda has come to stand beside the interpreter and defendant; she is conveying the judge's words to the interpreter and explains that unless the defendant can pay today he has to serve a jail sentence as he has no address to which the fine can be sent (the Inspector had said he was not happy the defendant could be contacted without an address).

INTERPRETER: Can he say something? Can he put his address at the old one for correspondence?
JUDGE: [Asked Inspector if he would be happy with that]
INSPECTOR: [He would have concerns]
JUDGE: All right, payment forthwith. In default, prison sentence of thirty days. I certify with some reluctance for the interpreter present.

The Garda continues to explain what Judge Z is saying, but the judge also continues talking, explaining the fourteen days to lodge an appeal.

The interpreter appears not to be listening to the judge as he continues to interpret for the Garda.

> JUDGE: Court is adjourned.

This is the only time Judge Z has adjourned in the middle of a session. He leaves the courtroom and various people, including a solicitor and other Polish defendants, approach. There is an air of concern.

Court resumes

The solicitor that had approached the defendant stands up and addresses the judge, expressing concern that the defendant had not fully understood what was happening, and noting that he is still unrepresented. Judge Z becomes extremely angry, and shouts:

> JUDGE: I take grave umbrage and exception to [what you are implying]. If you want to take over the administration of justice … It is completely unethical and unprofessional to engage with a defendant who is in custody when you have no authority to do so.

The monologue continues for some time; then the interpreter and defendant are re-called:

> JUDGE: May I ask him, did he approach her, or did she approach him?
> INTERPRETER: She approached him.
> JUDGE: And what did she say …?
> INTERPRETER: He can have the solicitor with no money …
> JUDGE: And when I was explaining that to him in the most simple way possible, through you the interpreter, did he not understand?
> INTERPRETER: He says he didn't understand.
> JUDGE: And what is your competence [as an interpreter]?
> INTERPRETER: It is just a translating word to word.

The judge says that he had spent a long time, and gone into great detail, about the defendant's right to a solicitor and to apply for legal aid.

> JUDGE: Did you tell him that?
> INTERPRETER: [That he had]
> JUDGE: I am not fluent in the Polish language. I am reliant on you, the interpreter, to translate …
> INTERPRETER: He said he couldn't understand the legal terms.
> JUDGE: Well, 'free' is very simple. What did he not understand about 'free'?
> INTERPRETER: He only understand …
> JUDGE: [Interrupting] Now listen! I expressed my dissatisfaction with you earlier on. What agency are you from? What agency?

INTERPRETER: [Agency].
JUDGE: It appears to me, Sir, that you are incompetent ... must be dismissed ... in the field of interpretation for the purposes of the administration of justice. Please leave the court.
[To solicitor] I am absolutely appalled [at the] suggestion that I had not discharged my duty line by line. ... Your conduct ... is grossly offensive and ... irresponsible. ... To approach the defendant in the manner you had ... You could have conveyed your concerns to a member of the Garda Síochána. ... Your conduct suggests that I have failed miserably in my duty.

Court is adjourned until further notice. The judge leaves the courtroom for a second time – even more unusual. There is a buzz as people discuss what has happened. The adjournment lasts a considerable amount of time. Finally court resumes. Judge Z announces that he deems it appropriate to vacate the earlier order based on the interpreter's lack of competence.

JUDGE: It's not for me to choose the interpreter, but from now on, Ms. [interpreter] from [Town] is the only interpreter to attend in future. ... With regard to the competency of [Agency] to assign interpreters to this court ... his incompetence to speak English was of concern to me from the very beginning.

He talks about whether to certify for the interpreter and finds there is no reason he should not be paid for his attendance.

JUDGE: Any interpreter from [Agency] shall not assist the court with any defendant before the court from now on. I am concluding my order.
[To the defendant] I don't have one word of Polish – the assigned interpreter was totally incompetent to deal with the sensitive issues before this court.

The judge says he had believed the interpreter to be conveying the correct information; he had informed him at length about his rights with regard to legal aid and representation, and so on.

JUDGE: I will invite you to come back next Thursday. Do you understand that?
DEFENDANT: [Shakes head].
GARDA: [That had been helping] Judge, there is another Polish national in court; he can understand and tell him – if that's acceptable.

The said person arrives and it is established that the defendant will come back the following Thursday.

JUDGE: Does Thursday or Friday suit him best?
FRIEND–GARDA–DEFENDANT: Thursday.

The judge formally requests an interpreter for this date, specifically the above-mentioned Polish interpreter.

> JUDGE: Mr. L, you are free to go.

The next week

The same case is called.

> JUDGE: Is there any appearance by or on behalf of Mr. L?
> SOLICITOR: Yes, Judge. I appear. He's speaking to the interpreter.
> JUDGE: [Reading] A Polish national. Is Garda W here?
> COURT PRESENTER: Yes, Judge.

As Garda W is coming to the witness stand, Judge Z asks her what Mr. L's understanding of English is. The Garda takes the oath.

> JUDGE: We're trying to ascertain if he had any understanding of English at all. You may or may not be aware of why the court is seeking this information. I'll take you back to [date], [Street] at midnight. What happened? Why did you come into contact with this [man]?

The Garda testifies that she had observed him driving; she stopped him and spoke with him.

> GARDA: He understood, ... he understood me, ... he understand [sic] what I wanted; he didn't have a problem.
> ...
> JUDGE: Did he understand why you had stopped him?
> GARDA: I asked him to put out his cigarette; he put it out. I explained that I wanted him to take a deep breath and blow into the bag; he did it ...
> JUDGE: And arising from that [breath] test, something happened.
> GARDA: He was arrested and conveyed to [Town] Garda Station. And I had requested an interpreter for him.
> JUDGE: During this journey to [Town] [did you communicate with him]?
> GARDA: Yes. He said that he was a Polish national and that he'd eaten too many apples.
> ...
> JUDGE: I am absolutely satisfied that he proceeded in a methodical and premeditated fashion to mislead the court. ... I was watching the interpreter, and while I wasn't satisfied with his competence, I was satisfied that the defendant understood what was going on. ...

The judge goes over what had happened on the previous court date with the solicitor who had 'wittingly or otherwise' addressed the court on the grounds that she was not happy with proceedings. He explains that the press had proceeded to publish an article that was 'grossly offensive and misleading'.

JUDGE: Ms. [Solicitor] was physically and emotionally upset. The problem is this; if I had said to a solicitor representing a client at the end of their case that 'you have made a dog's dinner' of it, it should rightly be reported. ... Ms. [Solicitor] got up and intervened where she had no audience, and the court had to respond, because the implication was that I had not discharged my duties fairly and fully. I had timed the case, and I had spent forty minutes going over and over and over again, and I was absolutely satisfied that he had understood.

The judge says the reporters should go back 'and put right the wrongs they have stated'. He says he had asked the prosecution if time could be allowed to pay the fine, but the answer had been 'no'; if they had agreed, that would have been the end of the matter. Judge Z says it is not for him to comment on the prosecution's decision over which he has no discretion, but that issues arose by the conduct of the defendant. He says that he is clearly concerned with Ms. [Solicitor]'s behaviour, and believes her intervention to have been wrong. However:

JUDGE: I have no doubt in my mind that from the minute the interpreter started, the defendant understood what was happening; I am satisfied that he knew, chapter and verse, exactly what was happening.
...
SOLICITOR: Yes, Judge. ... There is just one issue I would like to address. The defendant did have some English that he had learned in school. He has what you might call 'survivor English'. He understood what the Garda was saying, and he certainly understood the process –

The court breaks for lunch.

SOLICITOR: [To defendant, smiling] Now go away!

After lunch, Mr. L is called.

SOLICITOR: Judge, I appear. This is the same case that was being heard before lunch.
JUDGE: You're not in a position to indicate a plea.
SOLICITOR: Oh, I am, Judge. There continues to be a plea. Just the interpreter –

He looks around, waiting for the interpreter.

JUDGE: Wait a moment for the interpreter.
...

A few minutes later the Garda is sworn in again and gives the facts: at 12.11am, the accused was stopped driving a vehicle with [registration]; he was arrested and a breath test was administered. The result was 46 µg/100ml.

JUDGE: Is legal aid a requirement?
SOLICITOR: I would like to reapply for legal aid. He moved here recently from Poland; his father is here in court with him. He didn't think he was over the limit. He is living with his father – who is behind him there – at that address again.
COURT PRESENTER: I am satisfied that he is at that address, Judge.
JUDGE: May I enquire before I complete the order of the court if he is unclear about any aspect of the proceedings here today?
INTERPRETER: He understood everything, Judge.

The judge convicts and fines the defendant.

SOLICITOR: I would apply for the release of his passport.
[Passport is handed over.]
JUDGE: He's fully discharged from his bond.

End of case.

Bibliography

Adler, F. (1983) *Nations Not Obsessed with Crime* (Littleton, CO: Fred B. Rothman & Co.)

Agriculture Produce (Eggs) Act (1939) No.2/1939

Albert Jarzebak v The Governor of Cloverhill Prison & MJELR [2010] I.E.H.C. 493

Anderson, N. (20 November 2008) 'The clock ticked on towards two before the legal sparring began', *Irish Independent*

Attorney-General v Joyce & Walsh [1929] I.R. 526

Australia Attorney-General's Department (1991) *Review of Commonwealth Criminal Law* (Canberra: Australian Govt. Pub. Service)

Bacik, I. (2007) 'Breaking the language barrier: access to justice in the new Ireland', *Judicial Studies Institute Journal* 2

Bacik, I., A. Kelly, M. O'Connell & H. Sinclair (1998) 'Crime and poverty in Dublin: an analysis of the association between community deprivation, District Court appearance and sentence severity' in *Crime and Poverty in Ireland* (I. Bacik & M. O'Connell, eds.)(Dublin: Round Hall Sweet & Maxwell)

Bail Act (1997) No. 16/1997

Baka v Romania (16 July 2009) App. No. 30400/02, Eur.Ct.H.R.

Bartholomew, P.C. (1971) *The Irish Judiciary* (Dublin: Institute of Public Administration)

Benmaman, V. (2000) 'Interpreter issues on appeal', *Proteus: Newsletter of the National Association of Judiciary Interpreters and Translators* IX:4

Berk-Seligson, S. (1990) 'Bilingual court proceedings: the role of the court interpreter' in *Language in the Judicial Process* (J.N. Levi & A. Graffam Walker, eds.)(New York/London: Plenum Press)

Berk-Seligson, S. (2002) *The Bilingual Courtroom: Court Interpreters in the Judicial Process: With a New Chapter* (Chicago/London: University of Chicago Press)

Black, F. (24 December 2009) 'Immigrants leaving in thousands: applications for PPS numbers by foreign nationals plunge', *Irish Independent*

Bottoms, A. & J.D. MacClean (1976) *Defendants in the Criminal Process* (London: Routledge & K. Paul)

Boyle, K.C. (1984) 'The Galway District Court study' in *The Criminal Justice System: Policy and Performance* (D.B. Rottman, ed.)(Dublin: National Economic and Social Council), Appendix II

Brozicek v Italy (19 December 1989) App. No. 10964/84, 23 Eur.Ct.H.R.

Bunreacht na hÉireann (Constitution of Ireland), 1937

Butler, I. & L. Noaks (1992) *Silence in Court?: A Study of Interpreting in the Courts of England and Wales* (Cardiff: School of Social and Administrative Studies, University of Wales College Cardiff)

Byrne, R. & J.P McCutcheon (2009) *The Irish Legal System* (Dublin: Bloomsbury Professional)

C. & Ors v RAT & Ors [2012] I.E.H.C. 4

Campbell, L. (2007) 'The Criminal Justice Act 2007 – a theoretical perspective', *Irish Criminal Law Journal* 17:2

Campbell, L. (2008) 'The culture of control in Ireland: theorising recent developments in criminal justice', *Web Journal of Current Legal Issues* 1

Campbell, L., S. Kilcommins & C. O'Sullivan (eds.) (2010) *Criminal Law in Ireland: Cases and Commentary* (Dublin: Clarus Press)

Canny, J. (2003) *Sentencing Penalties* (Dublin: Round Hall Ltd.)

Carey, G. (1999) 'Trial courts and legal language', *Irish Law Times* 17

Charrow, R.P. & V.R. Charrow (1979) 'Making legal language understandable: a psycholinguistic study of jury instructions', *Columbia Law Review* 79:7

Charrow, V., J. Crandall & R. Charrow (1982) 'Characteristics and functions of legal language' in *Sublanguage: Studies of Language in Restricted Semantic Domains* (R. Kittredge & J. Lehrberger, eds.)(Berlin/New York: Walter de Gruyter)

Children Act (2001) No.24/2001

Civil Law (Miscellaneous Provisions) Act (2011) No.23/2011

Clune v D.P.P. & Clifford [1981] I.L.R.M. 17

Coen, R. (2008) 'The decline of due process and the right to silence's demise', *Irish Criminal Law Journal* 18:1

Colin, J. & R. Morris (1996) *Interpreters and the Legal Process* (Winchester: Waterside)

'Concern at judge's call for foreigners to pay interpreters' (14 May 2005) *Irish Times*

Conley, J.M. & W.M. O'Barr (1977) *Behavioral Analysis of the American Criminal Courtroom* (Durham, NC: Duke University Law and Language Project (Research Report 4))

Conley, J.M. & W.M. O'Barr (1990) 'Rules versus relationships in small claims disputes' in *Conflict Talk: Sociolinguistic Investigations of Arguments in Conversation* (A. Day Grimshaw, ed.)(Cambridge: Cambridge University Press)

Conley, J.M. & W.M. O'Barr (2005) *Just Words: Law, Language and Power* (Bristol: University of Chicago Press)

Conley, J.M., W.M. O'Barr & E.A. Lind (1978) 'The power of language: presentational style in the courtroom', *Duke Law Journal* 6

Conroy v Attorney General [1965] I.R. 411
Constitution of the Irish Free State (Saorstát Eireann) Act (1922)
Conway, V., Y. Daly & J. Schweppe (2010) *Irish Criminal Justice: Theory, Process and Procedure* (Dublin: Clarus Press)
Coonan, G. & K. O'Toole (2011) *Criminal Procedure in the District Court* (Dublin: Round Hall)
Coulter, C. (10 March 2003) 'The trials of foreigners translate into a difficulty', *Irish Times*
Courts (Establishment and Constitution) Act (1961) No.38/1961
Courts (Nr. 3) Act (1986) No.33/1986
Courts of Justice Act (1924) No.10/1924
Courts Service, annual reports 2002–2012 (Dublin: Irish Court Service)
Courts Service (2005) *Strategic Plan 2005–2008* (Dublin: Courts Service)
Courts Service (2008) *Strategic Plan 2008–2011* (Dublin: Courts Service)
Courts Service (2012) 'Request for tenders ("RFT") for provision of managed interpretation services', www.etenders.gov.ie/ (accessed August 2012)
Courts (Supplemental Provisions) Act (1961) No.39/1961
Criminal Justice Act (1951) No.2/1951
Criminal Justice Act (1984) No.22/1984
Criminal Justice Act (2007) No.29/2007
Criminal Justice (Legal Aid) Act (1962) No.12/1962
Criminal Justice (Public Order) Act (1994) No.2/1994
Criminal Law Act (1997) No.14/1997
CSO (2002) Census
CSO (2006) Census
CSO (April 2010) Population and Migration Estimates
CSO (2011) Census
Cuscani v UK (24 September 2002) App. No. 32771/96, 36 E.H.R.R. 2
D.P.P. v Adriano Martins Costa & Jose Claudio Batista [2008] I.E.C.C.A. 1
D.P.P. v Ismet Ceka [2004] I.E.C.C.A. 25
D.P.P. v Stanislaus Stokowski (17 December 2009) unreported, Court of Criminal Appeal, Finnegan J.
D.P.P. v Valdas Valiukas (27 April 2009) unreported, Court of Criminal Appeal, Kearns J.
D.P.P. v Vasile Vardoshilli (9 February 2009) unreported, Court of Criminal Appeal, Finnegan J.
D.P.P. v Yu Jie [2005] I.E.C.C.A. 95
Danet, B. (1980) 'Language in the legal process', *Law & Society Review* 14:3
Danet, B. & B. Bogoch (1980) 'Fixed fight or free-for-all? An empirical study of combatitiveness in the adversary system of justice', *British Journal of Law & Society* 7:1
Daud Abdilahi Gilingil v RAT & Ors. (1 June 2006) unreported, High Court, Feeney J.
de Jongh, E.M. (1991) 'Foreign language interpreters in the courtroom: the case for linguistic and cultural proficiency', *The Modern Language Journal* 75:3

de Jongh, E.M. (2008) 'Court interpreting: linguistic presence v. linguistic absence', *The Florida Bar Journal* 82:7

del Valle, S. (2003) *Language Rights and the Law in the United States: Finding our Voices* (Clevedon, England/Buffalo, NY: Multilingual Matters Ltd.)

Diallo v Sweden (5 January 2010) App. No. 13205/07, E.Ct.H.R.

Directive 2010/64/EU of the European Parliament and of the Council on the right to interpretation and translation in criminal proceedings, L 280/1, 26 October 2010

District Court Rules, www.courts.ie/rules.nsf/DistrictRules?OpenView&Start=1&Count=30&Expand=3#3 (accessed June 2014)

Donaghy, K. (3 May 2004) 'Trying times for courts as translation costs soar', *Irish Independent*

Donaghy, K. (20 January 2006) '€15m is lost in translation by the courts', *Irish Independent*

'Donegal Democrat reports on lack of court interpreters' (25 October 2007) *Donegal Democrat*

Doyle, K. (29 December 2008) '100,000 workers leave Ireland as pressure on jobs grows', *Herald.ie*

Dueñas González, R., V.F. Vasquez & H. Mikkelson (1991) *Fundamentals of Court Interpreting: Theory, Policy and Practice* (Durham, NC: Carolina Academic Press)

Dwyer, P. (1991) 'The Garda as prosecuting advocate in the District Court', *Irish Law Times* 9

Eades, D. (2002) 'Evidence given in unequivocal terms: gaining consent of Aboriginal young people in court' in *Language in the Legal Process* (J. Cotterill, ed.)(Basingstoke: Palgrave Macmillan)

Edwards, A.B. (1995) *The Practice of Court Interpreting* (Amsterdam/Philadelphia: John Benjamins Publishing Company)

Ellison, L. (2001) *The Adversarial Process and the Vulnerable Witness* (New York: Oxford University Press)

Elwork, A., B.D. Sales & J.J. Alfini (1977) 'Juridic decisions: in ignorance of the law or in light of it?', *Law and Human Behavior* 2

European Convention for the Protection of Human Rights and Fundamental Freedoms (4 November 1950) 213 U.N.T.S. 221, 226 (entered into force 3 September 1953)

F. & Anor v RAT [2010] I.E.H.C. 134

Felle, T. (17 August 2005) '€550,000 payout for court interpreters', *Irish Independent*

Fines Act (2010) No.8/2010

Fines (Amendment) Bill (2012)

Fitzpatrick & Anor v K. & Anor [2006] I.E.H.C. 392

'From Irish to Urdu' (June 2006) *Courts Service News*

Fuehrer, U. (February 2008) 'Cowboys and Indians', *ITIA Bulletin*

Fuwa Oladale Olawale v ORAC, MJELR (3 October 2002) unreported, High Court, Smyth J.

Garland, D. (2001) *The Culture of Control: Crime and Social Order in Contemporary Society* (Oxford: Oxford University Press)
Gartland, F. (27 March 2010) 'Professional fees for criminal legal aid work cut by 8%', *Irish Times*
Gibbons, J. (2003) *Forensic Linguistics: An Introduction to Language in the Justice System* (Oxford: Blackwell Publishing Ltd.)
Goodrich, P. (1987) *Legal Discourse: Studies in Linguistics, Rhetoric and Legal Analysis* (London: Macmillan)
Gradidge v Grace Bros. Pty. Ltd. [1988] 93 F.L.R. 414
Granger, E. & M. Baker (2003) 'The role and experience of interpreters' in *Working with Interpreters in Mental Health* (R. Tribe & H. Raval, eds.) (Hove: Brunner/Routledge)
Griffin, G. (1979) *The Collegians* (New York/London: Garland)
'Growing demand exposes poor translation service' (27 April 2007) *Irish Times*
Guerin, S. (7 February 2004) 'Criminal practice: the use of interpreters and translators in the Irish courts', paper given at Bar Council Conference on Criminal Procedure, Dublin
Güngör v Germany (dec.) (17 May 2001) App. No. 31540/96, Eur.Ct.H.R.
H.S. v RAT & Ors [2013] I.E.H.C. 262
Hale, S. (1999) 'Interpreters' treatment of discourse markers in courtroom questions', *Forensic Linguistics* 6:1
Hale, S. (2002) 'How faithfully do court interpreters render the style of non-English speaking witnesses's testimonies? A data based study of Spanish–English bilingual proceedings', *Discourse Studies* 4:1
Hale, S. & J. Gibbons (1999) 'Varying realities: patterned changes in the interpreter's representation of courtroom and external realities', *Applied Linguistics* 20
Hamilton, C. (2005) 'Sentencing in the District Court: "Here be dragons"', *Irish Criminal Law Journal* 15:3
Hamilton, C. (2013) 'Punitiveness and political culture: notes from some small countries', *European Journal of Criminology* 10
Hayes, A. & S. Hale (2010) 'Appeals on incompetent interpreting', *Journal of Judicial Administration* 20:2
Hayes, E. (October 2007) 'Editorial', *ITIA Bulletin*
Heffernan, B. (6 June 2006) 'Recruitment of court interpreters is put in the dock!', *Irish Independent*
Herbert, J. (1952) *Manuel de L'interprète* (Geneva: Librairie de l'Université)
Hermi v Italy (18 October 2006) App. No. 18114/02, Eur.Ct.H.R.
Hertog, E. (ed.) (2001) *Aequitas: Access to Justice across Language and Culture in the EU* (Antwerp: Lessius Hogeschool)
Hertog, E. & J. van Gucht (2006) *Executive Summary: Status Quaestionis* (Antwerp/Oxford/Portland: Intersentia)
Hickey, E. (1999) *Irish Law and Lawyers in Modern Folk Tradition* (Cork: Four Courts Press in association with The Irish Legal History Society)

Holmquist, K. (14 March 2006) 'Act now, while times are good', *Irish Times*

Hood, R., S. Shute & F. Seemungal (2003) *Ethnic Minorities in the Criminal Courts: Perceptions of Fairness and Equality of Treatment* (London: Lord Chancellor's Department)

House of Commons Justice Committee (2013) *Interpreting and Translation Services and the Applied Language Solutions Contract* (London: Stationery Office)

Immigrant Council of Ireland (16 July 2010) 'Press release: Level of callers to ICI does not support rhetoric of migrants "going home"' (Dublin: Immigrant Council of Ireland)

International Covenant on Civil and Political Rights (16 December 1966) G.A. Res. 2200A (XXI), 21 U.N. GAOR Supp. (No. 16) at 52, U.N. Doc. A/6316, 999 U.N.T.S. 171 (entered into force 23 March 1976)

Interpretation Act (1923) No.46/1923

'Interpreters keep the message clear' (July 2008) *Courts Service News*

IPRT (2013a) 'Facts & figures', www.iprt.ie/prison-facts-2 (Dublin: Irish Penal Reform Trust) (accessed July 2013)

IPRT (2013b) 'Media advisory: radical action needed to address stubbornly high prison numbers and meet basic duty of providing safe custody for all prisoners', www.iprt.ie/contents/2508 (Dublin: Irish Penal Reform Trust) (accessed July 2013)

Iqbal Begum [1991] 93 Cr. App. R. 96

'Irish lead resistance to draft EU law on suspects' rights' (12 June 2007) *Irish Times*

ITIA (2002) 'Submission to the Working Group on the Jurisdiction of the Courts' (Dublin: Irish Translators' and Interpreters' Association)

ITIA (2008) 'Submission on the Courts Service Statement of Strategy 2008–2011' (Dublin: Irish Translators' and Interpreters' Association)

ITIA (2011) 'Submission to the Courts Service on the New Tender for Interpreting and Related Issues' (Dublin: Irish Translators' and Interpreters' Association)

Jackson, J. & S. Doran (2003) *A Study of the Jurisdiction of the Criminal Courts in Ireland: Report to the Working Group on the Jurisdiction of the Courts* (Dublin: Courts Service)

Jarmołowska, K. (2011) 'Translation of a book of evidence and its impact on a criminal trial: a case study' (PhD dissertation, DCU)

'Judge attacks low standards of translators' (28 January 2004) *Irish Independent*

'Judge dismisses "incompetent" Polish translators' (12 October 2007) *Irish Examiner*

'Judge refuses to appoint translator for man accused of handling stolen phone' (28 July 2005) *Irish Independent*

Kamasinski v Austria (19 December 1989) App. No. 9783/82, 168 Eur.Ct.H.R. (Ser. A)

Kilcommins, S., I. O'Donnell, E. O' Sullivan & B. Vaughan (2004) *Crime, Punishment and the Search for Order in Ireland* (Dublin: Institute of Public Administration)

Kotsonouris, M. (2011) *'Tis all Lies, Your Worship: Tales from the District Court* (Dublin: Liffey Press)

Krings, T., A. Bobek, E. Moriarty, J. Salamonska & J. Wickham (2009) 'Migration and recession: Polish migrants in post-Celtic Tiger Ireland', *Sociological Research Online* 14:2

L. v RAT [2011] I.E.H. 181

Lally, C. (29 April 2009) 'Interpreter system poor – GRA', *Irish Times*

Law Society of Ireland (2004) *Human Rights Law Manual* (B. Moriarty & A. Mooney Cotter, eds.)(Oxford: Oxford University Press)

Law Society of Ireland (2012) *Criminal Litigation* (M. Butler, ed.)(Oxford: Oxford University Press)

Loftus, E.F. & J.C. Palmer (1974) 'Reconstruction of automobile destruction: an example of the interaction between language and memory', *Journal of Verbal Learning and Verbal Behavior* 13:5

Luedicke, Belkacem & Koç v Germany (28 November 1978) 2 E.H.R.R. 149 (Ser. A No. 29)

M.A.W. v RAT & MJELR [2009] I.E.H.C. 330

McCabe, D. (1985) 'Magistrates, peasants and the petty sessions courts: Mayo 1823–50', *Cathair na Mart* V:45

McCafferty, N. (1981) *In the Eyes of the Law* (Dublin: Ward River Press)

MacCarthaigh v Ireland [1999] 1 I.R. 200

MacCarthaigh v MJELR [2002] 4 I.R. 8

McKinley, C. (2 August 2013) 'Cost of court interpreters down 57% since 2008', *Irish Times*

Maley, Y. (1994) 'The language of the law' in *Language and the Law* (J. Gibbons, ed.)(London: Longman)

Maniar, A. (2013) 'Shambolic and unworkable: outsourcing of court interpreting services', www.irr.org.uk/news/shambolic-and-unworkable-outsourcing-of-court-interpreting-services/ (accessed August 2013)

Mattila, H.E.S. (2006) *Comparative Legal Linguistics* (Aldershot: Ashgate)

Melling v Mathghamhna [1962] I.R. 1

Mellinkoff, D. (1963) *The Language of the Law* (Boston: Little, Brown & Company)

Montgomery Hyde, H. (1964) *Norman Birkett: The Life of Lord Birkett of Ulverston* (London: Hamish Hamilton)

Morawetz, T. (ed.) (2000) *Law and Language* (Aldershot: Dartmouth)

Morgan, D. (1982) 'The life of a court interpreter', *Graya* 51:2

Morris, R. (1996) 'Interpreters and the legal process', *New Law Journal* 146:6759

Morris, R. (1999a) 'The gum syndrome', *Forensic Linguistics* 6:1

Morris, R. (1999b) 'The face of justice: historical aspects of court interpreting', *International Journal of Research and Practice in Interpreting* 4:1

Morris, R. (2008) 'Taking liberties? Duplicity or the dynamics of court interpreting' in *Interpreting in Legal Settings* (D. Russell & S. Hale, eds.) (Washington, DC: Gallaudet University Press)

Morris, R. (2010) 'Court Interpreting 2009: An Undervalued and Misunderstood Profession? Or: Will Justice Speak?' (Monographs in Translating & Interpreting 2), Universitat de Valencia

Muhammed Saleem v MJELR [2011] I.E.H.C. 223

MVA Consultancy (1996) *Foreign Language Interpreters in the Scottish Criminal Courts* (Edinburgh: Scottish Office Central Research Unit)

NCCRI (2007) *Interpreting, Translation and Public Bodies in Ireland: The Need for Policy and Training*, Advocacy Paper 5 (Dublin: National Consultative Committee on Racism and Interculturalism)

NCCRI (2008) *Developing Quality, Cost-Effective Interpreting and Translating Services for Government Service Providers in Ireland* (Dublin: National Consultative Committee on Racism and Interculturalism & Office of the Minister for Integration)

Nee, M. (8 January 2009) 'Murder case postponed for interpreter no-show', *Galway Advertiser*

ní Dhonnachadha, M. (2000) 'Irish language interpreting in the courts since the 1850s' (MA dissertation, DCU)

Noxious Weeds Act (1936) No.38/1936

O'Barr, W.M. (1982) *Linguistic Evidence: Language, Power, and Strategy in the Courtroom* (New York/London: Academic Press)

O'Barr, W.M. & J.M. Conley (1976) 'Subtleties of speech can tilt the scales of justice: when a juror watches a lawyer', *Barrister* 3:8

O'Brien, C. (4 April 2006) 'Are we lost in translation?', *Irish Times*

O'Brien, C. (7 June 2010a) 'No quality controls laid down for courts and Garda translators', *Irish Times*

O'Brien, C. (7 June 2010b) 'Hundreds of court, Garda interpreters have no qualification', *Irish Times*

O'Brien, J. (3 July 2007) 'Courts body to fork out £2m on interpreters as demand rises', *Irish Independent*

O'Donnell, I. (1998) 'Challenging the punitive obsession', *Irish Criminal Law Journal* 8:1

O'Donnell, I. (2005) 'Crime and justice in the Republic of Ireland', *European Journal of Criminology* 2:1

O'Donnell, I. (2008) 'Stagnation and change in Irish penal policy', *The Howard Journal* 47:2

O'Donnell, I., E.P. Baumer & N. Hughes (2008) 'Recidivism in the Republic of Ireland', *Criminology and Criminal Justice* 8

O'Donnell, Judge T.E. (2007) 'The Constitution, the European Convention on Human Rights Act 2003 and the District Court – a personal view from a judicial perspective', *Judicial Studies Institute Journal* 2

O'Mahony, P. (1997a) *Mountjoy Prisoners: A Sociological and Criminological Profile* (Dublin: Stationery Office)

O'Mahony, P. (1997b) 'Punishing poverty and personal adversity', *Irish Criminal Law Journal* 7:2
O'Mahony, P. (2002) 'The courts: introduction' in *Criminal Justice in Ireland* (P. O'Mahony, ed.)(Dublin: Institute of Public Administration)
O'Malley, T. (1991) 'Principles of sentencing', *Irish Criminal Law Journal* 1:2
O'Malley, T. (2009) *The Criminal Process* (Dublin: Round Hall-Thomson Reuters)
O'Malley, T. (28 June 2010) *Time Served: The Impact of Sentencing and Parole Decisions on the Prison Population* (Dublin: Irish Penal Reform Trust)
O'Monachain v An Taoiseach [1986] I.L.R.M. 660
O'Nolan, C. (2011a) 'New boundaries of justice in a world in motion: assessing the impact of global citizens in the Irish District Court' (PhD dissertation, Trinity College Dublin)
O'Nolan, C. (2011b) 'Penal populations in a world in motion: the case of the Republic of Ireland (ROI)', *The Howard Journal* 50:4
Official Languages Act (2003) No.32/2003
Öztürk v Germany (21 February 1984) 6 E.H.R.R. 409 (Ser. A No. 73)
Pérez, A.B. (2000) 'Interpreting in the Irish courtrooms: the impact of lack of regularisation on the quality of the interpreter's performance' (MA dissertation, DCU)
Petrea Stefan v MJELR, the Refugee Appeals Authority Ireland & the Attorney General [2002] 2 I.L.R.M. 134
Petty Sessions (Ireland) Act (1851)
Phelan, M. (9 June 2006) 'Letter: interpreting in the courts', *Irish Times*
Phelan, M. (October 2007) 'Court interpreters in the news (for the wrong reasons)', *ITIA Bulletin*
Phelan, M. (2011) 'Legal interpreters in the news in Ireland', *Translation & Interpreting* 3:1
Prison Service, annual reports 2001–2012 (Dublin: Irish Prison Service)
'Proposal to bolster defendants' rights to interpretation' (15 March 2010) *Irish Times*
R. v Burke [1858] 8 Cox C.C. 44
R. v Kwok Leung & Others [1909] Hong Kong L.R. 161
R. v Lee Kun [1915] 11 Cr. App. R. 293
R. v Tran [1994] 2 S.C.R. 95
R. v West London Youth Court, Ex p. N [2000] 1 W.L.R. 2368, [2000] 1 All E.R. 823
Radmann, J.A. (2005) 'Do you speak English?: a study on English language proficiency testing of Hispanic defendants in U.S. criminal courts' (MA dissertation, Louisiana State University)
Radzuik v MJELR & RAT (24 July 2009) unreported, High Court, Cooke J.
Reilly, J. & P. McArdle (20 June 2010) 'Pilot scheme aims to slash €3m court translation bill', *Irish Independent*
Riegel, R. (14 May 2001) 'Translator shortage causes havoc in court schedules', *Irish Independent*

Rigney, A.C. (1999) 'Questioning in interpreted testimony', *Forensic Linguistics* 6

Riordan, Judge D. (2007) 'Immigrants in the criminal courts', *Judicial Studies Institute Journal* 2

Rottman, D.B. (1984) *The Criminal Justice System: Policy and Performance* (Dublin: National Economic and Social Council)

Ryan, A. (1997) 'The Criminal Justice (Drug Trafficking) Act 1996: decline and fall of the right to silence?', *Irish Criminal Law Journal* 22

S.I. No. 565 of 2013 – European Communities Act 1972 (Interpretation and Translation in Criminal Proceedings) Regulations, 2013 (Dublin: Stationery Office)

S.I.M. v RAT & Ors [2009] I.E.H.C. 323

S.O.A. v MJELR & Anor [2009] I.E.H.C. 137

Sales, B.D., A. Elwork & J.J. Alfini (1977) 'Improving comprehension for jury instructions' in *Perspectives in Law and Psychology: The Criminal Justice System* (B.D. Sales, ed.)(New York: Plenum)

Saville-Troike, M. (2003) *The Ethnography of Communication: An Introduction* (Oxford: Blackwell)

Schane, S. (2006) *Language and the Law* (London: Continuum)

Solan, L. & P.M. Tiersma (2005) *Speaking of Crime: The Language of Criminal Justice* (Chicago: University of Chicago Press)

Spronken, T. & M. Attinger (2005) *Freedom, Security and Justice: Procedural Rights in Criminal Proceedings: Existing Level of Safeguards in the European Union* (Brussels: European Commission)

State (Buchan) v Coyne [1936] 70 I.L.T.R. 185

State (Healy) v Donoghue [1976] I.R. 325

Storey, K. (1998) 'The linguistic rights of non-English speaking suspects, witnesses, victims and defendants' in *Language Legislation and Linguistic Rights* (D.A. Kibbee, ed.) (Amsterdam/Philadelphia: John Benjamins Publishing Company)

T.D. v RAT & Anor [2010] I.E.H.C. 125

Tiersma, P.M. (1993) 'The judge as linguist', *Loyola of Los Angeles Law Review* 27

Tighe, M. (29 March 2009) 'Interpreters in court pay row', *Irish Times*

Trechsel, S. (2005) *Human Rights in Criminal Proceedings* (Oxford: Oxford University Press)

Tribe, R. (2005) 'Working with interpreters' in *Race, Culture, Psychology and Law* (K. Holt Barrett & W.H. George, eds.) (Thousand Oaks, CA/London: Sage)

UK Association of Police and Court Interpreters (2010) 'Position paper: outsourcing of language services in England and Wales', www.eulita.eu/uk-plans-outsource-language-services (accessed August 2013)

United States ex rel. Negron v the State of New York (1970) 310 F. Supp. 1304 (1970) and 434 F.2d 386 (1970)

Vrahimi v Turkey (26 September 2002) App. No. 16078/90, Eur.Ct.H.R.

Wadensjö, C. (1998) *Interpreting in Interaction* (New York: Addison Wesley Longman)
Waldron, J. (1993) *Maamtrasna: The Murders and the Mystery* (Dublin: Edmund Burke Publisher)
Waterhouse, K. (2010) 'Limited English Proficient (LEP) immigrants in Ireland's District Criminal Court' (PhD dissertation, Trinity College Dublin)
Wodak-Engel, R. (1984) 'Determination of guilt: discourse in the courtroom' in *Language and Power* (C. Kramarae, M. Schulz & W.M. O'Berr, eds.) (Beverly Hills, CA: Sage)
Working Group on the Jurisdiction of the Courts (2003) *The Criminal Jurisdiction of Courts* (Dublin: Stationery Office)
Young, P., I. O'Donnell & E. Clare (2001) *Crime in Ireland: Trends and Patterns, 1950 to 1998* (Dublin: Stationery Office)

Index

Note: 'n.' after a page reference indicates the number of a note on that page; page numbers in **bold** refer to discrete sections of text on the topic